Palgrave Macmillan Studies in Banking and Financial Institutions

Series Editor: **Professor Philip Molyneux**

The Palgrave Macmillan Studies in Banking and Financial Institutions are international in orientation and include studies of banking within particular countries or regions, and studies of particular themes such as Corporate Banking, Risk Management, Mergers and Acquisitions, etc. The books focus on research and practice, and include up-to-date and innovative studies on contemporary topics in banking that will have global impact and influence.

Titles include:

Yener Altunbaş, Blaise Gadanecz and Alper Kara
SYNDICATED LOANS
A Hybrid of Relationship Lending and Publicly Traded Debt

Yener Altunbaş, Alper Kara and Öslem Olgu
TURKISH BANKING
Banking under Political Instability and Chronic High Inflation

Elena Beccalli
IT AND EUROPEAN BANK PERFORMANCE

Paola Bongini, Stefano Chiarlone and Giovanni Ferri *(editors)*
EMERGING BANKING SYSTEMS

Vittorio Boscia, Alessandro Carretta and Paola Schwizer
CO-OPERATIVE BANKING
Innovations and Developments

Santiago Carbó, Edward P.M. Gardener and Philip Molyneux
FINANCIAL EXCLUSION

Allessandro Carretta, Franco Fiordelisi and Gianluca Mattarocci *(editors)*
NEW DRIVERS OF PERFORMANCE IN A CHANGING FINANCIAL WORLD

Dimitris N. Chorafas
CAPITALISM WITHOUT CAPITAL

Dimitris N. Chorafas
FINANCIAL BOOM AND GLOOM
The Credit and Banking Crisis of 2007–2009 and Beyond

Violaine Cousin
BANKING IN CHINA

Peter Falush and Robert L. Carter
THE BRITISH INSURANCE INDUSTRY SINCE 1900
The Era of Transformation

Franco Fiordelisi and Philip Molyneux
SHAREHOLDER VALUE IN BANKING

Hans Genberg and Cho-Hoi Hui
THE BANKING CENTRE IN HONG KONG
Competition, Efficiency, Performance and Risk

Carlo Gola and Alessandro Roselli
THE UK BANKING SYSTEM AND ITS REGULATORY AND SUPERVISORY FRAMEWORK

Elisabetta Gualandri and Valeria Venturelli *(editors)*
BRIDGING THE EQUITY GAP FOR INNOVATIVE SMES

Munawar Iqbal and Philip Molyneux
THIRTY YEARS OF ISLAMIC BANKING
History, Performance and Prospects

Sven Janssen
BRITISH AND GERMAN BANKING STRATEGIES

Kimio Kase and Tanguy Jacopin
CEOs AS LEADERS AND STRATEGY DESIGNERS
Explaining the Success of Spanish Banks

M. Mansoor Khan and M. Ishaq Bhatti
DEVELOPMENTS IN ISLAMIC BANKING
The Case of Pakistan

Mario La Torre and Gianfranco A. Vento
MICROFINANCE

Philip Molyneux and Munawar Iqbal
BANKING AND FINANCIAL SYSTEMS IN THE ARAB WORLD

Philip Molyneux and Eleuterio Vallelado *(editors)*
FRONTIERS OF BANKS IN A GLOBAL WORLD

Anastasia Nesvetailova
FRAGILE FINANCE
Debt, Speculation and Crisis in the Age of Global Credit

Dominique Rambure and Alec Nacamuli
PAYMENT SYSTEMS
From the Salt Mines to the Board Room

Catherine Schenk *(editor)*
HONG KONG SAR'S MONETARY AND EXCHANGE RATE CHALLENGES
Historical Perspectives

Andrea Schertler
THE VENTURE CAPITAL INDUSTRY IN EUROPE

Alfred Slager
THE INTERNATIONALIZATION OF BANKS

Noël K. Tshiani
BUILDING CREDIBLE CENTRAL BANKS
Policy Lessons for Emerging Economies

Palgrave Macmillan Studies in Banking and Financial Institutions
Series Standing Order ISBN 978–1–4039–4872–4
(*Outside North America only*)

You can receive future titles in this series as they are published by placing a standing order. Please contact your bookseller or, in case of difficulty, write to us at the address below with your name and address, the title of the series and the ISBN quoted above.

Customer Services Department, Macmillan Distribution Ltd, Houndmills, Basingstoke, Hampshire RG21 6XS, England

Capitalism Without Capital

Dimitris N. Chorafas
Member of the New York Academy of Sciences

palgrave
macmillan

First published 2009 by
PALGRAVE MACMILLAN

Palgrave Macmillan in the UK is an imprint of Macmillan Publishers Limited, registered in England, company number 785998, of Houndmills, Basingstoke, Hampshire RG21 6XS.

Palgrave Macmillan in the US is a division of St Martin's Press LLC, 175 Fifth Avenue, New York, NY 10010.

Palgrave Macmillan is the global academic imprint of the above companies and has companies and representatives throughout the world.

Palgrave® and Macmillan® are registered trademarks in the United States, the United Kingdom, Europe and other countries

ISBN: 978–0–230–23346–1

This book is printed on paper suitable for recycling and made from fully managed and sustained forest sources. Logging, pulping and manufacturing processes are expected to conform to the environmental regulations of the country of origin.

A catalogue record for this book is available from the British Library.

A catalog record for this book is available from the Library of Congress.

Printed and bound in Great Britain by
CPI Antony Rowe, Chippenham and Eastbourne

"A slave is he who cannot speak his thoughts."

Euripides

Contents

List of Tables and Figures

Tables

Figures

Preface

Warren Buffett called the worsening economic and financial crisis, which started in July/August 2007 and reached an intermediate summit in September/October 2008,[1] "an economic Pearl Harbor." Everywhere there is devastation. One looks at the right side of the balance sheet of banks, their *liabilities*, and nothing is right. Then one looks at the left side of the balance sheet of banks, their *assets*, and nothing is left.

While finance as a profession is much more an art involving people, politics, and market psychology than one dealing with numbers, the numbers, too, are important. Hundreds of billions of dollars, pounds, and euros have been wiped off banks' balance sheets in recent months because of fears that some complex financial instruments may be backed by assets which are nearly or fully worthless. These include:

- Housing loans that may not be paid back as a result of foreclosures,
- Corporate loans because defaults are rising, and
- A great lot of poorly understood and incorrectly valued structured products.

The underlying of many structured financial products is *debt* of households and of companies, often of dubious creditworthiness. According to at least one estimate, global household debt has reached the astronomical figure of $60 trillion. *If* so, *then* the prosperity of capitalism's last three decades rests on the fact that people have been living way beyond their means.

The other major factor behind the current crisis is the excesses promoted by lust for power, greed, and scant supervision. Banks and other financial companies have out-thought and out-organized the virtual economy by trading among themselves and by accumulating toxic waste. Over 95 percent of financial trades are bank-to-bank with no commercial needs in the background. They are done mainly in derivative instruments, over the counter (OTC) and off-exchange. The market for derivatives boomed during the past decade as banks sought new ways to make profits and pay fat bonuses by parceling out risk, with the aftereffect that:

- Capital is now scarce, and
- Confidence has taken a leave, pulling liquidity along with it.

On 15 November 2008 an international economic conference was held in Washington, DC, reviewed in this book. It brought together the heads of government of 21 nations and those of 4 supranational organizations, with the goal of finding a solution to the crisis. "This is a necessary but not sufficient condition" to give confidence to financial markets, said Michel Camdessus, a former president of the International Monetary Fund (IMF).

The emergency was underscored by the statement of George W. Bush, who said that he had agreed to the recent $700 billion rescue plan for US financial institutions only after being told the nation was at risk of falling into "a depression greater than the Great Depression." In the background of this new descent to the abyss are mountains of debt and plenty of toxic waste; in the foreground are:

- Extravagant salaries, bonuses, and other self-gratifications by bankers;
- Excessive leverage combined with other vulnerabilities;
- Weak underwriting and lending standards;
- Unsound risk control practices; and
- Increasingly complex and opaque derivative financial instruments.

Few people really appreciate the risks embedded in derivatives and other structured securities, which those who know them call financial weapons of mass destruction. Yet these risks are the reason why bankers, traders, investors, and regulators do not trust the value of assets warehoused in the vaults of credit institutions, to offer market-clearing prices. In addition,

- Banks do not trust one another to do business together, and
- There is definitely no trust that Washington, London, Paris, Berlin, and Tokyo would avoid creating costly new moral hazards as they attempt to bail out the global financial system.

It is almost amusing how the unstoppable accumulation of debt at every level of society, namely households, businesses, and the state – in short the borrowing and leveraging of the economy – is engineered precisely by those politicians and financiers who say that their credo is capitalism and free enterprise. What they really mean is not capitalism but the *State Supermarket*, and we have seen the results.

* * *

Written for professionals, but in a way the educated man in the street (a fast-growing breed) can understand, this book explains why – unlike many previous emerging-market crises – today's mess began in the rich world and spread all over the globe. *If* emerging economies start to collapse,[2] *then* the wisdom of globalized finance will come under intense questioning, though it would be difficult to measure:

- How much has been each country's fault, and
- What's the contribution of the free movement of capital.

Today, there does not even exist a reliable estimate of the amount of losses not only by countries and big banks but also by high net worth individuals. The former chairman and CEO of AIG and his counterpart at Lehman Brothers are said to have lost between them, from the two meltdowns, $7 billion. A single investor, Kirk Kirkorian, reportedly lost $12.7 billion from equity price collapses in two of his investments, MGM Mirage and Ford – while Russian oligarchs have put the three Americans to shame.

The way the financial news had it, between 1 May and 10 October 2008, the 25 richest Russian oligarchs lost $240 billion between them.[3] But they did not necessarily become penniless; neither did Kirkorian. Apart from the rest of their fortune, which is hidden away, what the Russian oligarchs lost was money that silly European and American banks had lent them. As for Kirkorian, the losses were registered in the name of Tracinda, his private firm, which had benefited from the banks' generosity in good times.

At the end, it is the whole economy and not just the banking industry that pays the bill. As one financial institution after another finds its balance sheet capsized, and descends into crisis, *capitalism is left without capital.* Instead of capital markets being vibrant, governments are called into action and (with taxpayers' money) they become the world's economic firefighters – dispatching tens of billions of dollars, pounds, and euros to banks as different as Bank of America, Goldman Sachs, Morgan Stanley, Royal Bank of Scotland, HBOS, Fortis, ING, and Hypo Real Estate.

Neither are big banks the only ones to suffer. If the week of 15 September 2008 is now called a "historic week" on Wall Street, on 6 and 13 October there began the two black weeks for middle-class investors who trusted their nest eggs to the markets. Many investors fretted, some were wiped out, and the most clear-eyed appreciated that:

- A crisis is a matter of *trust*, and
- The financial markets' trust of corporate governance has been badly shaken.

Since the mid 2007 meltdown, the big banks, the global companies, the US Treasury, the Federal Reserve, and their European or Asian counterparts have not been able to recreate the trust the market needs in spite of massive bailouts. Instead, the psychology worsened with the news that banks stood to lose another trillion on corporate loans; more CDOs turned toxic, the market for CDSs was shaken, and institutional investors were now asking for structured products to be treated on-exchange and not off-exchange.

* * *

Based on intensive research and written in a comprehensible manner, the book divides into three parts. Part One presents to the reader the multiple sense of money as an asset, a means of exchange, a unit of measurement (including that of inflation), an accounting standard, and generally a tool of management planning and control. In this discussion emphasis is placed on macroeconomics, money supply, the value of money, interest rates and money allocation to satisfy society's needs.

The text explains why in terms of macroeconomic risks financial market turmoil gives rise to sources of uncertainty, adding to the more familiar exposures novel ones stemming from global imbalances, a widespread real estate market collapse, and the rapid rise and fall of the prices of oil and other key commodities. It also describes how weaker borrowers find difficulty in obtaining credit, which deepens the downturn.

Credit matters. Without a functioning system of intermediation people cannot finance their mortgages; and companies cannot meet their payrolls, make investments, or honor the bills of their suppliers. The problem is that massive handouts have been made by governments to banks without guarantees that they would come forward with loans rather than use the money only to rebuild their balance sheets. Strains on the financial institutions' liquidity and capital base come from:

- Undercapitalization,
- Leveraged balance sheets,
- Downgrades of portfolio positions,
- Illiquidity of warehoused instruments, and
- Higher refinancing costs as trust wanes.

Part Two examines the positive and negative aspects of debt and of leveraging, taking practical examples to demonstrate that in the longer run superleveraging hits not only its addicts but also the overall economy. It is as simple, and brutal, as that. "Our independence depends on our ability not to overstep our limits," said Helmut Schlesinger, a former president of the Bundesbank.

Deleveraging is the answer, but it does not come free of cost. It also poses crucial questions regarding central banks, regulatory authorities, and asset allocation decisions. The leaders of the 21 nations who met in Washington for an international conference on the economic crisis and the bust of the banking industry issued an appeal for confidence; but will they be believed by business and by the public?

Another vital question is: who will have the moral authority to redress the balances? The western central banks' unique ethos has given them distinction. The events of 2008 have however proven that a great institution whose authority rests on its:

- Reliability, and
- Predictability

can hurt itself by being taken by surprise.[4] In addition, many of the unprecedented challenges of 2008/2009 have been traps set by the State Supermarket, which wants to be a friend to everyone – and therefore has treated central banks and regulatory authorities with mistrust, afraid that they might stop its bailouts.

Part Three is dedicated to case studies. In the US and Britain household debt has reached astronomical levels. The economy's troubles are pushing a growing number of already struggling consumers into bankruptcy, often with far more debt than those who fled previous downturns. Governments, however, are busy filling the empty coffers of big banks, even if they are now suffering from self-inflicted wounds. Banks are guilty:

- Of not having provided for timely and comprehensive measurement as well as management of risk, and
- Of having depended too much on dubious, leveraged financial instruments, while paying too little attention to internal control.

The market's vulnerability has been increased by the abuse of the virtual economy's freedoms, which hurt investor confidence, disrupted markets and changed the rules of the game. This gave a lift to the few while it hurt most severely the many.

It is a rare event for the economy to be hit by so many problems in such a short space of time, and this is a reason why piecemeal approaches will not work. The US government cannot solve the problems of Wall Street without solving those of Main Street. To rebuild confidence it must greatly strengthen bank regulation, as well as finding ways of keeping the people in their homes. Sheila Bair, who chairs FDIC, is right when she criticizes the $700 billion rescue plan for not addressing foreclosures.

Many economists argue that financial innovation, and the quick reallocation of capital that it promoted, was one reason why America's productivity accelerated in the mid 1990s. Innovation is always welcome, but because of its unknowns it must be matched by rigorous oversight. To the contrary, however, regulation has been reduced rather than strengthened. It was a very bad decision to do away with marking-to-market the banks' toxic waste, as was voted into US law in early October 2008 by tying it to the Troubled Asset Relief Act (TARA) which authorized the $700 billion handout.

Accounting standards setters have been arm-twisted into relaxing rules that force banks to be honest. The European Union lost no time in following up with bending the marking-to-market rules of IFRS, and on 20 October 2008 Shinsei's chairman also called for emergency change in Japanese accounting rules. Instead of increasing transparency, cooking the books is on the way to becoming the government-authorized universal practice.

* * *

Had this book been written even a few months ago, its central theme would have been that *credit* is what the crisis is all about. Today the keyword is *trust*.

With confidence at a very low point, capitalism is left without capital and this is hitting the real economy like a brick.

The irrational exuberance of living beyond one's means has been made worse by the fact that central banks did not respond to the first alerts about impeding trouble dating back to 2005, and they misjudged the further-out effects of the glut of cheap money. For their part, bank supervisors looked the other way as capital adequacy deteriorated, the liquidity of off-balance sheet instruments and vehicles disappeared, and (in several jurisdictions) the management of big banks seemed no more to be in control of credit allocation and trading – or of risk.

Thales, one of the foremost mathematicians of all times, had said that what one fool could do another fool could, too. This remained to be proved, but 2,500 years after Thales bankers, traders, homeowners, investors, regulators, and the political leadership at large have provided evidence that he was right.

* * *

I am indebted to a long list of knowledgeable people, and of organizations, for their contribution to the research which made this book feasible. Also to several senior executives and experts for constructive criticism during the preparation of the manuscript, Dr Heinrich Steinmann and Dr Nelson Mohler being among the most important contributors.

Let me take this opportunity also to thank Lisa von Fricks for suggesting this project, Keith Povey for seeing it all the way to publication, and Mark Hendy for editing the manuscript. To Eva-Maria Binder goes the credit for compiling the research results, typing the text, and making the camera-ready artwork and index.

Valmer and Vitznau DIMITRIS N. CHORAFAS

Part One
Money

1
The Destruction of the American Dream

1. Smith, Marx, and the debt society

The main theme in Adam Smith's classic *The Wealth of Nations* is *self-interest,* which its author considers to be the underlying motive of social and economic life. "It is not from the benevolence of the butcher, the brewer or the baker that we expect our dinner," Smith wrote, "but from their regard to their own interest."

Indeed, it is the combination of many self-interests of individual entrepreneurs that feeds great cities like London and New York, doing so without any central planning of what should be bought and sold at which price, from where, and why it is essential to have "this" or "that" commodity on the racks. Self-interest is also the basis of market behavior – which is as much political as financial and economic.

"A weakness of all economists," says Dr Roger van Zwanenberg, "is that they fail to make the connection between wealth and power. The early political economists, *à la* Adam Smith, were not fooled. Today, economics is taught without history and without politics, as if it was objective. Result: they fail to understand what is going on."[1]

The Wealth of Nations describes wealth creation in a competitive mercantile economy dominated by the market's invisible hand. This is the concept appropriated by right-wing politicians and economists. By contrast, the left-leaning prefer Smith's *Theory of Moral Sentiments,* which speaks against materialistic desires "of frivolous utility," and states that man has some principles "which interest him in the fortune of others and render their happiness necessary to him, though he derives nothing from it."[2]

This dualism in Adam Smith's thought was missed by Karl Marx when he mounted his formidable challenge to the economic theory of a market economy. Though a brilliant thinker, Marx lived a quite secluded life in London, leading him to the belief that human nature could develop beyond self-interest and therefore capitalism was nothing more than a passing phase in social and economic behavior – a notion disproved by Lenin and his pals in the October Revolution and the regime which impoverished Russia during the seven decades of its reign. Hernando de Soto says:

> [Marx] did not quite grasp that formal property was not simply an instrument for appropriation but also the means to motivate people to create real additional usable value. Moreover, he did not see that it is the mechanisms contained in the property system itself that give assets and the labor invested in them the form required to create capital.[3]

Contrary to Marx's social analysis as well as to Smith's mercantilism, de Soto's thesis is that:

- *Assets* become transcendent, and
- They serve wider social uses when they are exchangeable.

Yes, but which assets? His answer is "property titles," which he considers to be the visible tip of an iceberg consisting of the economic potential of assets. *If* growing property assets is the criterion of social uplift, *then* in its effort to outdo Marxism and defy human nature the Russian communist state proved to be of little service to the town's proletariat and an unmitigated disaster to the peasants.

Neither was the increasingly more complex economy of post-World-War-II communist states able to prosper by following plans from above, established in a way unstuck from day-to-day realities. The Soviet system of command and control did not work, and Gosplan broke at its seams, as I was able to observe in 1969 when I spent time in Moscow and Leningrad lecturing at the Academy of Sciences.[4]

The more complex the global economy became, the more the planners were at a loss:

- What their superiors typically asked them to do was to massage the input to obtain an output they theoretically needed or wanted at any particular time, and
- Their contribution was practically reduced to changing the answers they were getting from plans and mathematical models to please the party machine.

The irony is that, as we will see in this and subsequent chapters, such an unwarranted and futile exercise has found a counterpart in the first years of the twenty-first century in western society. As in Soviet times, with orders "from above" risk managers engaged themselves in the same sort of futility characterized by wishful thinking and disrespect for evidence of mountains of toxic exposure.

One could argue that the Soviet Union was not really a socialist state. Far from being the guardian of theoretical socialist doctrine Lenin, or more precisely Trotsky, organized a *coup d'état* which was a workers' and peasants' revolt only in appearance. In fact, it was a takeover.[5]

Neither was Stalin a communist luminary; if anything he was a right-wing dictator educated in a religious seminary, who condemned to exile and death millions of people. But Cuba has undoubtedly been a laboratory of communist doctrine for 50 years and life was and is not much better than in the Soviet realm; as for the North Koreans, they are dying of famine under the iron hand of their communist state.

In addition, let no one think that if socialism failed in economic terms it has at least been a powerful humanistic solution. Here is what Golda Meir says about the latter:

> One day, weeks after the [Yom Kippur] war, I phoned Willy Brandt, who is much respected in the Socialist International, and said: I have no demands to make to anyone, but I want to talk to my friends. For my own good I need to know what possible meaning socialism can have when not a single socialist country in all of Europe was prepared to come to the aid of the only democratic nation in the Middle East.[6]

All this criticism of socialism is not of course a eulogy of capitalism, because capitalism too has hit the rocks because of its excesses. Dean Atcheson, secretary of state under Harry Truman, once said that capitalism cannot afford another crisis like that of the 1929 Great Depression. If it happens, Atcheson pointed out, it will be the end of capitalism. We are precisely at that point.[7]

As the severe credit and banking crisis of 2008/2009 documents, working in unison George W. Bush and Alan Greenspan made an experiment to see if Atcheson was right. At the roots of the twenty-first century's crisis[8] of what is still but incorrectly called "capitalism" is the huge and fast growing level of debt by:

- Governments,
- Companies, and
- Families.

Whether we talk of federal, state, corporate (particularly those of banks), or family balance sheets, assumed financial obligations far exceed real assets. Luca Pacciolo's famous principle of balancing assets and liabilities has been awfully skewed to the latter's side, a situation which is made worse day after day, month after month, and year after year. When it crashed on 15 September 2008 Lehman Brothers, the big Wall Street investment bank:

- Had "assets" of $640 billion, of which about 40 percent were believed to worth between 5 and 20 cents to the dollar, and
- Had a long list of liabilities that were real, with debt at the 96 percent level and equity at about 4 percent, which was consumed in no time.

Enlightened people have foreseen this course of events and rung the alarm bell.

Bernard Baruch wrote:

> We must look upon the crucial trial we now face as, in essence, a test of our ability to govern ourselves.

He added that:

> This test of our ability to govern ourselves is really threefold.
>
> First, it is a test of values, of what things we will give up in order to make other things secure,
>
> Second, it is a test of our reasoning powers, of whether we have the wit to think our problems through to an effective solution,
>
> Third, it is a test of self-discipline, of our ability to stand by our values, and see our policies through, whatever the personal cost.[9]

Let's face it. Our debt society has flunked all three of Baruch's tests. Red ink aside, its values are wanting, its ethics dubious, its reasoning powers have been diminished and its self-discipline has taken a leave. In America, family debt is now equal to the gross domestic product (GDP[10] – see Chapter 7), in many cases corporate debt is unprecedented, and national debt is ever increasing, taking along with it to the stratosphere current-account deficits (created by a negative trade balance). By contrast, savings are nowhere to be seen. It is so much easier to spend than to save.

2. Termites in the basement

We live at the change of an epoch. Whatever Adam Smith wrote in the eighteenth century and Karl Marx in the nineteenth was marked by the realities of a predominantly real-assets society, which has ceased to exist. Today, using the names Smith and Marx, as well as their concepts, is inappropriate because our *debt society* has little regard for real assets:

- One can find its beginning in the mid 1920s with the institutionalization of private credit,[11] and

- Its only precedent, and bible, are the events of 1929 with the economic and social nightmares they brought along.

"I awoke to find myself at the bottom of a pit without any known means of scaling its sheer sides," said Marrinner Eccles, a successful banker of the 1920s who was able to save his institution from bankruptcy, and under President Roosevelt became one of the best chairmen ever of the Federal Reserve. His father had taught him that: "A business, like an individual, could remain free ... only if it kept out of debt, and the West itself could remain free only it kept out of debt to the East."[12]

Alert analysts point out that one of the reasons the credit and banking crisis of 2008/2009 is lasting so long is the nature of the previous boom and excesses. Plenty of parties have been borrowing money from one another, each trying to leverage somebody else's liabilities to pocket more in illicit premiums, bonuses, share options, and other "profits." This has been true all the way:

- From homeowners buying houses they could not afford,
- To bankers buying and selling complex debt products they did not understand, and
- To investors running after high yields offered by junk debt instruments without measuring their risk.

In the end many people and companies got burned. Banks twice so, because even when they borrowed money from the market the lenders were often hedge funds, conduits or structured investment vehicles (SIVs) which themselves had borrowed money from credit institutions. Then, when banks got into trouble, they restricted their lending, making life more difficult for other banks, businesses, and consumers:

- Causing companies to cut their spending, and
- Making it harder for families to repay their debts and save their homes from foreclosure.

Post-mortem, some economists said that this explains the absence of bargain-hunting in debt markets and other sectors of the economy. Investment-grade debt might look attractive on a level test view if all one has to worry about is the risk of default, but at present most market players, and investors generally, simply cannot afford for things to get worse before they get better. They may be forced into repaying loans and having to put their assets on fire sale.

Market actors, whether professionals or consumers, have not learned a lesson from their exuberance in the overheated stockmarket of the late 1990s, where many lost plenty of money. Instead, they continued with the habit of amassing debt and of entering into dubious investments. Greenspan's dramatic drop in interest rates, as well as the banks' rock-bottom mortgage rate and waiving of equity requirements, enabled people to finance newly bought homes without thinking about tomorrow.

- The citizens were no longer living on what they could afford.
- They were living the lifestyle they dreamed of, and thought they deserved.

This has been the nirvana of the American dream reached by miracle through liabilities. To do so, many consumers pushed themselves over their debt limit, but they still did not reduce spending – which the government did not want them to do since it would have caused a dramatic slowing of the economy. It is not without reason that the years of the G.W. Bush Administration have been called the "Reign of Error."

Yet, it should not have been difficult to appreciate that a Second Great Depression would bring the United States to its knees, and that it might be difficult to recover without the stimulus of another world war, as the First Great Depression demonstrated. In addition, under the watch of George W. Bush, supposedly heading a conservative Republican government, the US has been in a borrowing and spending mood.[13]

This has had its aftereffect. According to some estimates, foreign interests own about $9 trillion of American financial assets, including 13 percent of all stock, 13 percent of government agencies, and 27 percent of corporate bonds. Fannie Mae, the government-sponsored agency for home mortgages, borrowed about a third of its investment funds from outside the United States.[14]

Rarely was a voice raised to say that getting deeper and deeper into debt was doing serious, long-term damage to the American economy, and that the day of reckoning could not be far away. Yet, as far back as the late 1980s Charles L. Schultze, former chairman of President Carter's Council of Economic Advisors, had warned that deficits were not so much like "the wolf at the door" as *termites in the basement,* eating away gradually at the economy and at American living standards.[15]

Playing host to termites is no policy fulfilling a social dream. It is as bad as loaning a pair of crutches to somebody to move himself a hundred yards further towards a precipice; the precipice of market panic.[16] "A panic exposes the essence of banking as no lecture, book, or diagram can do," says James Grant.[17] – but not all panics are the same.

The panic of 2008/2009 has been different than those of 1837, 1857, 1873, and 1907. The nineteenth-century and first twentieth-century panics in America were characteristic of an economy swinging forward, by creating more and more real assets. Therefore the intervention of bankers known for being serious, like J.P. Morgan and George Baker, was sufficient to save the day.

By contrast, in 2007 and thereafter it is a debt economy which collapsed, and the easy way out has been that of creating more debt. Confronted with over $500 billion of losses from loans and writedowns,[18] which increased by roughly 50 percent when on 15 September 2008 Lehman went bankrupt, and with a Basel I capital base of 8 percent, which proved to be awfully inadequate and illiquid, global banks found themselves hanging from a string. Their survival depended primarily on central banks' generosity (Chapters 9 and 10) and secondarily on severely tightened lending to keep whatever capital they could put their hands on as they:

- Saw their equity crashing to a third or a fifth of its value,
- Borrowed from Sovereign Wealth Funds (SWFs),
- Went hat-in-hand to their shareholders, and
- Dumped into the coffers of central banks – the Federal Reserve, the Bank of England, the European Central Bank and a couple of others, a great lot of their toxic waste.

Collectively this has added up to a vicious cycle of moral risk with plenty of unwanted aftereffects. No wonder therefore that the *Grandfather Economic Reports*, which compile and popularize data on US indebtedness, admit: "We have become a nation of debt-junkies, living beyond our means more than ever before." To put it mildly, this is a stark antithesis to the American Dream – and the political leadership is responsible for it.

3. The first thing in credit is character

While it is too early to draw final lessons from the ongoing turmoil in financial markets, the events associated with the banking and credit crisis of 2008/2009 have demonstrated that the risk of global contagion rises with greater integration and interdependence of the banking industry. With financial globalization, like the one experienced in the last 20 years, problems can spill across borders rapidly:

- The diffusion of risk can happen in an unpredictable manner, and
- The aftershocks of a big credit crisis may quickly lead to systemic instability.

Contrary to what the pros have preached, that financial globalization has enough thrust to take care of headwinds, the 2008/2009 crisis demonstrated that economic advantages, including the ability to transfer credit and credit exposure, can be realized only if they are accompanied by a rigorous system able to:

- Assess,
- Monitor, and
- Control credit quality.

This requires timely and decisive risk management able to cope with the new requirements posed by the international financial markets as these evolve. A "must" is the factual and documented assessment of creditworthiness: up to a point the 2008/2009 crisis has been due to fake AAA credit ratings of junk bonds and collateralized debt obligations (CDOs).

There is no better example of the need for reliable credit standards than Dr J.P. Morgan's statement to the investigation conducted in 1912 by the US Congress into the Money Trusts. During his deposition, Morgan uttered his famous remark about credit:

- "Is not commercial credit based primarily upon money or property?" Samuel Untermyer (the legal counsel of the Congressional committee) asked him.
- "No, sir; *the first thing is character,*" Morgan replied (emphasis added).
- "Before money or property?" Untermyer insisted.
- "Before money or anything else. Money cannot buy it," Morgan said.

Unconvinced, Untermyer came back to the same question, which Morgan answered even more emphatically: "Because a man I do not trust could not get money from me on all the bonds in Christendom." In different terms, the basis of credit is *character* – or what Socrates called *virtue*, which the ancient philosopher defined as knowledge that cannot be taught.

Character is not only important in lending but also in general management; in being in charge of the entity under one's watch. There is evidence that bank CEOs do not really understand, much less care about, what they are doing. Two different 2008 audits documented that chief executives comprehend only a part of the business they lead, and practically nothing of complex derivative financial instruments. Both audits centered on what went wrong with Société Générale's[19] internal control, a damning account of:

- CEO aloofness,
- Weak procedures,
- Poor implementation, and
- Bad management.

One of these audits was performed by the bank's own inspectorate, which placed the blame squarely on the trader's line managers and superiors for the gaping hole of €4.9 billion ($7.4 billion at the time) in losses revealed in early 2008. The internal investigation found no evidence that top managers were aware of allegedly fraudulent or concealed positions, and it established several reasons why Jerome Kerviel's (the trader's) superiors did not detect his highly risky trades.

Commissioned by Société Générale to evaluate the bank's control procedures, PricewaterhouseCoopers (PwC) did the second audit. Its conclusion was that the fast-growing and highly profitable Delta One team of traders, to which Kerviel belonged, regularly flouted the rules and colluded with each other to cover up their tracks. As PwC put it:

- This trading team developed a strong entrepreneurial culture based on trust,[20] and
- Its rapid growth was accompanied by the emergence of unauthorized practices, with limits regularly exceeded and results smoothed or transferred between traders.

Moreover, according to PwC the bank's internal control system was slow to react and remediate the most sensitive issues, despite the fact that some of the weaknesses in internal control had been identified by internal audit as an area in need of correction. To make matters worse, control functions were split between different units, and procedures were insufficiently explicit. This made it difficult for control staff to understand the significance of identified discrepancies, said the PwC audit. In a nutshell:

- That's the image of the go-for-broke bank twenty- first century style, and
- It's a ghastly culture of destruction of the institution itself and of its clients.

There are plenty of reasons why in mid May 2008 Dr Horst Köhler, Germany's president and former head of the International Monetary Fund (IMF), publicly held the global financial market and its players responsible for the severe banking and credit crisis, saying that it has become a monster chargeable for:

- Massive destruction of assets, and
- Grotesque remuneration of its executives.

Köhler has not been alone in that critique. Kenneth Griffin, founder and head of the $20 billion Citadel Investment Group, adds that international finance has been functioning on the judgment of 29-year-old kids straight out of business school who control the capital markets of America.[21] The reference to age, however, distorts the sense of the problem. Young scientists can have extraordinary accomplishments. The average age of the engineers who built Apollo was just 26, not 60-plus; and the dotcom industry was built by the unconstrained thinking of people in their early to mid-20s. It is unstoppable leverage, in whose chain the 29-year-olds have been cogs, which saw to it that:

- The dotcoms bubble crashed in 2000, wiping out billions in wealth, and
- The subprimes' collateralized mortgage obligations turned on their head at the cost of trillions, leaving the banking industry in tatters.

Young doers don't know what is impossible, and they have less to risk when proposing bold solutions. At the same time they have much less experience in regard to risk control. That is why regulatory rules and limits play such an important role, and these are usually set by men of experience rather than by 29-year-olds.

The men of experience have failed in their job. In January 2008, in an article in *Executive Intelligence Review* (*EIR*), Lyndon LaRouche painted a somber picture by saying:

> [W]e are at a point not of an ordinary crisis, not of a financial crisis, not of a mere depression, but of a global breakdown crisis, centered in the trans-Atlantic community, especially the English-speaking trans-Atlantic community, which will radiate, if it's not stopped, to bring every part of the world into a *general breakdown of their respective social systems*.[22]

A torrent of public money thrown to the market by central banks has delayed that day of reckoning, but nobody can assure us that it will not come. The biggest risk today is the loss of confidence in the US government, said one of the American experts interviewed on CNBC on 19 September, 2008 – during the now famous "historic week" on Wall Street. The Yankee economy (section 6) has been turned by incompetent politicians into a State Supermarket (section 7) and Washington has found that once authority is lost it is nearly impossible to regain it.

4. A road toward major banking crises

From July/August 2007 to the "historic week" on Wall Street (mid September 2008) and beyond, market sentiment became increasingly grim. Apart other indicators, risk aversion towards questionable assets has been exemplified by the fact that more than a year after the crisis the prices of junk bonds and home equity loans have implied a default rate consistent with unemployment of around 20 percent rather than the prevailing 6.5 percent in the US – and the rout of the housing market extended to Britain, Ireland, and Spain as well as (to a lesser extent) Italy and France:

- With millions of homeowners having lost their home or being near the day of reckoning, there has been panic in the housing market, and
- Governments, particularly in the US and Britain, proved to be at a loss as to how to stop the housing market from descending into the abyss.

The globalization without limits of the financial industry, which for more than three decades grew like wild cacti, contributed significantly to the panic of 2008/2009. Governments have not been distinguished by their ability to be quick and decisive in righting the balances, by obliging banking firms under their watch to be transparent, and by removing uncertainty about future losses and writedowns.

The last example of sound central bank policies dates back to the early 1990s and it concerns the handling of the Swedish banking crisis. From that same period, however, comes one of the worst examples of central bank indecisiveness, namely that of the Japanese government, which took too long to act.

Hit by the 1990/1991 deep crisis, Japanese banks scaled back their international operations, but this did not avoid a prolonged period of generally negative growth in Japan itself, which was accompanied by a dramatic shrinkage in the Japanese banks' share in international claims. The latter fell from 38 percent in 1990 to less than 8 percent in 2007,[23] in what seemed like a repetition of World War II Japanese gains and losses.

Delays in getting hold of a bad situation and turning it around are against good business sense because, as economic and financial history teaches, not only is panic a distinct possibility but also the frequency of downturns has increased. Practically everybody remembers the year 2000 as a time of great alarm, with bankers and investors rushing to sell dotcom securities with a huge sacrifice of value; 7 years later this has been followed by another ruthless time.

Bernard Baruch wrote:

> Both my failure in whiskey and my success in copper emphasized one thing – the importance of getting the facts of a situation free from tips, inside dope, or wishful thinking. In the search for facts I learned that one had to be as unimpassioned as a surgeon. And if one had the facts right, one could stand with confidence against the will or whims of those who were supposed to know best ... Later in public life I found this rule equally valid and applicable.[24]

Bitter examples abound, not only from the 1920s, which led to the First Great Depression, but also from the 1980s, like the case of Seattle's SeaFirst and Chicago's Continental Illinois, which demonstrated the profound vulnerability of the banking system.

> With Continental Illinois, when you get right down to it, here was a \$40 billion[25] bank with only \$4 billion in deposits [Governor Partee said].[26] The core of the bank was very, very small ... it was the extreme case but it was not that unusual. Citibank has a small core too. Lots of big banks do.[27]

There is evidence that, as the dust of the subprimes and of the CDOs hecatomb started to settle, at least some central bankers and regulators foresaw the coming catastrophe and warned about it; but their call for urgent measures and controls was not heard. One such call came from the Bank for International Settlements (BIS) which repeatedly warned policymakers that they were not paying enough attention to the rapid growth of *leveraging*.

The credit and banking crisis which followed the many excesses and failures in business judgment also confirms the analysis by William White, BIS's chief economist, who has long argued that interest rates were held too low. Cost-free money (let alone living on debt rather than on owned assets) sees to it that leveraging becomes dope – a practice repeated in October/November 2008, and again in March 2009, by the Fed, and the Bank of England.

In an interview he gave to the *Wall Street Journal* on 21 June 2008, George Soros made the point that Greenspan kept interest rates low too long:

> And he did not heed the warnings that lending standards were being lowered, that deceptive practices were being used.[28] He was too much of a market fundamentalist. He believed that if you leave it to markets, everything will be all right. That's initially self-reinforcing, but eventually self-defeating.[29]

In the years which preceded the First Great Depression as well as in the years of Greenspan's watch (particularly after Bush decapitated the Securities and Exchange Commission), virtually all of the American big banks were resting precariously on very small foundations. They

- Operated on a disproportionately tiny core of depositors,
- Diluted their equity with hybrids, mortgage-related securities, and deferred tax assets (DTAs), and
- Featured a huge pool of borrowed money in the liabilities side of their balance sheet.

When the markets turned sour, vulnerability arose quite suddenly. Not only a golden horde of investors but also correspondent banks, who lent the funds on which other banks operated, closed their purses. The market suddenly woke up to the fact that commercial bankers, investment bankers, central bankers, and regulators collectively disregarded the principles of banking, going instead for:

- Rapid asset growth through gearing,
- Concentrations in certain assets and liabilities,
- Increases in mismatches in different commitments, and
- Positions approaching or breaching internal as well as regulatory limits.

All this occurred in spite of the fact there had been early warning indicators: credit rating downgrades, rising debt costs, widening credit default swap (CDSs) spreads, declining equity prices, negative publicity, counterparties requesting additional collateral, correspondent banks decreasing or eliminating their credit lines, and more.

CDS spreads on Wall Street banks remained volatile well after the July/August 2007 crash. Year-on-year, in August 2008 they pushed much higher, having fallen in March after the Federal Reserve extended emergency lending facilities to investment banks. (Reportedly, Morgan Stanley has been monitoring its own CDS spreads to assess the market's perception of its corporate health and if it rose too high it intended to cut back its lending.)[30]

Worst of all, while prior to the 2007 credit crunch the financial industry paid little or no attention to sound banking principles, after the market panic it has been toying with the idea that *capitalism without capital* is the best possible solution. It is hard to find evidence underwriting that assertion, other than the fact that the taxpayer is asked to foot the bill (Chapter 10).

5. "Capital insurance" and zero capital adequacy

Organized by the Federal Reserve Bank of Kansas City, the annual economic conference in Jackson Hole, Wyoming, is one of the foremost annual banking and financial events attended by central bankers, commercial and investment bankers, economists, academics, and journalists from all over the globe. It is a place to exchange thoughts and experiences, as well as listen to research papers supposed to be cutting new ground.

One of the papers presented in the late August 2008 Jackson Hole conference was titled "Rethinking Capital Regulation."[31] In a nutshell, its message is that compelling banks to hold more capital, and most particularly equity, goes against shareholders' interests – because it results in a lower return on equity. Instead, the "solution" is buying *capital insurance*, which will guarantee an infusion of fresh equity during a crisis.

Alan Blinder, of Princeton University and former vice chairman of the Fed, referenced in response to this argument that crises hurt almost everyone. Unless an insurer can be found who generally benefits from a global financial crisis – a species yet to be discovered – the bank expecting to get big money from an insurer when a major crisis hits is in for big surprises.[32] The story of MBIA, Ambac, and the other municipal insurers who guaranteed subprimes and got burned will be repeated at gale force, and at an order of magnitude (or more) greater.[33]

Still, it is always beneficial to listen to contrarian opinions, because they open new horizons that can never be found by following the beaten path. But at the same time such opinions must be documented with evidence that on one hand supports and on the other contradicts one's ideas. Anything short of this, however provocative, may be flawed, leading to loss of trust in the suggested approach.[34]

KRS (Kashyap, Rajan, and Stein, the writers of the aforementioned paper) are not the first to talk about banks holding *zero capital* (or so little that it can be seen only with a magnifying glass). In the 1970s and 1980s Walter Wriston, then the mighty CEO of Citibank (which later became Citigroup), argued that capital was wasted. "The only reason we keep any capital is some of the old fogeys on my board insist that we do," Wriston told Paul Volcker, then president of the New York Fed, in the 1970s.[35]

That's not altogether a positive reference for the KRS zero-capital thesis. While it is true that Wriston was a brilliant person and that under his reign Citi led the other American big banks in terms of growth and diversification, this emphasis on growth at any price, steady expansion, and disregard for the capital basis led Wriston to lend excessively, particularly to Latin America. The result has been a disaster, with:

- Massive losses and write-downs, and
- A capital crisis that brought Citibank to its knees and having to fight for its life.

At the end of the 1980s Wriston had to quit; John Reed took over (adopting capital conservation policies), and in 1990 Jerry Corrigan, who was then the chairman of New York Fed, had to authorize a major capital injection by the son of King Fahd of Saudi Arabia – in a twelfth-hour attempt to save the big American bank for going under. Citibank's stockholders were practically robbed, not rewarded, by a policy of inadequate (let alone zero) capital.

In short, it was those "old fogeys" on Citibank's board who insisted on the need for capital reserves, and not the luminary Walter Wriston, who were right. (When in the late 1960s George S. Moore, then chairman of Citibank, picked Wriston as CEO he gave him some advice: Be brave enough to scare Chase but not so brave as to scare me. Wriston disregarded Moore's advice at the cost of the bank he was heading, of its stockholders, and of his own.)[36]

Neither is there any evidence that Kashyap, Rajan, and Stein examined the case of cross-investments and its aftereffect. AIG, the huge international insurer whose stock descended to the abyss in the week of 8 September 2008 because of its billions in writedowns with subprimes, had also invested $600 million in Fannie Mae and Freddie Mac equity which sold that same week at 6 cents to the dollar. Just think what would have happened if AIG had also provided capital insurance to the two giant mortgage firms and to a couple of global big banks.

The irony goes further than that. Not only are insurance companies not immune to economic slowdown and to red ink, but they are also forbidden from damaging their balance sheet with silly investments and very risky trades. But they don't care. On 16 September 2008, 10 days after having rescued Fannie Mae and Freddie Mac from bankruptcy,[37] the US Treasury found itself obliged to:

- Inject $85 billion in cash into AIG, becoming 79.9 percent owner of the insurer (an amount increased to $173 billion), and
- Guarantee $441 billion of its liabilities (in notional amount).[38]

This adds up to over $600 billion of taxpayers' money to just one company which in March 2009 paid $220 million in "bonuses" to members of its financial products division that brought down the whole firm in flames.[39]

Had AIG provided capital insurance for global banks and had the US Treasury not moved to throw the lifesaver, the world would have been confronted with a full-blown systemic crisis. And had the Treasury moved, then the American taxpayer would have had to pay a couple of trillion dollars to save the day.

Granted, AIG's example was not present when the zero-capital paper was written; there were however other cases. Therefore, if members of the KRS team truly wanted to make a name for themselves, they should have used real-life adversities to inject some *ifs* and *buts* into their *capital insurance* theory. They should also have searched for facts about how banks, particularly big banks, have always sought ways around regulatory rules on capital adequacy.

- The 8 percent of regulatory capital required by the 1988 Basel Capital Accord (Basel I) has been more than halved through the use of hybrid capital, fake AAAs, DTAs, and other junk, and
- The use of off-balance-sheet vehicles, like conduits for commercial paper and structured investment vehicles (SIVs) for securitized mortgages, has been driven largely by the fact that these opaque structures required little or no capital.

Rajan said in the 2008 Jackson Hole conference that since the business of banking is to take on and manage risk, any broad-based attempt to thwart risk-taking is likely to see it reappear in less transparent form. Quite so. Therefore if he and his two colleagues wanted to contribute to the health of the banking industry they should have come up with an effective way to plug that hole, rather than making it wider. The crisis came not because of Basel I capital rules but through:

- Waste and imprudence, and
- Growth for growth's sake,[40] for higher and higher commissions, bonuses and golden parachutes.

Neither is it certain that Kashyap, Rajan, and Stein have paid due attention to the fact that *if* it were practical (it is not), a capital insurance premium is going to be extremely high – because it is akin to taking exposure with people who time and again have proved to be drunk drivers.[41]

Moreover, to be able to pay the high premiums associated with capital insurance and still enjoy fat bonuses, bankers will become even greater risk takers than they have been, thereby creating a vicious cycle. Confronted with all these weaknesses in KRS's logic, one is led to the opinion that rather than being cancelled out capital ratios for banks should be significantly strengthened, with added requirements for:

- Liquidity (Chapter 9), and
- A ceiling to leveraging.[42]

The way Mario Draghi, governor of the Bank of Italy and president of the Bank for International Settlements (BIS) Financial Stability Forum,[43] puts it, today bankers are not hoarding capital because they have hit their minimums. Rather, they are worried that markets will punish them where capital buffers become inadequate. I might add that when the market senses banks have inadequate capital, plenty of leverage and too many illiquid positions, it has no more confidence in those banks' governance. That's the way market discipline works in a regime of free enterprise.

6. Is the Yankee economy too big to fail?

The origin of the word *Yankee* – famous nickname of the New York folk – is Anglo-Dutch. Probably because they were eating plenty of cheese, the first settlers from Holland in New Amsterdam (today's New York) were called "John Cheese" by the English settlers, paraphrased as "Jankese" in broken Dutch. (By contrast, the word *Dixie* has French roots. In Louisiana's 10-dollar bills, the word "Dix" (Ten) was written on the face of the legal tender.[44])

Yankee economy is used in this book as a generic term transcending Adam Smith and Karl Marx, and describing the debt society which defines our way of living. I could as well have used the term "western economy" but the latter often means different things to different people while it has been a deliberate choice to focus on only one specific economic model (and its travails) in this discussion: *the interminable screw of debt*.[45]

Take as first example the American public debt. Contrary to loans taken from banks, funds and foreign governments, a country's public debt is not supposed to be repaid (at least not wholly). Even so, the level of national debt – largely an accumulation of budget deficits, entitlements, and one-tantum events like war bonds or the salvage of Fannie Mae and Freddie Mac – is a significant statistic because:

- It tells a lot about a nation's internal indebtedness relative to gross national product, and
- It has to be served over a long stretch of time, absorbing financial resources that might have gone to infrastructural, educational, and other projects.

Indeed, with so much money thrown left, right, and center through a fire brigade approach, America scarcely builds a new infrastructure or seriously revamps the existing one, investing 2.4 percent of GDP in infrastructural projects as compared with 9 percent in China (albeit from a smaller base). Even on occasions when projects are suggested they are met with outrage by nearby cities, suburbs, and neighborhoods because they disturb the status quo.[46]

The US is not alone in steady budget deficits. Japan, Italy, Greece, France, Belgium, and Canada (to name a few) are on the same track a the Yankee economy. Japan has the dubious honor of being ahead of everybody, with a public debt about 172 percent of GDP. The public debt of Italy and Greece is over 100 percent of GDP. That of France is 68 percent;[47] servicing it absorbs practically all direct personal taxes (not corporate taxes or value added tax) paid by French citizens

American public debt has not yet reached 100 percent of GDP, but with some more Fannies, Freddies,[48] Bears, AIGs, Citigroups, and Banks of America, as well as the repeated interventions and injections of huge amounts of money into the coffers of zombie banks, it might.[49] As of 1 November 2008, American national debt is equal to 80 percent of GDP, to the tune of $11.3 trillion[50] – and if current Yankee deficit policies continue it is projected that it will reach between 230 percent and 240 percent of GDP by 2040, which means that a disaster will befall the nation.

In fact, all of the aforementioned current public debt figures are underestimates because they deliberately don't account for all government commitments. In the case of the US, *if* social security and medicare are included *then* the national debt swallows up to $53 trillions, which corresponds roughly to $175,000 for every American man, woman, and child – an amount which:

- Is totally unmanageable, and
- Continues growing by leaps and bounds because politicians have not the guts to make hard choices.

Quite to the contrary of what they should be, politicians are big spenders. To get re-elected, they spend and spend (the so-called pork barrel) without worrying about the aftereffects on the economy, or even how new commitments are going to be honored. What they fail to recognize is that at the end of the day the options are limited and stark. A booming national debt Yankee style:[51]

- Dumps the current generation's leverage on future generations,
- Destroys the tax system, as high taxes lead the citizen to duck them, and
- Brings the economy to its knees while leaving no money to better the quality of life.

Some economists call the zooming national debt a *fiscal cancer*. In 2008 David Walker, a former head of the US government's internal auditing authority,[52] made it his mission to get the citizens and their leaders to understand and acknowledge the threat, and appreciate the fact that the nation's financial condition is much worse than generally admitted. The same is practically true of all western nations.[53]

(A movie , *I.O.U.S.A.*, financed by Pete Peterson, secretary of commerce in the Nixon Administration and former CEO of Blackstone, brought that message coast-to-coast. The film features interviews with prominent businessmen and officials such as former Federal Reserve chairmen Paul Volcker and Alan Greenspan, as well as former US Treasury secretaries Paul O'Neill and Robert Rubin. Greenspan warns in the movie that the nation cannot continue consuming more than it produces indefinitely. "Without savings, there is no future," he says in the movie, forgetting that his 1 percent interest rate has been a monster enemy of savings.)

As if these woes were not enough, the Yankee economy is confronted with the meltdown of the banking system, which is adding to the questions of solvency. To be able to see through that mess, former Treasury secretary Hank Paulson assembled a "Plunge Protection Team" (PPT), but answers about a strategy for coming up from under have been loaded at the liabilities side of the balance sheet:

- Greenspan piloted the Yankee economy onto the rocks,
- Bernanke opened the gates to big failed bank nationalizations,[54] and
- Paulson tried to pull the US economy up from its shoestrings by betting on mountains of new debt, and by paying lip service to regulation.

It looks as if the Bush Administration had been living on the hope that nothing would hit it, which resembles the five-year credit default swaps (CDS) spreads of AIG on 15/16 September 2008. As Figure 1.1 shows, CDS spreads rose from trivial in January 2008 to 500 basis points (5 percent) in mid-September and then to 3,500 bp (35 percent) within a couple of days. The panic also spiked the CDS spreads of Morgan Stanley and Goldman Sachs,[55]

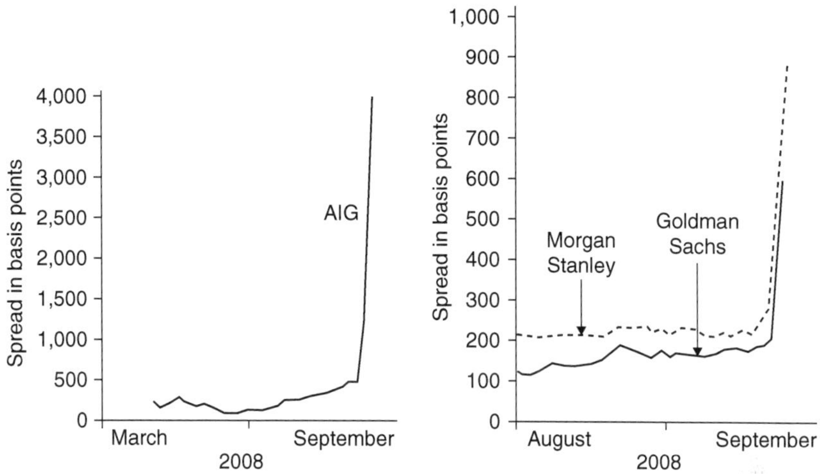

Figure 1.1 Spread of 5-year credit default swaps in Wall Street's "historic week."

followed by a run on their equity. (Credit default swaps are discussed in Chapter 5.)

Bankruptcy was the foregoing conclusion for AIG, until after initial reluctance the US Treasury and Federal Reserve poured in over half a trillion dollars to stabilize the troubled global insurer. But who will come up with at least $28 trillion (corresponding to two years of US GDP[56]) to stabilize the Yankee economy?

7. The State Supermarket

Debt is not reaching for the stars and deficits are not inflated simply because of big spending projects to please political friends, and myriads of handouts in entitlements. The *State Supermarket* of the debt society is topping that with its saving of companies from their own mistakes.

"[This] was not supposed to be part of the government's job description," says Peter Goodman:

> [It] was the sort of thing that happened in other shores, where sentimental commitments to social welfare trumped sharp-edged competition:
>
> - Using government largess to lift inefficient firms to safety
> - Sparing jobs and limiting pain
> - But keeping their economies from reaching full potential.[57]

Forget the now gone Soviet menace. The State Supermarket is destroying from within the American free enterprise system. Right after the virtual nationalization of the Federal National Mortgage Association and Federal

Home Loan Mortgage Corporation by the US Treasury, Republican senator Jim Bunning put his thoughts this way: "When I opened my newspaper yesterday, I thought that I woke up in France. But no, socialism reigns as master in America.[58]

Right? Wrong. The State Supermarket is not a kind of classical socialism. It is the kid of two strange bedfellows. The one came into timid existence in the early 1930s with the New Deal in the US and got a backbone in 1936 with the Popular Front in France – growing up to become the *nanny state*. The other was born a decade earlier, in the 1920s, with Ponzi games[59] reaching adulthood with bank-to-bank trades in derivative instruments where big institutions turn themselves into mean gamblers.[60]

Working largely for the government, the State Supermarket's priests are the species *Homo bureaucraticus*. That's neither socialism nor communism, at least not according to the books. (To see what is in a true socialist's mind, all one needs to do is read the speeches of Jean Jaurés,[61] the French socialist and humanist.) But it is the model of the State Supermarket that gave birth to a generation of largely corrupt and often incompetent public servants and politicians.

Thanks to their efforts, a great deal of the economy's jobs which made America's strength migrated abroad, automobile and other companies lost their momentum, railroad lines have been uprooted, the infrastructure has been left to perish, and elected leaders are no more as watchful of the economy as they used to be. In addition to all this, in the State Supermarket failure is not an option. Everybody has to "succeed," particularly those who game the system.

Like any salvage plan, the mammoth $700 billion handout that has been aimed to pull up from under big banks and their inept managers is subject to "What is in it for me?" questions. If the government is ready to bring under the State Supermarket's wings one sector of the economy, why not another? Why "them" and not "us"? This sort of request for funds is expanding like an oil spot, and to succeed Barack Obama must have the courage to:

- Say: "No!"
- Put discipline first,
- Assure proper management,
- Establish top priorities, and
- Set a long-term budget path.

It is not possible to do everything at the same time. As Golda Meir put it when elected prime minister of Israel:

> The government cannot do everything all at once. It can't wave a magic wand and meet everyone's demands simultaneously: eradicate poverty without imposing taxes ... develop the economy and still give everyone his due. No government can do all this at one and the same time.

She added:

> In the first place, those among us who are poor mustn't permit themselves to be turned into the passive objects of other people's concern. They must be active in their own behalf.[62]

This evidently includes General Motors, Citigroup, and plenty of others asking for handouts. In addition, those who engineered the Financial Pearl Harbor should be brought to justice and from there to prison. This has happened with the Savings and Loans scams of the late 1980s, but two decades down the line, instead of apt punishment:

- The malfeasants have been protected by the Bush Administration's cronyism, and
- The incompetent have been allowed to reward themselves lavishly, using taxpayers' money for that purpose.

On 9 September 2008, just 48 hours after the US Treasury took over Fannie Mae and Freddie Mac, the giant government-sponsored mortgage institutions, it was stated that their accounting was a house of cards – and that that's what had prompted the Treasury's action.[63]

Over long years, nobody among the supervisory authorities and other government officials seems to have seen that; therefore nobody was "responsible."[64] The road to hell was paved with red ink. Year-on-year, 1 July 2007 to 30 June 2008, Fannie and Freddie had lost $14 billion. Eventually investigations will be launched to find out what went wrong, but the way to bet is that these investigations will focus on the trivia and not on the real culprits. In an interview with Bloomberg news on 9 July 2008, former St. Louis Fed president William Poole made the point about Fannie and Freddie explicitly: "Congress ought to recognize that these firms are insolvent, that it is allowing these firms to exist as bastions of privilege, financed by the taxpayer."[65]

This is not the only evidence on the State Supermarket's irresponsibility. The way an article in *Executive Intelligence Review* had it, after a recent House Agriculture Committee hearing in which he testified on the need to rein in speculation, representative Bart Stupak of the US Congress reported that a "Wall Street warroom" had been set up to block any action by the government against speculation. Later, Stupak told *EIR* that:

- This warroom was being run by investment banking giant Morgan Stanley, and
- The banks and other financial companies were doing all they could to stop any action aimed at ending speculation in food, oil, and other commodities.[66]

The practice resembles that of Generalissimo Chiang Kai-shek, nicknamed "Cash-my-check" by those who really knew him. In 1927 he had used the fear of communism to extort millions from Shanghai merchants. Then, in the late 1930s and early to mid 1940s "Cash-my-check" and his pals used the fear of communism to extract $3.8 billion from the American government[67] (roughly $60 billion in today's money).

Today, it is no more the fear of communism but the fear of the Second Great Depression that is being used to spend public money in order to fill pockets. Those who say "the government can pay" forget that the government (you name it) has practically no money of its own. What it has comes from two sources:

- Taxes, and
- The printing press – which feeds inflation (Chapter 3).

This is a vicious cycle because the State Supermarket is inventive in its tax and spend policies. The Federal Reserve and other western central banks now accept a wide range of collateral, including junk securitized mortgages for loans, giving commercial banks the opportunity to dump their bad paper on the taxpayer in exchange for cash (Chapter 9). This way the government is taking Mickey Mouse money off the banks' books and helps them out of insolvency under the guise of averting a credit crunch – which continues unabated, thank you:

- On 30 April 2008, credit tightening at US banks stood at 30 percent.
- On 31 August 2008, credit tightening had surged to 65 percent.

Additionally, while officially the Fed had brought the interest rate to practically zero, that demanded by banks for giving mortgages stood at 6.5 percent while institutions used public money to rebuild their balance sheets. It does not take a genius to appreciate that one way or another this is going to come to an end, and the end may well be the self-destruction of the American dream.

2
Macroeconomic Challenges

1. A common thread in financial crises

There is a common thread in practically all financial crises, and this is *irrational exuberance*. Even if in 2003–6 interest rates were at rock bottom, it was irrational to believe that house prices would continue going up. In the end homeowners and investors turned themselves into speculators, betting against not only economic theory but also the evidence from past booms and dooms.

Investments other than houses and office buildings might have been more rational in the longer term, but under a short-term perspective they were not appealing to bankers and investors. A good example of a sector of the economy which is hungry for large amounts of money is the oil business, though admittedly in the short to medium term attractive opportunities in the oil sector have been hard to find:

- During the last half dozen years some 70 percent of important oil discoveries were located in complex deep-water and ultra-deep-water areas;
- The cost of oil exploitation has soared while there is tight supply of qualified labor and engineering capacity; and
- The largest holders of reserves in the world like Russia, Saudi Arabia, and Iran remain closed for western exploration, therefore attracting little foreign capital.

To the contrary, large budget deficits in many western countries, Japan and the main up-and-coming emerging markets, coupled with savings which have grown extremely large in developing economies, have produced a glut of money looking for a comfortable home with immediate return. First US real estate then that of other developed countries seemed to be offering that home.

Post-mortem, economists say that China's integration into the global economy – together with a high propensity to save, an undervalued dollar exchange rate, and persistent very low dollar interest rates – created a major money glut. China now has the highest deposits-to-GDP ratio of any major economy, while the United States, Mexico, Brazil, and Russia have the lowest. China's savings policy is also characteristic of other emerging economies, where gross national savings as a share of GDP have grown tremendously, adding to the global money supply (Chapter 3).

In conjunction with the waning, and often absent, bank supervision in America this trend has led to a very rapid increase in leverage and assets among US financial institutions, who made profits by recycling the money of developing economies. Recycling meant buying money in markets that had plenty to offer, rather than depending on deposits for their lending and trading activities. By 2007,

- The ratio of total loans to deposits in the US approached 400 percent.
- By contrast, that ratio ranges between 80 percent in Japan and 110 percent in Britain.

The US, Britain, and Japan also differ in per capita gross domestic product (GDP). This stands at $45,000 in the US, somewhat less than that in Britain, but only $35,000 in Japan. At the other end of the income distribution spectrum, with $2,000 to $3,000 per capita, are China, India, and Indonesia – whose loans-to-deposits ratios stand at 60 percent to 70 percent, below that of Japan.

A loans-to-deposits ratio of 60 percent to 80 percent is affordable without the need for gearing. To the contrary, one of 110 percent, let alone of 400 percent, is not without a pyramid of debt, which significantly weakens the banks' financial staying power. Eventually, both credit institutions and the US and British economies were hit by the headwinds of:

- A credit crisis,
- A banking crisis,
- A rise in defaults,
- A rise in unemployment,
- Falling house prices,
- Falling equity prices, and
- A rise in inflation.

A direct result has been the increase in central bankers' concerns that the intermediation of credit in the financial system would be hampered to such an extent as to bear on the performance of the real economy. In addition, a protracted disruption in the money and credit markets leads to a persistent hoarding of liquidity by banks and further tightening of availability of credit. This exposes vulnerabilities among those households, companies, and nations that are highly indebted or particularly dependent on short-term external financing.

Economists now predict that in the longer term the most negative force of them all will be the weakening of the United States balance sheet because of the massive commitments made by the Treasury and Federal Reserve to save the markets from their self-destruction. With the salvage from bankruptcy of Bear Stearns, Fannie Mae, Freddie Mac, and AIG, plus the $700 billion put at the Treasury's disposal to buy toxic waste and lift other financial institutions, the US government debt has been ballooning to stratospheric heights (Chapter 1). Critics say:

- Central banks are at present inflating another credit bubble;
- They may be saving the economy from short-term disaster, but they are bringing nearer the next big crisis.

Some economists suggest that, added to the spending spree of George W. Bush – from Iraq to the economic stimulus at home – this spike in debt will have detrimental macroeconomic effects on America. And *as if* the aforementioned uncertainties were not enough, there is the new US fund that will buy mortgage-backed securities in order to "support the market." The first purchase will be $5 billion, but this is an open-ended commitment and the sky is the limit. It will be hard to stop such purchases from setting a disturbing precedent: *If* the government can buy mortgages, *then* why not credit-card debts, car loans, or any other receivables whose value has sunk?

Neither does it help that financial instruments are now so complex that it is very hard even to guess about their real value, let alone that of the whole bank, which is partly responsible for the fact that in late 2008 banks suddenly found themselves in a state of borderline insolvency. The fire-brigade intervention of the Treasury secretary has got mixed reviews. Investment and commercial bankers who were quick to grasp the lifesaver saluted it as a "giant step." A number of economists, however, expressed exactly the opposite opinion:

- Characterizing the government's torrent of red ink as the worst possible solution, and
- Predicting that not only the US but also the world is facing a macroeconomic nightmare with Japanese-type stagflation.

In two words, this was the west's economic picture as 2008 came to an end, and therefore the central bankers' dilemma: their mandate for price stability and sound economic policy versus doing something to please the markets and their players, whose definition suddenly became very flexible. First, not without reason, it was the commercial banks' fate that attracted the reserve banks' attention; then investment banks were added to the list, and with them mortgage outfits and insurance companies. But on 18 September 2008, the Fed said that it will help money funds in their redemption woes, while homeowners are waiting in the wings; and a month later in an obscure statement the Fed hinted that hedge funds, too, might qualify for good money sometime later.

2. Macroeconomic challenges: the macromarkets

The salient macroeconomic challenge for the Obama Administration is to put the American economy back on its feet. In a moment of frankness during the 15 November 2008 G20 international economic conference in Washington, President Bush admitted that he had agreed to the $700 billion rescue plan for financial institutions (Chapter 10) only after being told the nation was at risk of falling into "a depression greater than the Great Depression."[1]

The Washington conference's communiqué (Chapter 9) reflected on this statement. Under the heading "Actions Taken And To Be Taken," it stated that: "Against this background of deteriorating economic conditions worldwide, we the 21 participating nations agreed that a broader policy response is needed, based on closer macroeconomic cooperation ..." It also brought into the picture the IMF, "given its universal membership and core macrofinancial expertise ..."[2]

This has been a sensible approach because the deep banking and credit crisis of 2008/2009 has practically hit all countries. However, the communiqué of the Washington conference also had weaknesses, and Chapter 9 explains why. One of them is the lack of a definition of financial institutions with an inordinate systemic risk (Chapter 6), including how to:

- Redress them in the near term, and
- Effectively supervise and control them in the longer term.

The variables that affect a business entity like a credit institution are both endogenous and exogenous. The endogenous ones are generated and (up to a point managed) inside the institution's system; such is the case of risk appetite and leverage. Those that are exogenous emanate from the environment, to a large measure escape the reach of the bank's management (even if the institution is affected by them), and are the subject of central-bank comments and projections.

The December 2007 *Monthly Bulletin of the European Central Bank* commented as follows on euroland's exogenous macroeconomic variables:

> In the Governing Council's view, the risks surrounding [the] outlook for economic growth lie on the downside. They relate mainly to the potential

for a broader impact from the ongoing reappraisal of risk in financial markets on financing conditions and confidence and on world and euro area growth, possible further oil and commodity price rises, as well as concerns about protectionist pressures and possible disorderly developments owing to global imbalances.

The *Bulletin* further noted references that:

- Fiscal policy assumptions are based on national budget plans in the individual euro area countries, and
- With regard to short-term interest rates ... *market expectations*[3] are derived from forward rates, reflecting a snapshot of the yield curve.

As the reader will appreciate from this quotation, the macroeconomic landscape is made up not only through government action, such as monetary policy and interest rate decisions of the central bank, but also by factors which affect, and are in turn affected by, the *macromarkets*. Under this heading come, among other issues, market-implied interest rates, currency exchange rates, stock indices, and bond futures, as well as all sorts of derivatives. Though these instruments and their markets are diverse, they have at least two things in common:

- Their *macro* dimension, and
- Their ability to sidetrack prudential regulation.

Among themselves, the macromarkets are large enough to accommodate many investors. But there is a significant difference between maintaining momentum in them and gaining momentum in them. After a downturn or profitless period, each big player's size is a hindrance to regaining momentum. Moreover, momentum must be gained with profits commensurate to the risks being taken, of which there are plenty.

Additionally, while at least theoretically longer-term trends in financial markets are ordinarily underpinned by macroeconomic fundamentals, in practical terms trading, hedging, and speculative activities play a most important role in driving short-term trends – including volatility. Even if unexpected consequences are short-lived, the vulnerability to shocks and potential for disruption:

- Significantly increases, and
- Alters the premises under which a given position has been taken.

Investors can improve their prognostication by studying the most likely behavior of macroeconomic factors and trends. But to improve their accuracy investors need to learn hard lessons by examining analytically what has succeeded and what has failed in macroeconomic policy, and which forces have opposed monetary policy and fiscal policy initiatives.

The Japanese bubble of 1990/1991 and subsequent 18 years is an often-quoted example of policies that went astray. While no two bubbles and their background factors are the same, it is not unlikely that the analysis of one of them provides valuable insight in studying another. There are, for instance, several similarities between the woes that hit the Japanese economy in the early 1990s and those that damaged the American economy in 2008/2009 – from the causes of the economic downturn to the subsequent dysfunctioning of the banking system:

- With regard to economic downturn, in both cases the financial industry was more concerned with maximizing profits than with the health of its balance sheet, and
- After the bubble burst, both banking industries were bent on restructuring their balance sheets rather than offering public service, making the easing of monetary policy ineffectual.

Four and a half decades after WWII ended the Japanese central bank and government confronted a different set of questions from those dominating the post-war years. Their priority became to stop deleveraging from gaining momentum and wrecking the economy. For this they used conventional macroeconomic tools which proved to be ineffectual:

- Cutting interest rates to nearly zero, and
- Increasing public spending to unprecedented levels to give the economy a shot in the arm.

Because, like old soldiers, traditional thinking never dies, it is not surprising that economic history repeated itself when in 2008/2009 in America the Fed employed the interest rate medicine, while banks (and to a lesser extent households) made it their priority to regain financial health. Credit institutions slashed lending, leading to a significant credit crunch that has not been solved by central banks' monetary easing and liquidity injection. To the contrary:

- The more the Fed cut interest rates,
- The higher went the overnight interbank lending rate, as well as the mortgage rate charged to homeowners.

The fact that positive effects from the central bank's easing were nowhere to be seen where it counted is an object lesson taught by the credit crunch experience. When the banking sector is concerned primarily with its own wounds, to avoid bankruptcy, banks don't act any more as financial intermediaries and much of the classical notions in macroeconomics becomes irrelevant. This was observable in the Japanese government's borrowing and spending, which has nearly quadrupled the national debt but did not move the Japanese economy.

By contrast, a more positive lesson to learn from Japan's effort to regain economic power is that by mobilizing fiscal policy it kept its problems within its borders, using the sharp increase in national debt as an alternative to further weakening the yen and harnessing foreign demand. This was, however, only one country's woes. If all countries affected by the credit crunch in 2007/2008 tried to export their way out of recession, they would export the very ills they were confronting at home.

The macroeconomic problems described in the foregoing examples carry with them social and political risks. Political instability could lead to legal, fiscal, and regulatory changes all the way to the reversal of globalization's effects. At the same time, a country's inability to service its external debt position raises the risk of import and exchange controls. Moreover, a country that is heavily dependent on its commodity and natural resource exports becomes vulnerable to lower prices and other factors weakening the global economy when asset bubbles unwind (section 5).

3. Macro-prudential analysis[4]

A tool integrating different perspectives in targeting financial stability is known as *macro-prudential analysis*. Its aim is to provide integrative approaches to macro- and microeconomic studies, as well as experimentation aimed at measuring the ability of the banking system to withstand shocks. The interest in macro-prudential analysis has been increased by the costly banking crises of the 1980s, 1990s, and early twenty-first century, which revealed the need to examine:

- The conditions created by bubbles,
- The implications connected to the credit cycle, and
- The risk absorption capacity of the banking system.

Since 2000, the European System of Central Banks (ESCB) has been carrying out a macro-prudential analysis on a regular basis, including the production of macro-prudential indicators. The latter consist of data that gauge macroeconomic developments, including the financial situation of firms and households, as well as, most evidently, conditions prevailing in financial markets at large, and in the banking sector in particular. The goal is that of:

- Assessing the stability of the financial system, and
- Describing threats to it that could result from common shocks affecting either many or all financial institutions at the same time.

Sources of risk can also materialize through turbulence in financial markets, infrastructural reasons, and the aftermaths of failure of one or more major counterparties that propagate through the system. The macro-prudential studies of ECB also include a number of forward-looking indicators, aiming at capturing expected outlook for key institutions over the short to medium term. An example is the distance to default of the major players in the banking sector.

Among key factors in assessing possible external macroeconomic sources of risk are market fragility and the prevailing situation of the banking system. This is being studied through backward-looking indicators, often based on income statements and balance sheets, a reverse-engineering approach. One of the objectives of this exercise is to capture possible internal fragilities like:

- Inadequate provisioning,
- Low capital buffers, or
- Insufficient risk management skills and tools.

Moreover, the likelihood of instability in the banking industry is examined by identifying the most probable transition channel for future shocks to the banking system. Examples are significant exposures to credit risk, interest rate risk, and foreign exchange risk. The risk of contagion also includes the likely aggravation of assumed exposure should a liquidity crisis in one financial market segment spread to another.

More recently, particularly as a result of the severe credit crunch, central bankers and economists have added other risk factors – such as cyclical and countercyclical credit events. In the background of this enlargement in factors of exposure lies the global repricing of risk in the credit market, which started in July/August 2007 and has been more severe and longer-lasting than recent previous cases of market turbulence. This first resulted in material income and investment losses for banks, leading to:

- Tighter credit availability, and
- Increased risk of downturn in the global credit cycle.

Classical economic theory suggests that banks protect themselves against financial consequences of normal credit cycle fluctuations by including a premium in their lending rates, and by making impairment charges. This is too simplistic however in an environment where bank loans are widely used as collateral for asset-backed securities. In this case, a sudden increase in corporate default rates and household delinquencies may well have unexpected implications for the financial performance of credit institutions.

Central bankers are also worried by the fact that traditional approaches to the credit cycle simplify, and therefore abstract from, complex channels of monetary transmission. Therefore, they are providing an incomplete picture focusing much more on the expected credit and income losses of banks than on the unexpected. Yet events in the long leg of the risk distribution play the most important role in terms of credit market disruptions in a deleveraging cycle:

- As expectations of increased default probabilities rise, they contribute to a widening of credit spreads and a lowering of the market value of securitized credit products; while
- To the extent that the positions of banks and investors are incompletely hedged (which is by no means the exception) they face higher collateral requirements and eventually forced liquidations.

As far as mortgage-backed securities (MBS) are concerned, residential as well as commercial, the reason that the macroeconomic consequences are likely to be much bigger than those suggested by classical economics is that many of these losses will be borne by banks and other leveraged financial institutions that hold approximately half of all outstanding mortgage debt – at least in America. And such losses are never really spread evenly.

Furthermore, the scale of income erosion or outright losses for banks that may result from the financial sector's deleveraging depends on many factors, including the degree of leverage not just in the system but at each individual institution. A role is also played by the extent of spillover to other markets, and whether the process of adjustment takes place in an orderly fashion.

There exists, therefore, no simple answer to the question: for how long will writeoffs and writedowns dampen lending? The response is further conditioned by how easily will banks be able to rebuild their capital, and which strategy they will follow in response to weaker balance sheets, as well as credit demand in the globalized economy – including emerging markets.

With the ability to raise money in the debt markets severely restricted because of the credit crisis, emerging market banks and companies could struggle to roll over between $110 billion and $150 billion of maturing debt. Not only corporates and banks but also governments in emerging markets are highly leveraged without cash to fall back on. Prices of Argentina's credit default swaps, a gauge of credit risk, rose to their highest ever level after the country's 2001 bankruptcy, and Argentina is once again on the sick list of countries prone to fail.

As of November 2008, macroeconomic signals from the bond and loans markets indicate there will be defaults. Countries, banks and other companies which accumulated plenty of debt before the credit crisis are likely to be among the casualties in a climate where even an apparently investment-grade institution like Lehman Brothers was quickly forced into default.

The reader should also notice that banks are not the only institutions suffering from excesses like the subprimes debacle. The insurance industry is exposed to severe credit problems as investors, guarantors, and providers of capital. Because they are large institutional investors, insurers may hold mortgage-backed securities as well as issues by monolines like MBIA or Ambac – which also means that insurers can be exposed as providers of insurance coverage.

As guarantors, insurers may find themselves confronted with large losses because of having underwritten mortgage guaranty policies, provided financial guaranty insurance policies, or offered directors and officers errors and omissions insurance policies to mortgage and other banks which went to the wall. Legal risk is usually a very expensive proposition. Over and above that, insurers holding subprime products in their portfolio are faced with writedowns with the result that their treasury is significantly affected.

4. Effect of the credit crunch on macroeconomics

The 2008/2009 crisis started with the earthquake of the subprimes, and it revealed its toxicity when the shadow banking systems of structured investment vehicles and conduits started to unravel. In September and October 2007, two months after the crisis began, the equity market was rising and it continued doing so for another month, though by the end of the year it had started losing weight and it nosedived from July to October 2008.

Yet equity prices were not the main concern of the markets. *Credit* was the real macroeconomic earthquake. It needs no explaining that the credit system melted down no matter how much money central banks threw to the markets for liquidity purposes.

This lender-of-last-resort liquidity did not help the main street, as small and medium enterprises were deprived of access to credit, finding it difficult to meet their payrolls and pay their suppliers. It did not help big banks either, even if these were the intended beneficiaries. In March 2008 Bear Stearns lost its liquidity in days, obliging the Fed to extend its support to systematically important investment banks because of their huge exposure to credit default swaps (CDSs).

The effect of the Fed's action, however, was short-lived. Even this did not prevent a run on other US investment banks given concerns about their solvency. Lehman Brothers collapsed; Merrill Lynch might have faced the same fate had it not been bought by Bank of America; the pressure moved to Morgan Stanley and to Goldman Sachs. Leveraged institutions that were both illiquid and quite likely insolvent like Fannie Mae, Freddie Mac, and AIG were taken over by the US government:

- In violation of free-market principles, and
- In the name of avoiding systemic risk.

But the credit crunch did not ease, because the crisis has been broad and deep and a global issue. Apart from the United States, two other examples underline that message. One is from Asia, where in August 2008 one of the region's largest banks reported a negative earnings surprise because of its exposure to CDOs and SIVs. The other instance is from Europe, whose banking system started melting down in August/September 2008, slightly over a year after the beginning of the credit earthquake. Funding pressures tightened the screw:

- The European Central Bank's auction of three-month loans on 24 September was more than three times oversubscribed, and
- After the 3-month euro interbank offered rate (Euribor) surged to a record high the ECB found itself obliged to make additional funds available to banks through to the end of the year.

The large majority of European financial institutions have not been originators and distributors of subprimes, Alt-As, and other poisonous mortgages. In spite of this, however, many experienced huge losses and many more are at risk of sharp losses because of the toxic US securitized products they bought in the go-go years 2003 to 2007. They are also hit by:

- A massive increase in leverage following aggressive risk-taking, and
- A severe liquidity crunch exacerbated by a dollar shortage.

Both are examples of poor governance. Other woes include the bursting of domestic housing bubbles; household and corporate defaults in the recession; big loans to Russian oligarchs; and large exposures to the Baltic states and Iceland as well as southern Europe, where housing and credit bubbles were financed in foreign currencies through the carry trade.

Big names in European banking found themselves on the sicklist and had to be rescued by governments to avoid bankruptcy. Bankers and plenty of investors had significantly underestimated both the breadth and the depth of the credit bubble, as well as its consequences. Many decisions made in boardrooms away from the market place rewarded financial manipulation instead of sound business practices. Excesses, greed, and corruption on Wall Street passed on to the European landscape, causing a situation affecting every citizen. Just as pervasively, market sentiment was becoming depressed. A September 2008 poll of global fund managers by Merrill Lynch found risk appetite to be at its lowest level in over a decade.

Beyond the European financial industry's overleveraged balance sheets, an estimated $1.4 trillion of bank debt was falling due in Europe in the fourth quarter of 2008 and in 2009, just as bondholders had received their first big blow of the crisis thanks to Lehman's bankruptcy. Banks in Iceland, Ireland, Scandinavia, and Spain had been highly dependent on the wholesale markets and analysts suggested some of them might find it difficult to roll over their obligations – with Iceland being the first bankruptcy victim.

A mid-2008 IMF study argued that the pain of deleveraging (section 5) would be felt more keenly in "Anglo-Saxon markets," because highly leveraged investment banks exacerbate credit bubbles. But even if the news from the banking industry had been bleak, not only in the two shores of the Atlantic but also all the way to Russia, an outright depression was still unlikely.

This is by no means certain. A great deal depends on whether the rout of the global banking industry and the weakening of the American, European, and Asian economies turns out to be much more severe than suggested by evidence up to the end of October 2008. All counted, there is real and present danger to financial stability, defined as the condition in which the financial system comprised of:

- Central banks,
- Capital markets,
- Other financial markets,
- Financial intermediaries, and
- Market infrastructures

continues functioning or starts falling apart. The big question is for how long the global financial system will be capable of withstanding severe shocks and of avoiding dangerous imbalances getting out of hand. A criterion of the robustness of financial stability is the system's ability to mitigate the likelihood of disruptions which impair the market's functioning or lead some sectors to a full stop. This can be best observed in the longer term.

Avoiding a disastrous outcome requires not only the identification of risks and vulnerabilities as well as the steady monitoring of inefficiencies in allocation of capital, pricing of risk, and risk control, but also a thorough understanding of what went wrong, in order to establish policies and procedures able to prevent similar shocks from having a disruptive impact. Also, and most importantly, a meaningful and rigorous strengthening of regulations and control, including a powerful model for reliable risk measurement, will require to be instituted.

5. The unwinding of asset bubbles

The unwinding of asset bubbles is related intimately to the aftereffects of overleverage in the financial sector and private households as well as to associated economic imbalances. The latter see to it that deleveraging is always taking a toll. The immediate effect is risk aversion, all the way to a market psychology that is raising volatility and hitting currencies, credit, and equity valuations. Longer-range effects are the risk of inflation, negative impact on growth, and more.

In the years after World War II, periods of financial market volatility have been a signal that leadership in the markets, and growth stories associated with it, have been changing. Securities analysts believe that following the 2008/2009 events emerging economies, residential real estate, commodities, small caps, hedge funds, and private equity will not resume their past role. Instead of credit-driven motors, the new leaders will be:

- Defensive, and
- Relatively cash-flow-stable sectors of the economy.

Deleveraging will call the tune, and this is contractionary. An example is provided by scarcity in consumer credit, which feeds through many parts of the economy, from travel and motor car sales to construction. The effects of reduced lending and borrowing because of tighter lending criteria:

- Have a negative impact on goods prices, and
- Impact default rates, which tend to increase.

At the same time, higher borrowing costs can lead to a decline in asset prices held by the private sector, representing a negative-wealth shock to consumers, decreasing company profits and affecting the economy. This leads to so-called second-round effects in finance, from credit cards to corporate investment and corporate debt.

The way to bet is that the negative-effects magnitude, resulting from unwinding asset bubbles, is proportional to how these bubbles built up and for how long. In connection with the credit quake of 2008, the credit cycle which preceded it had gone parabolic, with the proliferation of zero-equity house financing schemes (and the same in car sales), and literal explosion of subprimes, Alt A mortgages, cov-lite loans, no-documentation loans, liar loans, piggyback loans, and ninja loans. The last listed were given to people with no income, no jobs, and no assets. In the aftermath:

- In America asset deflation is evident in housing, equities, and commercial real estate, with an estimated $50 trillion of balance sheet items deflating,[5] and
- The formerly booming consumer credit volume growth turned negative, leading some economists to suggest that it is impossible to have inflation in a credit contraction.[6]

The result has been a consumer recession, capital goods recession, and stockmarket crash *all in one*, with experts arguing that there is no antidote for a deflationary debt liquidation process. Past experience with deflationary processes suggests that it overwhelms the government's efforts, and leads economists to predict that while the central banks' 2008 "bailout mania" might save some institutions it will lead to no fast turnaround of the economy.

(For example, on 18 September 2008 in one day the Fed, the ECB, the Bank of England, the Bank of Japan, the Bank of Canada and the Swiss National Bank injected $247 billion into the market, after having already spent $1.5 trillion for market liquidity reasons. And even this was peanuts compared with the jumbo $630 billion the Federal Reserve also made available in one day, right after the initial rejection by the US Congress of the Treasury's request for $700 billion on 29 September 2008.)

What the reader should retain from these references is that in spite of such an unprecedented injection of money, the decline in overall economic output does not come to a dead stop. The proof is that it has continued in America and Europe, spreading towards emerging markets which recoupled to the western economies for the occasion. Other indices too pointed to the fact that one after the other economies weakened and continued to weaken. As of mid September 2008:

- The Baltic Dry Index for shipping had collapsed by 57 percent.
- Oil prices were down 30 percent from their July 2008 peak.
- Increases in unit labor costs slowed to a mere +0.5 percent year-on-year.
- Gold sank 26 percent from its highs, though it recovered with the new wave of banking bankruptcies in the week of 22 September 2008 and moved again towards 1000 dollars per ounce in late February 2009.

Equally dismal has been the effect of unwinding asset bubbles on financial reporting. With the 2008/2009 credit crunch, the already low transparency worsened. Mario Draghi said banks and other financial institutions must restore trust in each other by not concealing unpleasant facts about their condition, adding that "The less transparent is the banking system, the more the market will require capital."[7]

Draghi is right, but where and how to find capital at a time of unwinding asset bubbles had become an insoluble problem, with the most unthinkable "solutions" going the rounds among senior bankers. After the bankruptcy of Lehman Brothers and the purchase of Merrill Lynch by Bank of America, it was the turn of Morgan Stanley, second largest US investment bank, to feel the credit earthquake. The first "solution" heard on Wall Street was nothing more than the product of desperation.

The notion of Morgan Stanley merging with Wachovia was based on the premise that the very different funding risks faced by a struggling retail bank and a besieged investment bank somehow cancel each other out. Senior bankers should have had the knowledge to appreciate that merging two banks that are short of capital does not make one that is rich.

On 29 September 2008, to save Wachovia from bankruptcy, the Federal Deposit Insurance Corporation (FDIC) acted as midwife in its proposed sale for a mere $2 billion to Citigroup,[8] but it was bought finally by Wells Fargo. Morgan Stanley fared better. After converting to a bank holding company it received an injection of $9 billion from Mitsubishi UFJ, Japan's biggest bank, in exchange for 21 percent equity, and another $25 billion by the US Treasury taken out of the taxpayers' pockets. None of these developments:

- Benefited from a thorough study,
- Has been part of a longer-term business plan.

In Britain, in connection with the merger of Lloyds TSB and HBOS, the Lloyds management made token attempts to convince the market it was planning it all along. The fact was that this had been a shotgun marriage, so that the government had to override the competition authorities' objection to a near monopoly in mortgage loans. But the British government, too, was generous (with taxpayers' money) to Lloyds/HBOS.

The British Treasury did not play Santa Claus with Bradford & Bingley. On 29 September 2008 it was seized by the British authorities and after some talk that it would be merged with Northern Rock its branches and retail operations were sold to Santander while the rest was nationalized. (Rumors had it that between B&B and Northern Rock the British government had "nationalized" some £65.5 billion ($119 billion) of financial ashes.)

Meanwhile in continental Europe on 29 September 2008 Hypo Real Estate slid down the drain, its stock dropping 35 percent in value. It was pulled up by a €35 billion ($51 billion) credit line from German banks. But the French, Belgian, and Luxembourg governments had to inject €9.2 billion ($12 billion) to save Dexia from bankruptcy because of its exposure to financial toxic waste.

The Belgian, Dutch, and Luxembourg governments were thriftier with Fortis, which they nationalized and dismantled to save it from itself. Into a €900 billion ($1.2 trillion) bank they injected just €11.2 billion, or 1.24 percent of its assets – surely a timid first installment. Rumor had it that Fortis would sell for €10 billion the remains of ABN Amro, which it owned, to ING, for which it had paid €24 billion. In the end the Dutch government paid the money and also gave ING €10 billion to improve its finances.

6. Macroeconomic risks in a globalized economy

Based on a study which included 181 countries and data since 1980, a recently published research paper[9] sustains the thesis that low- and middle-income countries had a roughly 20 percent chance of suffering a banking crisis and a 30 percent likelihood of a currency crisis, external debt default, or spike in inflation. Along with the fact that foreign direct investments (FDIs) reverse direction, these statistics are among the main *macroeconomic risks* in a globalized economy.

Foreign direct investments are a double-edged weapon. They contribute to the capital of local companies and finance infrastructural projects, but they also increase currency crises, contribute to inflation spikes, and are themselves exposed to debt defaults. Foreign inflows help local stockmarkets as shares rise in good times, but when bad times loom in the horizon:

- Foreign investors run for the exit, and
- Equity prices drop relentlessly, often ending below where they started.

Neither are industrial countries immune to ups and downs induced by globalization. After its spectacular global surge in the 1970s and 1980s Japan has been in the grip of a low-level banking squeeze for nearly two decades and in that time there have been business cycles. In addition, the Japanese macroeconomic experience puts in doubt the statement by the US Treasury secretary that the real revival will start only when house prices stop falling. Rather, it looks like time alone will tell.

In addition, as far as macroeconomic risks are concerned, at both the national and international levels the actions of the banking sector influence the outcome not only in financial terms but through intensifying lobbying too. When George W. Bush fired William Donaldson, the experienced investment banker who headed the Securities and Exchange Commission, he created the precondition for scant supervision. In the course of a few years the risk dynamics have changed:

- In 2000/2001 the top macroeconomic risk was the stockmarket collapse.
- In 2002 it was deflation.
- In 2004, it centered on the jobs market and on debt instruments.
- In 2008/2009 the top macroeconomic risk has been the self-inflicted wounds of the banking system.

Both endogenous and exogenous factors were present in all of the above crises. Looking back to 2004, endogenous has been the risk of financial industry shock due to the likelihood of massive liquidation of leveraged hedge fund positions, amidst geopolitical tensions that were exogenous. Risks associated with the shadow banking system of hedge funds and other non-banks were underplayed in the economy, yet they have been present and real.

In 2004, as now in 2009, the banking system was open to a stress in exposure emanating from highly leveraged hedge funds, and this not only from the unraveling of the banks' positions. After a rather brief lock-up period, investors can redeem their investments on a quarterly basis. This makes a bank-like run on hedge funds highly possible, even if these entities neither have the capital base to withstand a run on their treasury nor can (normally) get money from public authorities.

Taking a look at the years which followed the 2004 crush of debt instruments, largely due to consecutive interest rate increases by the Fed, we see that after a period of stress the global economy entered a growth cycle tending to become one of its most dynamic since the 1950s. A major part in this was played by the ongoing rapid pace of expansion in the emerging market economies, even if the cyclical momentum of the industrial countries also picked up (both exogenous factors). Rock-bottom interest rates in the US, the lowest in 50 years, were the US economy's endogenous factor.

In the late 2004 to early 2007 timeframe, the financial markets were lifted by a generally brighter economic climate. The stockmarkets were buoyant with share prices climbing; by contrast, credit risk management became lousy, with the risks being taken leading to a decidedly pessimistic assessment of the economy, and from there to the subprimes mess and credit crunch.

In terms of macroeconomic risks, there is an ironic similarity between what has happened in 2008/2009, and what took place in the 1997/1998 crisis in Asia. At that time, hot money from western banks and hedge funds created financial bubbles and spread inflation across the region. When the hot money pulled out, the more stable western financial institutions snapped up Asian assets on the cheap.

In 2007 sovereign wealth funds returned the compliment; money from Asia and from the petro-economies has been picking up the best pieces of the wreckage left by the US credit bubble – but they let go after suffering severe losses as the equity of the banks where they injected funds continued to drop. The slack was taken on by governments, which did not want to see some of their bigger banks file for bankruptcy protection. Central banks were ready to oblige by injecting liquidity.

As the crisis spread from the US to Europe, it revealed hidden weaknesses in euroland's monetary union. In the European repo market, during the so-called "historic week" on Wall Street (15–19 September 2008) many banks were only accepting the highest-quality collateral such as German bunds in exchange for cash. They were refusing to accept bonds of the so-called peripheral nations of euroland like Italy and Greece, while some were said to be refusing to accept British gilts.[10]

Theoretically, the role governments and central banks play in macroeconomics, and by extension in the macromarkets, is more or less centered on *financial stability*, which is the domain of central banks. Practically, this is only half-true because governments influence the economy through many channels[11] – from lender of last resort to the recycling of worthless financial paper brought by wounded banks to the monetary institution's discount window.

Financial stability, of course, has to be steadily monitored as well as reassessed. The aim of financial stability studies is to provide a link between macroeconomic modeling of an economy's behavior and information on the way macromarkets function, including the impact of key financial intermediaries. Such studies require a broad view of economic environments, including:

- Conditions of the macroeconomy,
- Behavior of macromarkets' segments, and
- The weight attributable to different sources of financial stability, or instability.

The behavior of macromarkets' segments can have important implications for financial stability, *if* the entities behind crucial market positions are highly leveraged; leveraging always tends to have a systemic impact. This makes it necessary to complement a macroanalysis with microeconomic financial studies, as well as a stress test of balance sheet assets and liabilities. To this list of issues under examination the 2008/2009 events have added the quality of credit ratings.

In a macroeconomic sense, stress tests take into account that some plausible though unlikely shocks to the financial system would entail a high cost if they were to happen. The banking system's ability to withstand low-frequency but high-impact (LF/HI) shocks must be evaluated by estimating the expected size of losses generated under a shock, comparing the outcome to existing buffers in the financial and economic system within the perspective of a macro-prudential analysis.

7. The macroeconomic crisis may morph but it will not disappear

In the course of April 2008 supposedly leading financial lights at Goldman Sachs, Morgan Stanley, JPMorgan Chase, and BlackRock proclaimed that the worst of the crisis was over. Blackstone too told investors that there were signs of recovery in once-moribund markets. But real life in financial markets, and in the macroeconomy at large, has been a totally different story. Among other woes, housing troubles moved up the food chain from subprime borrowers to the rich and famous.

In an interview he gave on 7 August 2008 to Bloomberg Financial Services, Dr Henry Kaufman pointed out that the American economy will eventually have a shallow recovery after the ongoing recession. There seem to be no reasons for a dramatic takeoff as unemployment is rising, corporate profits are under pressure, consumer income is stagnant, and so are other factors whose impact defines the way an advanced economy leverages or deleverages itself.

Apart from the macroeconomic facts discussed in preceding sections there is the issue of US dual deficits – internal and external. With foreigners significant holders, and continuing buyers, of American financial assets (primarily fixed-income) there is the risk of a current-account deficit crisis. Nearly half of outstanding Treasuries are held by foreigners, and some 90 percent of foreign inflows into US agency debt has been from foreign official institutions. But not all facts are bleak. The pros say they feel more positive because, at least according to their opinion, by end of October 2008 sentiment was better than it was in early parts of the year. In their judgment global capitalism has pulled back from the brink:

- The collapse of Bear Stearns, Fannie Mae, Freddie Mac, AIG, and Lehman did not spread far and wide.
- Some assets that had been left for dead, like big leveraged loans, started showing some signs of life.
- Big banks round the world have raised billions of dollars to shore up their badly wounded balance sheets, or have been pulled up by their governments.

Critics answer that not only have the optimists got their facts wrong, but their logic also is at fault. Liquidity plays hide-and-seek; the markets are still in the doldrums, including the bond market; wrongdoers have not been punished; tougher regulation has not shown up; and there is plenty of evidence the big banks will use the taxpayers' money they got to start lending again to "reward" their top managers and traders with big bonuses for 2008.

That some other things might be a little better does not mean they are good. If the US housing market continues to worsen, then the financial sector will be in for much more pain. Banks have already lost billions on mortgages, credit cards, and home equity loans, and still historical trends suggest worse is to come. As portfolios of securitized mortgages and of other structured products are wound down, or sold at steep discounts, lenders will be forced to recognize losses, leading to further major writedowns.

At the heart of issues intimately connected to consumers is the *negative wealth effect*: homeowners tend to spend more when they feel wealthier owing to higher paper values of their assets. On the contrary, the effect of negative wealth is to bend consumer confidence. A sharp fall in house value, particularly when this falls below the homeowner's mortgage, leads people to abandon their house altogether:

- As it has become apparent that many citizens (not only in the US) were given mortgages they could not afford, the first question has been how many would eventually default.
- Then, a new and greater danger emerged: that many family homes will be simply abandoned, with unknown ultimate damage to the financial industry, and corresponding knock-on effects for the economy.

One of the great miscalculations by banks in the go-go years of 2003 to mid 2007 was their disregard for *negative equity*, where the value of the equity left in the house is less than the loan. Therefore, it is reasonable to suggest that the ultimate default rate on the "toxic" debt issues that have caused big problems in the credit market also depends on house prices.

In spite of all the talk about the contribution of mathematical models to asset pricing, nobody seems to have modeled the historical experience of default rates in response to negative equity. This is only partly a negligence, because indeed there are no historical data on national house prices falling so sharply in nominal terms[12] as they did in 2008/2009, while available evidence suggests prices could fall further.

Known as a *black swan*, a national fall in nominal house prices is an exceptional event that has not been covered in historically based valuation models. Such events can lead to unpredictable extreme responses in financial markets being found at the long leg of the risk distribution.

In an interview he gave to Bloomberg in the week of 29 May 2008 George Soros made a case for US government intervention to keep house prices from falling too far:

- In Soros's opinion this would limit harm to society and to capital markets.
- But at the same time government intervention in a market's natural clearing mechanism opens the risk of unpredictable distortions.

There is as well the question of how it will be enacted. On one hand there is the $700 billion bailout by the US Treasury, the mechanics of which are still unclear, at best (Chapter 10). On the other, Congress wants to see homeowner support by the Federal Housing Administration (FHA), whose financial resources are meager. If FHA recycles these wounded mortgages through Fannie Mae and Freddie Mac, the two big US-government-sponsored entities already taken over by the Treasury, the size of the bill will be such as to have a serious negative impact on the government's balance sheet, with macroeconomic consequences.

In order to avoid tunnel vision, both immediate and further-out unwanted consequences must be analyzed under the perspective of the ongoing American and European banking crisis, which is unfolding much faster than its Japanese, Korean, and other Asian equivalents in the 1990s. The way a Merrill Lynch study puts it:[13]

- The Asian crises teach us that it is imperative US policymakers tell us which financial institutions will survive and which not, and
- Until this uncertainty is resolved, financial institutions will be reluctant to deal with each other, and therefore will continue aggravating the credit crunch.

A method frequently used is to set up bank restructuring agencies and asset management companies, with banks recapitalized by the government under certain conditions. But as the same Merrill Lynch study points out, net fiscal costs from banking crises are substantial, averaging 13.3 percent of GDP while average recovery rate is just 18 percent of gross fiscal costs, and there is a negative correlation between output losses and fiscal costs.

Beyond this, because the banks' excesses hit whole economies, some jurisdictions are grappling with domestic macroeconomic imbalances and fears over the viability of their banking sectors, made worse by global aversion to risk. An example is Iceland. By mid May 2008 the three Scandinavian central banks extended a €1.5 billion helping hand to the North Atlantic island nation in its struggle to fend off the effects of the global credit crisis. The plan did not succeed, with the result that not only the three largest banks but the whole Icelandic economy went to the wall.

Iceland's downhill slide was aggravated by the fact that its currency was under pressure from the carry trade, its banks had overplayed their hand in expansion, and its monetary policy had not been working. Iceland had Europe's highest interest rates, at 15.5 percent, and inflation hit a 20-year high of 11.8 percent in April 2008 – a possible precursor to other similar events, and a warning to the Federal Reserve, the Bank of England and the European Central Bank that once the inflation's genie gets out of the bottle it is tough to put it back in again.

3
Money Supply and Inflation

1. Economic policy, fiscal policy, GNP, and GDP

Decisions made by governments and central banks deeply affect macroeconomic factors, and through them households, companies, and generally the economy's financial agents. Such decisions may be social in nature with economic aftermath; or they may primarily concern monetary and fiscal policies, the two discretionary tools available for the management of:

- Economic activity, and
- Financial infrastructure.

The making of a successful *economic policy* requires extraordinary attention in analyzing and understanding what takes place within society in connection with past and present decisions affecting people and companies,[1] as well as the likely aftereffect of decisions contemplated in the future. At the end of the day, the results of economic policy will be measured by the way and extent to which people and companies mobilize real and financial means to achieve the ends a society thrusts upon itself.

In this, monetary policy[2] acts precisely as both a stimulus and a regulator, defining how much money will be in circulation (section 2), what interest money should earn (Chapter 4), what the acceptable level of inflation (sections 3 and 4) is, how high the household debt-to-income ratio could or should become (Chapter 7), whether a long consumption boom is getting out of hand, and when to take the drinks away while the party is still going. A fundamental economic fact, and macroeconomic factor, is that resources are not unlimited. Hence, there must be a choice about what to produce, how and for whom:

- From agricultural produce, to mining, energy sources and materials, manufacturing capacity, and transportation, real goods are limited by definition.

- To the contrary, money supply must be managed *as if* it were scarce, because the value of money is the inverse function of its availability.

Easy money leads to spoilage, and money available at low cost promotes financial bubbles and brings economic catastrophes like the 2008/2009 credit and banking crisis. Too much money chasing a limited supply of goods results in inflation and/or leads to surges of current-account deficits.

Money is valuable not only because we can buy things with it but also because it is a store of value, a unit of measurement, an accounting tool, and a means for contracting transactions as well as for making settlements and payments. Properly managed capital contributes to economic development and growth.

The alternative to using money is barter. The barter economy, which preceded the money economy, has no established and generally recognized unit of exchange or of quantitative means of account. Nearly everything needs to be renegotiated. The invention of money simplified matters. The downside is that money loses value because of excesses leading to inflation, while in the globalized economy currency exchange rates are volatile.

Like monetary policy, *fiscal policy* is a powerful economic weapon. Unlike monetary policy, which should be the domain of an independent central bank, fiscal policy is established by the government and it consists of two parts which must work in unison:

- Direct and indirect *taxation*, and
- *Expenditure* whose financial plan is the government's budget.

Under good governance the two contribute toward maintenance of a progressive high-employment economy, development and sustenance of infrastructure, social services, the educational system and, in collaboration with monetary policy, the control of the inflation and deflation (section 7).

While monetary policy is supposed to be objective, fiscal policy is largely political and therefore subjective. Moreover, not every country has clear fiscal (or monetary) targets, and many of those who have them have not achieved them. Even if they know that a rigorous budgetary implementation and the avoidance of expenditure slippages are crucial, politicians rarely stick by their commitments.

For instance, deficit reduction plans are not backed by specific measures on the expenditure side; there are no automatic stabilizers contributing to the smoothing of cyclical economic fluctuations, there is an absence of structural policies needed to reduce adjustment costs, and so on. Similarly, efforts to promote moderate unit labor cost growth are wanting or non-existent, and shortsighted measures do not result in real economic growth while feeding inflation. The two measures of sound monetary and fiscal policies are:

- Financial stability, and
- The value of goods and services produced and consumed.

The total value of goods and services being produced in an economy is known as the *gross national product* (GNP), or simply *national income*. This is measured as the total output by people and firms. As a production-side metric it can also be seen as total income received by households in the form of wages, salaries, fees, rent, interest, and profits.

By contrast, the *gross domestic product* (GDP), which is presently being employed more than GNP, is a supply-side measure based on money spent by households. The easier, nearly accurate way to look at it is as GNP minus exports plus imports.

(Notice that the definition of what is in and out of GDP is not unique. In the globalized economy there are many different reporting standards. For instance, American statisticians count firms' spending on software as investment; in Europe this is treated as intermediate consumption. As a result, the surge in spending on software in recent years has inflated America's growth statistics, but not Europe's.)

The growth of GDP per capita is generally interpreted as evidence of spreading wellbeing. This is only partly true, but it still constitutes an approximate guide to average living standards. Summary GDP growth figures don't tell the whole story in terms of relative performance, because much depends on how wealth is distributed.

To appreciate what may be right and what may be wrong with the different GDP measures, the reader should remember that during the period when GDP was developed, in the 1930s and 1940s, the economy of western countries was much more industrially and agriculturally oriented. GDP was designed to indicate whether the economy was headed:

- Upward, or
- Downward.

Today, the old GDP is a system based on axioms and postulates that downplay the mammoth service economy; it is as obsolete as the value added tax (VAT) invented in the late 1950s by the French taxmen to simulate the benefits the German *Konzern* derived from vertical integration – which is another illusion because vertical integration has been wiped out by globalization's insourcing and outsourcing.

There is as well the fact that measurements expressed in monetary terms are altered by inflation. Hence, many economists prefer to focus on Nominal Gross Domestic Product (NGDP)[3] growth. *If* the desired inflation rate is, for instance, 2 percent and the long-term growth that can be sustained without pushing up inflation is about 2.5 percent, *then* monetary authorities should aim to accommodate NGDP growth of about 4.5 percent. This, too, is an assumption.

Nominal GDP and potential GDP tend to correlate. The latter is a prognosticator of the former, provided all goes well with the economy. Critics say however that this is not the way to bet. They also point out that, in their judgment, gross domestic product has never been a metric to measure real, physical economic growth. From the outset:

- GDP has been an accounting-type measurement expressed in monetary terms, and
- There is no correspondence between what it is claimed that GDP measures and what it actually expresses.

One issue where GDP is valuable in spite of its shortcomings is as an indicator of too-fast economic growth due to leverage. Financial crises usually don't happen without underlying economic problems. Big budget deficits and other imbalances underpin financial crises, but politicians do not always appreciate that one cannot inflate one's way out of current economic problems. Too rapid an economic growth – like Mao's great leap forward – is no indicator of a better position but of a lack of stability which ends by hurting the economy.

2. Money supply and monetary base

The amount of money in an economy has to be measured. This is the role of the monetary base: MB or M0 and M1, M2, and M3, the money supply (MS) metrics (more on them later) developed for the national economy but not yet adjusted for global conditions. This creates a distortion in the measurement and management of money in circulation, particularly in regard to the first basic principle: don't let money supply growth spiral out of control.

Many economists mistakenly assume that global monetary conditions are set by the big industrial countries' central banks. Yet since 2006 a staggering three-fifths of the world's broad money supply growth has flowed from emerging economies whose printing presses work overtime. Goldman Sachs reckons:

- Growth in China's broad money measure has quickened by a striking 51 percent per year along with a 15 percent inflation, and
- In India and other emerging countries the broad money supply has increased by an average of 24 percent a year, between two and three times as fast as it has in the developed world.

The second basic principle of sound economic management is that money supply affects the rate of spending. Ideally, we need an MS large enough to give us a gross domestic product that represents nearly full employment at stable prices and to stimulate growth. It never happens that way, because in practice things are not that simple.

Adjusted for inflation, money growth has accelerated alarmingly with the result that the entire world's money supply is growing at its fastest for decades, in real terms. One might expect emerging economies' money supply to outpace that of the western world, because their GDP growth is faster. But their surplus money growth over and above the increase in nominal GDP (section 1) is exporting inflation. Over and above that, China and India have real interest rates (Chapter 4) among the world's lowest, even though they have the fastest-growing economies.

Another powerful reason why money supply has been overshooting targets set by western central banks is that the commercial banks have been leveraging the financial system. "There is no limit to the amount of money that can be created by the banking system," Marriner Eccles, the chairman of the Federal Reserve in the Franklin Roosevelt years, warned, "but there are limits to our productive facilities which can be only slowly increased, and which at present are being used at near capacity."[4] This is particularly true when politicians pressure the central bank to keep interest rates low, both to hold down the cost of government borrowing and to encourage private economic activity – leading to a conflict of responsibilities and disabling monetary policy of its role of:

- Regulating money and credit, and
- Maintaining economic stability.

Speedy monetary growth can have disastrous consequences in the medium to longer run. Do we have the necessary measurement tools to help us in distinguishing between right and wrong economic policy? A compass to navigate between too slow and too fast money supply growth? Or, is all this uncharted territory?

This section has started with reference to the *monetary base* (MB), a measurement valid within a jurisdiction but not internationally. For instance, cross-border financial flows, which can be substantial, are not reflected in it. Another example of what is not factored in MB is liquidity going into global financial markets from different jurisdictions – such as huge purchases of US Treasury bonds by Japanese and Chinese central banks.

Down to basics, the monetary base is paper money and coins in wallets, drawers, under mattresses, and in vaults. That's the money over which the central bank has 100 percent control. Typically,

- 6 percent to 8 percent is in coins,
- The rest is in paper money.

The British call it M0 and it provides a good way to measure the outstanding currency. Still, it is a very partial metrics because there are many things not included in it that evidently expand the money supply, and therefore how much money is in existence. The increase comes by steps representing parts of the banking system's liabilities. The first step up is:

M1 = M0 + Overnight deposits

That's the European Central Bank's definition of M1. The Fed's is more complex; its M1 includes currency outside banks plus demand deposits at commercial banks and at savings and loans, plus other checkable deposits at banks and thrifts, plus traveler's checks.

Even this M1 is no perfect measure of how much money is in existence one step up from M0. For instance, it does not include an estimate of bank overdraft facilities which, in fact, is not accounted for in the next higher step up, the M2. According to the ECB:

M2 = M1 + Other short-term deposits

These other short-term deposits include those with an agreed maturity of up to two years, and deposits redeemable at notice of up to three months. The Fed's M2 definition is somewhat more elaborate, incorporating small-denomination time deposits plus passbook savings deposits at all depository institutions, money market mutual funds shares, bank overnight repurchase agreements, and Eurodollars. One more tick up comes M3:

M3 = M2 + Marketable instruments

That's the ECB definition. To get M3 the Fed adds to M2 large-denomination ($100,000 and over) time deposits at all depository institutions, plus bank long-term repurchase agreements. The Federal Reserve also distinguishes an "L" class that adds to M3 long-term Eurodollars, bankers' acceptances, commercial paper, Treasury bills, US savings bonds, and other liquid Treasury securities.

As the careful reader will observe, M0, the monetary base, is the most fundamental measure while M1, M2, and M3 measure money supply at three different levels of reference. MB and the three MSs correlate, the latter being the product of MB and velocity of circulation of money which is created by central bank policies affecting the banking system and other factors like companies' and households' propensity to consume – reflecting credit availability effects.

More money in circulation means more spending. Subject to central bank policy (and sometimes contrary to it), lenders may increase the amount of funds offered to borrowers, thereby allowing them to expand their spending plans. On the other hand, in exceptional cases such as the 2008 credit crunch they may decrease the amount of funds offered to borrowers.[5]

Also known as the "money multiplier," the velocity of circulation of money is an important macroeconomic factor. Dividing the total GDP (not just the increase in it) by the total money supply gives us the average number of times a jurisdiction's monetary unit (dollar, pound, euro, and so forth) turns over during the year:

- In the longer term, the velocity tends to fluctuate between 5 and 8, though it does not need to stay in that range.
- Other things being equal, the higher is the velocity of circulation the faster is the short- to-medium-term growth and the greater the push of inflation.

Central banks care most dearly about money supply conditions. Here in a nutshell is how the ECB analyzed them in mid 2008:

> The latest monetary data continue to support the view that the underlying pace of monetary and credit expansion in the euro zone area remains strong, pointing to the persistence of upside risks to price stability over the medium to longer term. The annual growth rate of M3 moderated somewhat further in June, but remains high at 9.5 percent ... The impact of the flat yield curve is leading to substitution within M3 and this contributes to explaining the further decline in annual growth of M1 to a historically low level in June.[6]

There is no international authority looking after the growth of M3 in the global economy; even statistics on M3 from different jurisdictions are

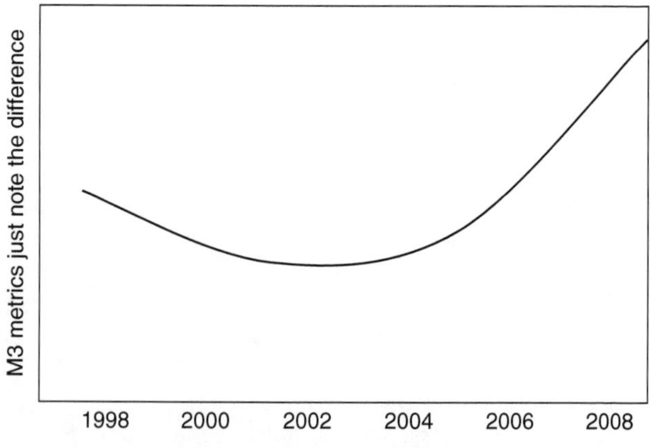

Figure 3.1 Trend line of growth in the world money supply over the 1998–2008 time frame.

Note: The trend line is an average of estimates by different parties in connection to M3.

difficult to put together, because the definitions of money supply by different monetary authorities are not homogeneous, and statistics are not always dependable. Therefore, I am sticking my neck out by trying to draw a trend line like the one shown in Figure 3.1, which is based on partial evidence. The aim is to look at a pattern, and the pattern is not at all reassuring in terms of future inflation.

Within a given jurisdiction, M3 is frequently targeted by central banks in tuning their monetary policy. The ECB is doing so; in the Greenspan years the Fed was inclined to target inflation (a lagging indicator). Monetary analysts have good reasons for being interested in M3 because, as a leading indicator, it helps to identify the medium-to-longer-term trends in inflation and thereby provides relevant information for policy decisions aimed at the maintenance of price stability. However, in interpreting monetary developments, it is also important to distinguish transient influences from underlying trends.

3. Core and headline inflation

As far as households and companies are concerned, inflation means rising prices. When inflation escapes control it reaches exponential levels, as is dramatized by a recent example from Zimbabwe (Figure 3.2).

Central bankers are sensitive to inflation expectations, which have significant macro impact and are a leading indicator. Notice, however, that:

- Not all prices of goods and services rise by the same amount at the same time, and
- Not all factors contributing to the general rise in prices are included in an inflation index.

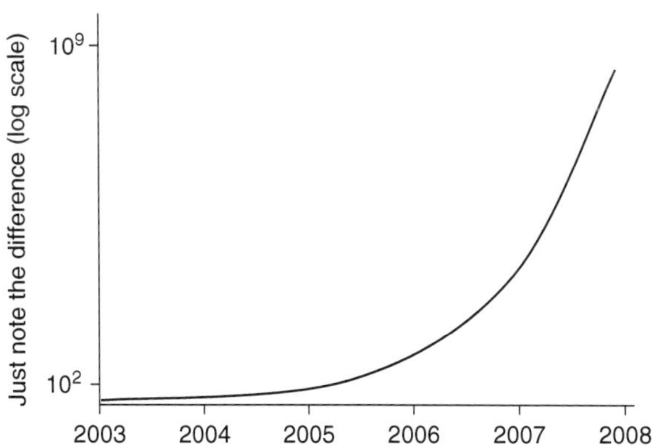

Figure 3.2 How to make a currency worthless: Zimbabwe's inflation should not be the model for political decisions and monetary policy.

Inflation is an average for the entire population and goods and services produced, sold, and consumed within a jurisdiction.[7] Averages are approximations because none of us is an exact average; each company and each consumer has a different attitude to inflation, and receives a different impact from it. What they all have in common is that it depreciates the value of money, which can no more be defined as:

- Having a fixed and invariable price in terms of a unit of account, and
- Being accepted on face value for payment of debt or for goods and services rendered.

Under monetary regimes that are founded on price stability, policymakers see to it that expectations of inflation are kept relatively low. By contrast, when there is lack of clear definition of price stability targets or, even worse, lack of trust that inflation will be kept under lock and key, inflation expectations tend to be revised upwards with new releases of adverse data or contradictory statements by the government.

The Federal Reserve follows two measures of inflation: *core* and *headline*, which tend to diverge. Core inflation – which typically rests on the consumer price index (CPI) components – is usually less, and sometimes much less, than headline inflation, which includes food and energy, but it can also be higher than headline inflation; for instance when food and energy prices tank.

Up to a point, however, core and headline elements of inflation impact upon one another. Increases in food and energy costs, for example, can squeeze spending on other goods and services with the result of depressing prices and artificially lowering core inflation. That may be the reason why in a June 2008 speech Mervyn King, the Bank of England's governor, referred to the practice of excluding price categories as highly misleading. A rational approach to classifying inflation factors is followed by the Deutsche Bundesbank, which distinguishes between *headline*, consisting of:

- Energy and
- Unprocessed food,

and *core*, divided between:

- Processed food,
- Industrial goods, and
- Services.

Increases in the cost of processed food should never be taken lightly. Between January and July 2008 in the European Union, Bulgaria, Latvia, and Lithuania saw a significant increase in food prices by 19.6 percent,

25.9 percent, and 17.0 percent respectively. These countries also reported the largest contribution of consumer food prices to inflation for the same period.[8]

The Fed suggests that core inflation is useful to gauge whether there are second-round inflation effects percolating through the system following shocks to food and energy, two items over which a central bank has no control. But many economists question how far core inflation alone may be a good guide for monetary policymakers.

There are also sectors of the economy which, as a matter of deliberate choice, policymakers don't include in an inflation index. One example is inflation (and deflation) in housing;[9] another is stockmarket inflation/deflation. (It is interesting to notice that level of inflation and stockmarket values tend to correlate. A study by HSBC shows that the best response from the stockmarket is obtained when inflation is between 2 percent and 4 percent:

- When inflation falls out of the bottom end of that range, the economy is flirting with recession and deflation.
- When inflation rises above 4 percent, and particularly when it reaches 6 percent, stockmarket valuations start to deteriorate sharply.)[10]

While many less-developed economies go through busts of inflation and deflation as a matter of course, in a developed economy inflation harms economic performance and once it sets in it feeds upon itself. Inflation in medical care and education, for example, does not go away in a recession, though discretionary spending is curtailed, leading to a consumer-led downturn without necessarily bending the inflation curve. In this case the economy enters a phase of *stagflation*.

Some economists and monetary policymakers suggest that mistakes such as those that caused the Great Stagflation in the 1970s are much less likely today because central banks in the industrial countries are now independent of politicians. By contrast, few of the main central banks in emerging economies enjoy full legal independence, and thus often face pressure from politicians to hold interest rates low to boost growth and jobs in spite of inflation or stagflation.

Poorly managed countries suffer persistently from stagflation. Argentina provides an example. The economy is growing no more and since January 2007 the official inflation rate has been massaged to remain in single digits, while the true figure has soared above 20 percent. When Cristina Fernandez de Kirchner succeeded her husband as president in December 2007, Argentineans hoped that she might help restore the government's computational credibility, as she had promised during her campaign. But those expectations proved too optimistic, even if:

- Company expansion plans and bank lending depend on a reliable benchmark of price increases, and

- Investors punished the Argentinean government by increasing its risk premium, forcing it to pay higher interest rates when it refinanced debt.[11]

Central banks under the thumb of the government become accomplices to doctoring the statistics rather than the economy's ills. Not long ago, an IMF study ranked 163 central banks according to their political autonomy based on factors such as how officials are appointed, the length of their terms, and whether interest rates have to be approved by the government. Some of the central banks that have been flooding the global market with money, for instance those in China, India and Russia, were said to be among the least independent, but this does not mean that western monetary policymakers:

- Always get it right on inflation.
- Are able to defy ministers of finance over long stretches of time.

In early 2008 in America the government enacted a deficit package for fiscal stimulus, and this exercise will be repeated in the coming months. In August 2008, the Bank of England Monetary Policy Committee (MPC) forecast that consumer-price inflation would fall back to its official 2 percent target, but only after a period of economic weakness had drawn its sting. "The more the government does, the more the MPC can't do," says Geoffrey Dicks, an economist at Royal Bank of Scotland.

4. The politics of inflation

André Tardieu, the high commissioner of France to the United States and French prime minister in the early 1930s, is famous for having said: "We must tax the poor. They are the most numerous." Inflation is the ideal taxation of the poor, as well as of the middle classes. It eats up the value of the most assets and by doing so it relieves indebted governments of a good deal of their contractual obligations.

There are other reasons too why higher inflation should not be off the table of monetary policymakers. For instance, it helps ease an immediate credit crisis as it shifts wealth from lenders to creditors. What is often forgotten, however, is that it also brings on another much bigger crisis because practically it penalizes the very creditors it is supposed to help by making their other monetary assets worthless.

Therefore, economists who truly care for the work they are doing advise politicians and central bankers to focus narrowly on price stability, which should not be confused with bailing out insolvent banks as happened in connection with the 2008/2009 crisis. In fact, it would probably be both moral and healthy for the global financial system if some of those reckless mortgage lenders and investment bankers were left to go bankrupt. In other terms, inflation should never be used as:

- The price of monetizing public debt,
- A way out of financial straits, or
- A means to get globalization moving again.

Monetizing public debt is bound to be inflationary, even if temporarily it would improve public finances. In 2003 when he was a Fed governor, Ben Bernanke, the Fed chairman, reportedly commended this course of action to Japan's policymakers.

The way an article in *The Economist* had it, Bernanke argued that one way out of a slump is for policymakers to commit themselves to a period of catch-up inflation to break deflationary expectations and heal the wounds from past price falls. That, the article says, is the *nuclear option*:

- Rescuing the indebted,
- But hurting those with savings.[12]

Confronted with facts and figures, a growing consensus among monetary policymakers and academics has been that, apart from its many other negatives, inflation exerts a systematic detrimental effect not only on savings but also on macroeconomic performance. It is causing misallocation of resources, negatively affects the factors of production, and leads to reduction in the rate of growth of capital accumulation.

Probably for these reasons the Japanese did not buy Bernanke's advice. At the same time, however, Japan's ballooning debt did not lead to inflation, as had been expected; falling prices were the rule until recently. Economists suggest that the reason Japan has so far escaped galloping inflation may well be its amazing appetite for public debt instruments, as private financial assets turned sour.

America and Europe may not be that lucky. A Merrill Lynch study looked at the current global bank bailout as *inflationary*:

> In the medium term, if the energy and credit crises are indeed linked to the same market failure, a massive government-led bank bailout may not help reignite the global economy and could bring about a second round of commodity price inflation. Whenever economic activity starts to recover, energy demand will likely start to strengthen and put upward pressure again on prices, as the ongoing bank bailouts will be inflationary in the long-term.[13]

Bailouts have been 90 percent a political issue.

- They have been misdirected, because they filled the big banks' treasuries rather than helping homeowners,[14] and
- They scarcely accounted for the fact that with rapid liquidity growth, past cost pressures that have not fully fed through would feed the fires of inflation.

This miscalculation may prove to be very costly because, in the middle of a banking and credit crisis, upside inflation risks limit the ability of policymakers to react to downside growth risks – and this not only in the United States, Britain, and euroland. High-growth countries in Asia and the Gulf as well as Russia have been testing their limits. In 2008, for example, China became a country with heightened inflation risks, large current-account surplus, and policymakers responding with a cocktail of not-so-effective tightening measures.

In Brazil, President Luiz Ignacio Lula da Silva described inflation, long a Brazilian bugbear, as a "degrading disease."[15] Lula added that he would prefer steady growth at 5 percent a year for 15 years to a faster, bumpier ride towards higher GDP. This is a concept other political leaders will be well advised to espouse.

An interesting aftereffect of a financial crisis in the globalized economy is the commercial impact that a crisis in one major market has on other major markets. While by late 2007 many American bankers, economists, and politicians had been debating on whether or not there would be a recession, and how far the Fed might aggressively cut rates to avoid it, clear-eyed experts looked at a recession as the way that might permit banks and other institutions to clear their balance sheets, some of them asking the question: "Will an American recession lead to rock-bottom interest rates, or will the Fed choose to fight inflation?"

The recession created a dilemma for the Federal Reserve, the European Central Bank, and the Bank of England. In late 2007 and early 2008 more expensive crude oil had pushed up consumer prices. To counterbalance this, central banks had to keep a lid on inflation in other sectors of the economy by holding interest rates higher than they would otherwise have liked, given the banking crisis and credit crunch.

(Oil shocks in the 2000s may have hurt less than they used to, but oil prices matter. With the 2008/2009 crisis US consumers had to absorb many punches: falling house prices, tighter credit conditions, rising unemployment, higher prices at the pump, and higher food prices. All this clouded the outlook for consumer spending, particularly as over the preceding two decades households had overspent, significantly increasing consumer debt and creating a huge trade deficit – all of them being events which made America's economy vulnerable.)

Textbooks say that inflation is a monetary phenomenon conditioned by both money supply and by credit policy (section 2), but as the preceding references document the commercial and political implications are wider. Therefore, the decision-makers' picture includes not only central bankers but also governments and parliaments. The politicians have not been alien to the fact that over a number of years in the United States and in several other countries monetary conditions have been loose, with real interest rates low and credit growth rapid:

- Credit is a leading indicator both of the economy and of inflation.
- Without printing an inordinate amount of money, betting on deficits, and promoting loose lending it is impossible to stimulate abnormal demand for goods.

It is however no less true that within a politically motivated environment the task of central bankers has become harder, particularly with globalization. As cannot be stated too often, western central banks, which dominated issues related to money supply, have lost that privilege – while the globalization process itself has shifted from being a disinflationary phenomenon to one that is increasingly inflationary.

5. Central banks and the control of inflation[16]

In an interview he gave on 7 August, 2008 to Bloomberg Financial Services, Dr Henry Kaufman stated that one of his main worries was the rise in inflation in 2009 and beyond. In his opinion, in 2008 there had been a creeping inflation, which had not been properly recognized by the authorities, and therefore had not had enough attention paid to it.

In 2007/2008 the Federal Reserve as well as other central banks and governments hoped that the inflation curve would bend of its own will, because of the ongoing economic recession. This is however a very narrow viewpoint, because it only accounts for what is happening in western economies. For inflation to subside, Kaufman said, the developing world, too, should curb its growth, and exercise restraint in the years ahead. To say the least, this is far from being certain to occur.

Kaufman was right. The inflation news in America was ugly. Year-on-year to July 2008, consumer prices rose 5.6 percent, the fastest since 1991. Producer prices rose 9.8 percent, the most since 1981. Fuel and food were mostly to blame, but even excluding them core consumer and producer inflation have both picked up. America's recession meant that the public's psychology was negative. In early July 2008:

- Consumer confidence was lower than in the last three recessions.
- House prices continued to fall,
- Wall Street worried about more huge losses at big banks, and

- Congress was pondering what to do next as the economy's signals were mixed.

According to the conventional view, monetary policy affects inflation through its impact on the real economy. Higher interest rates reduce demand relative to the economy's potential to supply goods and services. By contrast, a wage–price spiral develops if workers and companies conclude that higher inflation is here to stay and adjust wages to compensate. This has been a basic reason why the ECB has watched out for inflationary expectations. At least according to theory:

- When demand rises relative to supply it feeds the fires of inflation.
- But when unused slack accumulates, it forces firms, employees, and workers to compete for scarce customers and jobs by lower prices and wages.

In practice, however, unemployment and other measures of economic slack have a rather limited bearing on the transmission of monetary policy. Central bank actions affect inflation primarily by altering inflation expectations; for instance, a low funds rate in itself threatens to lift inflation, and government deficits amplify the inflation psychology, leading monetarists to fear that even a credit crunch will do little to contain it.

What government and many monetary policymakers often miss is that market psychology is further destabilized by the fact that central banks, and most particularly the Fed, have subscribed to one economic philosophy in an expanding economy and quite another when the economy is contracting. An asymmetric policy sees to it that:

- When the market is euphoric central banks leave the markets to their own devices.
- But the moment there is a hint of crisis, central banks respond by cutting interest rates to stimulate their economies and prevent asset prices from falling.

This distortion in policy finds its roots in the so-called *efficient market* theory, which rests on false premises. In reality, markets are far from efficient, as they often get locked into booms and busts. If markets were really as efficient as Alan Greenspan and some economists believe, why would economies need monetary policy in the first place? The efficient mechanism would see to it that:

- The market set the appropriate level of interest rates for the economy, and that
- It automatically rebalanced itself if a problem in the financial system came up.

The facts of life disprove this hypothesis. Letting the markets have their way has produced the major crises of 1929/1933, 2008/2009 and many intermediate ones. Moreover, the Bear Stearns, Fannie Mae, Freddie Mac, and AIG rescues show that the monetary authorities are desperate to avoid the economy descending to the abyss because of excesses during the uninterrupted years of free rein.

The results of an accommodating policy by central banks have been reflected in a study in August 2008, which suggested that consumers were going to be forced into retrenchment of the kind not seen since the six-quarter downturn of the mid 1970s. For a whole year after the start of the 2008/2009 crisis, American and European consumption held on remarkably well, but that was because of lags between shocks (energy, housing and credit) and the peak impact they inevitably exert on consumer spending behavior. The risk, that same study concluded, was that a consumer downturn would come next.

All this took place at a time (mid 2008) when 25 percent of the global economy was experiencing a two-digit rate of inflation, while year-on-year in the US prices increased by 5.6 percent – a 17-year high. In Japan, a country that over nearly two decades had been experiencing more deflation than inflation, the wholesale inflation rate rose to the highest level in 27 years.

In Latvia, which is part of the European Union but not of euroland, inflation remained high at 17 percent. For a country with a pegged currency that has been a scary statistic, though there were no signs of the contagion spreading from the troubled but tiny economies of the Baltic to the rest of the European Union.

In euroland, in July 2008, inflation accelerated to its fastest pace in more than 16 years after oil prices reached a record high (they did turn down a month later). The year-on-year consumer price index (CPI) increased by 4.1 percent while the unemployment rate reached 7.3 percent. Yet companies were ready to make inflationary strike settlements. On 1 August 2008 Lufthansa offered the strikers a 7.5 percent wage increase (a 5 percent immediate hike plus 2.5 percent in July 2009) which came on the heels of an even more inflationary settlement by the German railroads.

Upward pressure on pay led to more job losses in Italy and Spain, which were already struggling with poor competitiveness and rising unemployment. Accelerating wages also reinforced fears that inflation would prove hard to bring down, tying the European Central Bank's hands as it tried to fight inflationary pressure, aiming to keep the rise in prices below 2 percent. (Still, on two occasions, late October and early November 2008, the ECB cut interest rates by 50 basis points each time.)

The apparent seizure of euroland's economy had sat uncomfortably with the ECB's decision to raise interest rates to 4.25 percent in early July 2008. The bank's rate-setting council knew it was tightening policy during a sticky period for the economy, but it hoped the rate increase would send a message that it was serious about controlling inflation. (The bank's worry was that the current inflation, which inched up to 4.1 percent in July, might influence how wages and prices were set for the future.)

In conclusion, accommodating policies on interest rates and inflation have their limits. Even if a twelfth-hour central bank intervention sees to it that an outright depression is temporarily avoided, there is the danger that the financial system will become progressively less stable as higher risk-taking is encouraged and inflationary pressures set in. This also creates major public debt problems in the long run.

For their part, consumers and companies are encouraged to borrow. Families do not save because of the low level of interest rates and a belief that central banks and governments will always rescue them if things go wrong. They become debt addicts and this significantly increases their exposure in times of adversity.

6. The end of the non-inflationary consistent expansion: a scenario[17]

During most of the years from the stockmarket bubble of 2000 till the subprimes bubble and credit crunch of 2008/2009, the financial world prospered in an environment of low inflation and steady growth. But overleveraging saw to it that all that changed and tough times characterized market behavior and the value of financial assets. Calling this period of market volatility and turmoil the most difficult challenge yet for the British Monetary Policy Committee, in mid May 2008 Mervyn King declared that the decade of Non-Inflationary Consistent Expansion, or NICE, was over. In King's opinion the most likely scenario is that of:

- Tight credit and rising inflation,[18] forcing a rebalancing from consumption and borrowing to production and savings, and
- A choppier, less predictable economic growth with more uncertain company profits, and markets characterized by significant unpredictability.

During the preceding go-go years the sources of so-called cost-push inflation were commodities. Because of the steady rise of their price tags, consumers faced an upward spiral of costs while profit margins of many companies around the world were under pressure as companies sought to pass on all of the rising raw material costs. On the consumers' side, higher prices started to curtail demand.

Underscoring the global nature of the food price shock, in the first semester of 2008 food prices increased simultaneously in several major economies outside euroland. The food price components that contributed most to euroland's inflation were cereals and dairy products, which also rose in most other economies, suggesting a common shock behind the zoom in food prices.

For its part, investing was riddled with examples of poor monetary and fiscal policies leading to inflation. It is nevertheless interesting to note that the global market countries with lower rates of inflation have generally been outperforming those with higher inflation rates. Post-NICE, some economists suggested, the global economy found itself at the start of probably a decade of great instability with unknowns introduced by the fact that nowadays the cost of finance is decided outside the control of central banks:

- This is novel, leading to increased macroeconomic challenges, and
- The effects of the credit crunch are compounded by a rising asset price volatility.

Inflation, too, has escaped the central bankers' control largely because many of them were too preoccupied with calming the markets rather than with the longer-term effects of monetary policy easing. Economic history, however, has shown repeatedly that periods of high inflation have been systematically associated with sizeable redistributions of both income and wealth bypassing or even at the expense of large sections of the population. This:

- Increases social tensions, and
- Works to the detriment of social stability.

The stability of money is also put into question. When money turns into confetti every investment is risky, said Warren Buffett in an interview to CNBC on 26 May 2008. Even in a period when inflation is taken as being more or less subdued, like the decade and a half from 1992 to 2007, American inflation has eaten up the dollar for breakfast: a dollar in 1992 was worth 69 cents in 2007.

Central bankers and economists who hoped (and continue hoping) that inflation will return to low levels on its own accord have lost touch with reality, as risks to the outlook for inflation over the medium term remain clearly on the upside. They include not only the possibility of further rises in the price of goods as the benefits from globalization wane and companies try to regain pricing power, but also increases in administered prices and indirect taxes because cities and states can no more make ends meet.[19]

Most ominous among the rather mixed signals emanating from a broad set of indicators in post-NICE time is the risk that price- and wage-setting patterns will add to inflationary pressures, inciting labor unions and companies to push their pricing power harder than was initially expected. The brakes may be provided by the fact that consumer spending would bear the brunt if the unemployment rate rises significantly.

Economists working on scenarios wrapped around the aforementioned themes suggest that capital expenditures (capex) would decline, and that this would have a direct result on corporate profit forecasts as investment slacks hinder improvements in productivity. Opinions have however been divided regarding the dollar's behavior against a basket of currencies.

Reversing earlier expectations that the dollar will face major headwinds as a result of US current-account deficits and very low interest rates engineered by the Fed, some economists have been projecting that the dollar would strengthen against the euro if for no other reason than because euroland's economy, too, is in the doldrums. A currency's weaknesses are inflation's self-feeding system (see also Chapter 4).

Confronted with a falling currency, producers and traders demand an extra risk premium for holding goods denominated in that currency, while economic agents find it difficult to distinguish variations in relative prices from changes in general price levels. In the 2006 to mid 2008 timeframe, euroland provided an example of those aftereffects as soaring oil prices threatened higher inflation.

In 2008, euroland's economic growth slowed rapidly, despite Germany's robust performance, with the deceleration being sharpest in the service sector. The price shock in individual euroland countries differed considerably in terms of both speed and size. With all inflationary factors counted, the impact has been worst in Spain where in March 2008 annualized inflation hit 11 percent. At the same time Spain, like all other western countries, has been hit by a recession, house price deflation, and credit contraction. In this environment the European Central Bank had little room for maneuver.

7. Recession and deflation

Poverty is caused by incompetent economic policy, but inflation is by no means a guarantee of economic advance. Quite to the contrary, its presence sometimes serves to reveal the underlying problems of society in even harsher form. And as we saw in section 4, inflation which impoverishes everyone on a fixed income, or who holds money as wealth, is the most arbitrary tax of them all.

What about recession and deflation? *Deflation* reflects a slump in demand, leaving several sectors of the economy with excess capacity. Falling prices invite consumers to delay purchases of anything other than absolutely necessities, leading to still weaker demand and a further fall in prices. This is as well exacerbated by households which, confronted with the risk of unemployment, decide that it is time to save and, if possible, rebuild their finances:

- Debt deflation is welcome if done in an orderly manner,
- But without careful watch a deflationary environment can acquire its own momentum.

Defined in a very narrow sense as two consecutive quarters of negative growth, a *recession* might lead to deflation. The two terms, however, are not synonymous. In real terms, two consecutive quarters of economic contraction may or may not identify the beginning of a recession; and there also exist other criteria. A better definition of recession is a fall in average income per person. Merrill Lynch provides a good complementary definition:

Recession = Higher delinquency rates + Bond downgrades.[20]

Analogical thinking from recent economic travails that can be used to qualify recessions is provided by the lessons from Japan's economic contraction (which is still on). The *economic price* Japan has paid for past excesses has become of particular concern to monetary policymakers, as well as the global financial markets. Opinions diverge. Some economists have started to suggest that history can be very unkind to central bankers who keep monetary policies tighter than necessary during late-cycle periods in order to:

- Fight inflation, and
- Maintain the value of the currency.

Other economists don't buy this argument because it forgets that economic contraction, and therefore recession, is unavoidable *if* political and monetary policymakers want to rebalance the economic system and prune it of its *excesses* in terms of credit, leverage, and speculation. Moreover, a recession is not ended simply by pumping more money into the system. As Japan's case demonstrated, this makes matters worse because it prolongs the rebalancing period. Here are some points to keep in mind, as of late 2008, about the US, Britain, and Euroland.

- Core inflation has breached the comfort zone;
- Productivity has been slowing;
- Unit labor costs are trending higher;
- A housing bust continues;
- The equities markets remain jittery; and
- Geographical (read: political) uncertainty is on the rise.

The *comfort zone* has no unique definition, but several central banks equate it to an inflation equal to or less than 2 percent per year. Because nothing walks on a straight line – as the physicist Werner Heisenberg pointed out – monetary policymakers look at the ideal band for annual inflation as being between 0 and 2 percent (which is practically what the "up to 2 percent per year" means).

Keeping within this band of 0 to 2 percent is a difficult target for central banks. If monetary policy is too tight, they will be held responsible for creating a recession. If it is too loose then their grip on inflation slips, with markets and the public ceasing to believe that prices will remain stable; and, with this, inflation escapes prudential control.

The silver lining of inflationary excesses is that they inspire fear about a repetition of the same experience, and this lasts for a decade or two. For instance, in the early to mid 1980s thanks to rigorous Fed action the Great Inflation of the late 1970s gave way to an age of low, steady inflation during which central bankers learned how to steer policy. Moreover, inflationary expectations at moderate levels combined with globalization to support strong, steady economic growth.

It is surely no strange coincidence that by now more than twenty central banks have explicit inflation targets and all of them hope to avoid deflation. Critics however say that during the last half-dozen years inflation targets have been half-baked, because:

- Inflation can exist in a period of economic contraction, and
- During that period interest rate policies rarely compensate for it.

The Fed, some economists suggest, has been positioning itself in today's economic landscape with criteria that were valid in the past but are relevant no more. By pushing down the dollar (a situation reversed in August 2008), the Fed let down its vigilance over inflation because it fired up the price of dollar-denominated commodities – or at least gave an excuse to speculators for doing so. This is dramatized in the chart in Figure 3.3.

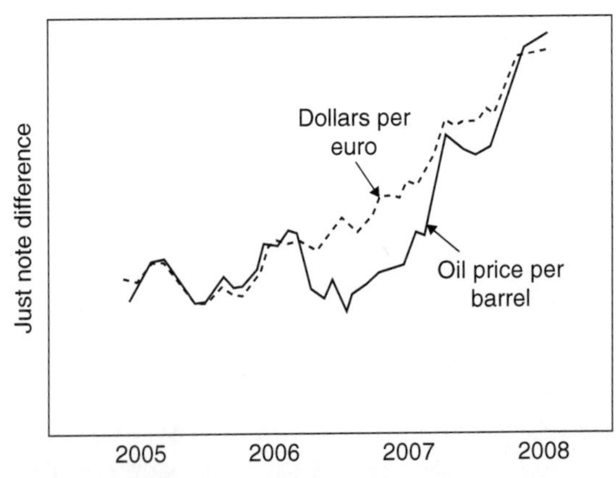

Figure 3.3 From 2005 to 2008 the trend lines of dollar weakness (vs. the euro) and the price of oil correlate.

From 2005 to 2006 the price of two commodities, the euro and oil, were perfectly correlated; then from late 2006 to late 2007 they got unstuck, but correlated again in 2008. Such correlation continued after both the euro's exchange rate and the price of oil bent; this was a trend rarely found between two commodities, which should give food for thought to economists and central bankers – the Fed's included.

According to some opinions, the reason for interest rate weaknesses on the part of the Fed – eventually followed in October/November 2008 by the Bank of England and the ECB – has been not the fear of deflation but the desire to allow the banking industry's self-inflicted wounds to heal gradually. But the wounds of the banking industry are so deep, and the doubts about the institutions' creditworthiness so pervasive, that the only visible result is the damage suffered by:

- Savers,
- Investors, and
- The whole economy.

An added irony is that globalization became an inflationary force instead of one of price moderation as in the late 1980s, throughout the 1990s and in the first years of this century. Higher inflation accompanied not only lower unemployment in the west but also an improvement in the standard of living of developing countries. (Two American economists, Milton Friedman and Edmund Phelps, both Nobel prize winners, had early enough pointed out that the trade-off from globalization was only temporary.)

By pushing down inflation for a while, globalization reinforced the credibility of western monetary policies but this could not last forever. Characterized by Ronald Reagan as more deadly than a hit-man, inflation is already in double digits in countries like oil-rich Venezuela (25 percent), Argentina (15 percent), and Russia (14 percent), while it hovers between 8 and 10 percent in Saudi Arabia, China, India, and Indonesia; and the produce these countries send to the west bears the cost consequences.

The monetary base is also zooming not only because American and European central banks keep the presses running for three shifts per day, but also because many countries, including China and Japan, micromanage their currency. When central banks intervene in foreign exchange to prevent their currency from appreciating, they have to print money to buy dollars, which boosts domestic liquidity.

There are two additional ironies. One is that the Fed's successive interest rate cuts have made it even harder for emerging economies to tighten their monetary policy. The other, which nobody seems to bother about, is the devastating effect *negative interest rates* have on savings.[21] Yet everybody says that savings are the cornerstone of economic development.

4
The Cost of Money

1. Interest rates[1]

Traditionally, the cost of money is the interest rate paid for deposits and loans. The payment of interest has been at the core of the capitalistic system, because as a store of value money mobilizes wealth for productive purposes, luring savings into new ventures that can multiply economic rewards. Higher interest rates attract savers, and the savings rate is a multiplier of wealth. But governments and other big spenders are penalized from high interest rates because they increase the cost of their debt. In short,

- Debtors gain from low interest rates, and
- Savers as well as institutional investors, like pension funds, lose.

Precisely for this reason, keeping money for too long at 1 percent – well below inflation, as the Greenspan Fed did for several years at the beginning of this century – destroys savings and by extension productive investments. Lowering the benchmark price of money makes other assets more attractive, including speculation, which increases the odds on a truly nasty economic meltdown (we had it).

Greenspan's and Bernanke's policy of rock-bottom interest rates may have been a gift to speculators but they were also anti-American because the US needs to create nearly 100,000 jobs a month merely to absorb the growing population. When growth in employment is stalled, the economy becomes vulnerable. Worse still, negative interest rates, which means rates below the level of inflation,[2] prod people and companies to take inordinate risks, with the likely rate of return a fraction of assumed exposure.

This can have disastrous consequences. As the 2008/2009 banking and credit crisis has shown, well-managed assets are not those of a casino society but those representing a hope for the future: promising a return to the wealth holder, and creating work for others. If successful, the new venture would produce its own surplus of wealth, which is fed back into the economy. This recycling process:

- Compounds the original value, and
- Produces a higher level of wellbeing.

In a nutshell, these few sentences describe the process of intermediation characterizing a properly run banking system. A commercial bank will get few or no deposits if it does not pay interest to the depositor commensurate with what the market offers and above prevailing inflation. When the central bank reduces interest rates nearly to zero, supposedly to stimulate the economy (or to give a helping hand to banks silly enough to wound themselves), it distorts the way a free market works and feeds up a bubble which will eventually burst.

It needs no explaining that under these conditions the market participants' expectations of impending interest rate moves by monetary policymakers, or governments, have a noticeable effect on the market. Moreover, not only the interest rate level but also the timing of decisions regarding changes is an integral part of the management of money supply. But which interest rate? Figure 4.1 shows that, as far as euroland is concerned, there is not one but several:

- At the center is the minimum *bid rate* for main refinancing operations.

This is set by the European Central Bank (ECB). Not shown in the graph are two other rates which tend to find themselves above the minimum: the marginal rate, which is typically above; and the euro overnight index average rate (Eonia[3]), which may be way above the minimum rate as in the 2008 credit crash, or a little above or a little below it as happened on several occasions in 2005 – but above the deposit rate:

- The lowest steady line in Figure 4.1 is the *deposit rate*.

Theoretically this is officially authorized, but practically it is not. Banks and their clients have the freedom to negotiate the deposit rate, which happens as a matter of course for large amounts but also for smaller ones in conjunction with other services like portfolio management. Companies usually negotiate with their bank the deposit rate in association with:

- The marginal *lending rate,* which is the upper line in Figure 4.1.

Negotiated rates tend to be volatile. Therefore, when studying developments in the money market it is important to analyze not only the level of interest rates but also their volatility, with at least two issues in mind: assessing the impact of monetary policy decisions on the money markets,

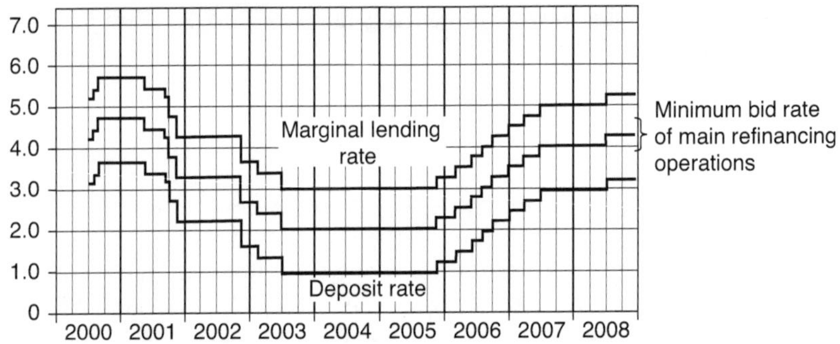

Figure 4.1 ECB interest rates and money market rates of euroland, 2000–8.
Note: According to a study by the Council on Foundations.

and examining how well the market functions – particularly in regard to the transmission of monetary policy to the long and short ends of the interest rate maturity band.

2. Monetary policy decisions and interest rate volatility

Monetary policy decisions impact upon the volatility of interest rates. Therefore, central banks try to make sure that their policy decisions, and associated communications, do not foster unnecessary uncertainty, which would usually manifest itself in higher financial market volatility. Analyzing volatility at the two ends of the maturity band at the same time can offer insight into:

- The money market structure,
- The way its mechanism ticks, and
- The efficiency with which it operates.

In this exercise, *realized volatility* reflects the perceived uncertainty prevailing in the market, while *implied volatility* is calculated on the basis of options based on forward-looking expectations. The latter aim to provide indications of volatility over the horizon covered by futures contracts.

What may be the reason for an increase in interest rate volatility? Take as an example the event of July/August 2007. Between the end of June and early August it became clear that a number of financial institutions had incurred substantial losses on their activities in the American subprime mortgage markets. As concerns about exposure to subprime mortgage defaults intensified:

- The ability of conduits to refinance themselves through commercial paper diminished, and
- Demand for liquidity on the part of banks needing to provide credit to these conduits increased.

These events were further exacerbated by difficulties in the valuation of structured financial products while the increased demand for liquidity, together with a loss of trust toward counterparties, resulted on a tendency to hoard liquidity by practically all big banks. The aftereffect has been that overall market liquidity declined significantly.

It did not take long before interest rates in the money market zoomed, particularly in the overnight segment, where the interest rate reached, on an intraday basis, levels almost 70 basis points above the minimum bid rate. The same events also caused a substantial increase in very short-term market interest rates.

In addition, as money market tensions persisted increases were observed in interest rates in the longer-term segments of the unsecured market – essentially interbank loans not secured by an exchange of collateral. This led to spreads against the secured segments of up to five times the historical average – a situation which continued over long stretches of time in spite of the fact the major central banks injected over a trillion dollars of liquidity into the market. Credit institutions:

- Were unsure of the credit quality of their counterparties, and
- Were more interested in using central bank funds to rebuild their balance sheets than they were in acting as intermediaries.

The Federal Reserve responded with a rapid succession of interest rate cuts, from 5.5 percent to 2 percent and then down to 1 percent in early November 2008. Each time, however, the effect on the markets did not last more than 24 hours. "Interest rate cuts have been complete nonsense, another unsound part of an unsound financial structure," wrote Martin Wolf in the *Financial Times* of 10 July 2008.

As several economists expected, interest rate cuts of the federal funds rate and of the discount rate did not help to revive the US housing market. Who would buy a property when property prices continued dropping? Neither did it help the money market at large. While the Fed rate went from 5.5 percent to 2 percent, the interbank interest rate went significantly higher and so did the mortgage rate because credit risk zoomed.

By contrast, till the second half of October 2008 both the European Central Bank and the Bank of England have been reluctant to cut interest rates. The ECB's decision to stick to its guns reflected not only the fact that till September 2008 the banking crisis did not hit euroland's economies with the force it hit the American but also, and primarily, the Central Bank's concern about inflation.

The Bank of England cut interest rates by 75 basis points while the ECB stood still. Then, on 8 October 2008 there was a coordinated rate cut by the Federal Reserve, the Bank of England, the European Central Bank, the Swiss National Bank, the Swedish Riksbank, and the Bank of Canada. With this, global yield curves steepened significantly, with one aftermath being that steeper yield curves open opportunities for the carry trade, increasing global exposure.

In addition, despite the rate cuts Libor spreads remained at elevated levels, underlining the unwillingness of financial institutions to participate in the interbank market. The Federal Reserve's announcement that it would create a special fund to buy US commercial paper was first judged as an important step, though it was taken without a legal mandate.

In no time this developed into a major controversy. On 10 November the news broke that the Fed had spent $2 trillion of taxpayers' money supporting different banks by accepting their toxic waste as collateral, but had refused to name the recipients. Congressman John A. Boehner requested that the Federal Reserve reveal who they were, and Bloomberg news did the same under the US Freedom of Information Act, also filing a federal lawsuit to force disclosure (Chapter 8).

Sound governance also requires that *forward interest rates* be looked after. The often-used assumption that longer-term nominal interest rates reflect expected economic growth is, at best, nearsighted. Apart the fact that they may be affected by population growth, time preferences of economic agents, and bias resulting from the current crunch, longer-term nominal yields can be broken down into three main parts:

- The expected real interest rate, often regarded as closely linked to economic growth projections;
- The expected long-term rate of inflation (Chapter 2), for which investors ask for compensation; and
- Risk premia of which the most important are related to uncertainty connected to future developments in real interest rates and other factors.

Longer-term interest rate changes may be influenced up to a point by central banks, but they are more intimately affected by re-evaluation of economic growth projects, inflation expectations, and changes in risk appetite. Typically, yield curve studies (section 5) look at implied forward overnight interest rates 10 years ahead extracted from the term structure of zero-coupon government bond yields, taken as a proxy of market participants' expectations about interest rates.

3. Central banks have lost their ability to use interest rates as a weapon[4]

Martin Wolf was not alone in his criticism of the Fed's policy of cutting interest rates to appease the markets. Many economists are now seriously questioning the wisdom of the Fed's policy of dramatically lowering interest rates every time the market gets nervous. Even partial success relies heavily on trust in the Fed's ability to keep inflation under control, and there were signs that the policy of rapid rate cuts had been undermining that trust.

Furthermore, there is evidence that the central banks of the major industrial countries have lost their ability to use interest rates as a way to influence the market. This is unprecedented, and while it is often credited or debited to globalization, in all likelihood there exist more profound reasons for it.

All by itself, critics suggest, cheaper money will not remove the source of the banking and credit crisis turmoil: worries about who holds the losses from the subprimes, Alt-As, and other dubious instruments' mess, and the uncertainties over banks' balance sheets, are not eased by cutting interest rates. Smoothing these concerns takes time – the time required to:

- Work out what illiquid securities are worth, and
- Better understand who bears the ultimate losses and how much capital banks will need to clear up the mountain of their financial debris.

This does not mean either that the opposite strategy of interest rate tightening is a better solution.[5]

The Great Depression of 1929 gives testimony to what happened after the ill-fated and ultimately aborted attempt to raise rates in the early 1930s. The counterevidence is that the Riksbank, the Swedish central bank, most successfully used a sharp increase in interest rate to pull the country out of a deep banking crisis into which it had fallen.

One of the reasons why in 2008 interest rating setting by central banks had become irrelevant is that the system of intermediation is no longer working. Banks used to borrow from each other at about 0.08 percentage points above official rates; on 30 September 2008 they paid more than 4 percentage points over that old benchmark.

What puzzled many experts is that interest rates scaled these extremes even as the Federal Reserve promised hundreds of billions of dollars in extra funding. The classical model of banking intermediation has been warped onto self-parody, with rising voices proclaiming that rates should be left alone for a while:

- Ring-fencing the central banks' independence, and
- Allowing them to use other means in trying to soft-land the economy.

All this is written in the understanding that the short-termism of politicians is much more likely to do harm than good. Indeed, one of the economic and financial fundamentals which in western countries assured the relative stability of the last three decades has been the central banks' independence, which has been put in question in the US, Britain, and euroland.

As the fortunes of the big global banks dived, because of their own mistakes, and given the effect this had on major economies, central bankers have been criticized by both chiefs of state and the press for being "insufficiently accountable," as well as politically insensitive to the ongoing financial disaster. The European Central Bank and the Bank of England became the target of politicians, while in Japan politicians vetoed candidates for governorship of the central bank, leaving the post vacant for several weeks.

In the US, the Federal Reserve went along with the Bush Administration's wishes to bend the rules to please the market, leading some commentators to compare (back in March 2008) the Fed's salvage of Bear Stearns with that of the US Congress's authorization of a big loan for bailing out Chrysler. In September 2008 this was followed by the salvage of Fannie Mae, Freddie Mac, and AIG – with little understanding of the fact that such bail-outs:

- Could mitigate the problems,
- But will not be able to avert new big bank crises.

One of the challenges facing governments and central banks is where precisely they should end the bailout packages. Should they sacrifice non-banking companies to save the banking sector? Should they pay an inordinate amount of attention to the risks resulting from the subprimes? Or should they do precisely the opposite?

Washington Mutual, America's largest thrift, and Wachovia, its fourth-biggest commercial bank, went bust because of bad loans, not because of the subprimes:

- Outside Wall Street, in the US, banks have lent 96 cents for each $1 of deposits, in violation of Basel I rules.
- Compared with this, European banks have done even worse; they lent roughly €1.40 for each Euro 1 of deposits.

Deposits were not enough to face this lending frenzy, so they had to borrow the rest from money market investors, who now lack the confidence to continue lending. In addition, British, Irish, and Spanish banks had housing busts of their own, not just the toxic American securities they bought by the billion.

Last but not least, globalization has been another reason why western central banks lost their ability to use interest rates as a weapon. In an environment where risk aversion is elevated, the currencies of countries with banking crises and recessions are penalized by investors no matter what was their interest rate – unless they become refuge currencies[6] (sections 7 and 8). Higher-yield currencies with large current-account deficits but no other pole of attraction:

- Soften in this environment, and
- The eroding yield support makes matters so much worse.

On the other hand, it is most positive that there exists such a diversity in market reactions. According to enlightened spirits, *if* there were one type of global money, the way promoted by some experts (who ask for a return to a Bretton Woods solution[7]), *then* it would be so much more easy for governments to manipulate personal wealth and pick up their citizens' money as they please.

4. Jeffrey Lacker's remarks on the Fed's policies

Since the beginning of the subprime crisis in July/August 2007 Ben Bernanke's Federal Reserve has been interested primarily in stimulating the economy through a tandem of sharp interest rate cuts. As we have seen, these brought the US dollar interest rate down to 1 percent and also had, over a period of time, a knockout effect on the dollar.[8] In parallel with this, the Fed became lender of last resort to a variety of financial companies outside its remit.

On 5 June 2008, in a striking insider's critique, Jeffrey Lacker, president of the Federal Reserve Bank of Richmond, said that programs the central bank had created to combat the credit crisis and banking crisis:

- Distorted private markets,
- Encouraged risky behavior, and
- Could endanger the Fed's independence.

Lacker's comments, made in a speech in London and amplified in a subsequent interview, show the concerns other central bankers, including former Fed chairman Dr Paul Volcker, raised about 2008 Fed policies, including not only interest rates but also the rescue of Bear Stearns, an investment bank which had never been under the Fed's supervision, of Fannie Mae and Freddie Mac as too big to fail,[9] and of AIG, the giant insurance company and derivatives outfit.

These concerns are said to be shared by several senior people inside the Fed, including some of the other regional Federal Reserve banks' CEOs. The way Jeffrey Lacker put it, the danger is that the effect of recent credit extension on financial market participants who were never before under the Fed's wings might introduce greater risk-taking, which in turn could give rise to more frequent crises.

The salvaging of Bear Stearns was a "first" and it created a precedent which can lead to a new type of exposure due to the danger that financial entities abiding by no regulatory rules and under no rigorous supervision, but supported by public money, will continue taking inordinate risks. Their management will work on the assumption that taxpayers' money will pull them out of the bad situation into which they bring themselves, no matter how bad this may be. As Lacker put it, before the Bear episode there were well understood and properly articulated boundaries around when the Fed would lend. These were mainly connected to:

- Managing short-term interest rates,
- Helping banks deal with temporary shortages of cash, and
- Facilitating the closure of the bank taken over by the regulators.

By contrast, the Bear Stearns action and other salvage actions brought the central bank beyond previously accepted boundaries, and it is now wrestling with the consequences. Indeed, not only the Fed but also the European Central Bank has taken many unconventional steps to improve conditions in credit markets, including a vast expansion of loans to financial institutions through repo agreements by exchanging Treasuries for much riskier securities (Chapter 9):

- Policy interventions in financial markets run the risk of increasing moral hazard and inhibiting price discovery.
- Novel central bank programs intended to quell instability can actually make instability more severe in the longer run.

With this change in policies which came in the wake of the 2007/2009 credit and banking crisis, by lending to financial institutions which have not been under its jurisdiction, and doing so on an unprecedented scale, the Fed is making decisions it long sought to avoid about the allocation of credit. And it has also acquired new powers of oversight, which fall outside its status. This:

- Enlarges and alters the structure of the time-honored cost of money equation, while
- The partial removal of credit risk from counterparty transactions increases market uncertainty about their proper pricing.

Equally unprecedented is the fact that in the months which followed events like the rescue from bankruptcy of Bear Stearns, there has been no attempt by the Bush Administration or US Congress to rein in the Fed, probably because the politicians themselves are unsure about which is the better response to a deep economic and financial crisis. Nowhere has this lack of political leadership become more felt than in the central bank's deployment of its balance sheet to restore liquidity to specific markets, like interbank loans, which had a significant effect on the composition of its portfolio:

- In early 2007, an estimated 91 percent of the Fed's assets were invested in government bonds.

- By early August 2008 that share shrank to just 52 percent,[10] the balance representing a mixture of dubious collateral.

Ben Bernanke seems to think that this returns the Fed to its roots as lender of last resort to prevent financial panics. But the question is posed: to whom should the Fed lend and on what terms? After all, the central bank's money is public money and, other things being equal, the reduction of government bonds under the Fed's wings from 91 percent to 52 percent means that three-quarters of its holdings is composed of low-creditworthiness assets.

In the meantime, interest rates have refused to obey the central bank's commands, making the cost of money a guessing game for market players. On 16 September 2008, during morning trade in London the overnight dollar rate rose briefly above 10 percent before it was fixed at 6.44 percent, more than double its setting of 3.11 percent a day earlier, and triple the previous week's rate of 2.13 percent.

The British Bankers' Association, which sets the daily official money market or London Interbank Offered Rate (Libor), said in a statement: "The Libor overnight rate recognizes that, in the current uncertain market, banks are looking to their own liquidity as the priority."[11] Critics however suggested that the way to interpret this statement is that:

- Monetary financial institutions and market makers have taken over some of the central banks' responsibilities,[12] and
- The central banks themselves are entering into new areas of activity, some of which are uncharted territory.

This extension of authority and responsibility by central banks, in the course of the 2008/2009 crisis, is far from creating unanimity; and the acceptance of low-credit-rating paper is even more controversial. "We have been able to keep a good separation between monetary policy and these other areas," Bernanke told Congress in July 2008, but two months earlier Paul Volcker had urged Congress, if it wanted to prop up favored sectors, to do so transparently, adding that poorly defined boundaries are the way to destroy the Federal Reserve in the long run.

The argument that other monetary institutions like the Bank of England and European Central Bank had also accepted low-rating CDOs and subprimes paper is not necessarily a justification for continuing with this practice; neither is the status of all central banks precisely the same. The ECB has had the ability to lend against a wide variety of government and private collateral, as the Fed now does; but the Fed's independence is more tenuous than the ECB's and it is also required to strive for both:

- Price stability, and
- Full employment.

By contrast, stable prices are the ECB's sole goal. Additionally, the Fed is vulnerable at times of economic turmoil. The Great Depression led to an overhaul of its original 1913 status, which shifted power to Washington. This has given the politicians a greater role in special authorizations.

5. Interest rates and yield curves

Supply and demand for credit, general market conditions, contract terms, maturities and other factors impact on the term structure of interest rates, and play an important role in shaping the *yield curve*. The *spot yield* on an interest rate product is yield in the cash market on that product at a particular point in time. The *forward yield* is the term describing the market's expectation about what the spot yield will be some time in the future on a particular interest rate instrument.

One of the examples in section 4 brought to the reader's attention that interest rates, and therefore yields, in a fixed-income investment or loan can change at a moment's notice. In a literary sense, forward yield starts seconds down in time, but this is not what we are after when we talk of yield curves that typically target the medium to longer term – up to 10 years or (by extension) 30 years.

The yield curve is built on a tandem of forward rates and is one of the financial industry's most powerful predictors. The pattern of bond price volatility, for instance, is expressed through the yield curve which reflects the time value of money:

- In normal times, long-term yields are higher than short-term interest rates.
- But just before recessions or sharp slowdowns, yield curves often invert (a process known as backwardation) and short-term rates can rise above long-term yields.

Stated in different terms, the structure of a yield curve is frequently but not always upward-sloping. Yield curves can also be flat or downward-sloping, depending on monetary policy and economic conditions. They may also have a tendency towards a complex format ranging from upward-sloping over some maturities while being flat over other maturities. A negative spread, or inverted yield curve, is typically interpreted as signaling a high probability of a recession.

The implied forward yield curve shown in Figure 4.2 is derived from the term structure of interest rates observed in the market. As such, it reflects the market players' expectation of future levels for short-term interest rates. In recent years, the data used for the curve's first 10 years have often been derived from swap contracts. Usually, though not always, the 10-to-30-years curve is an extrapolation.

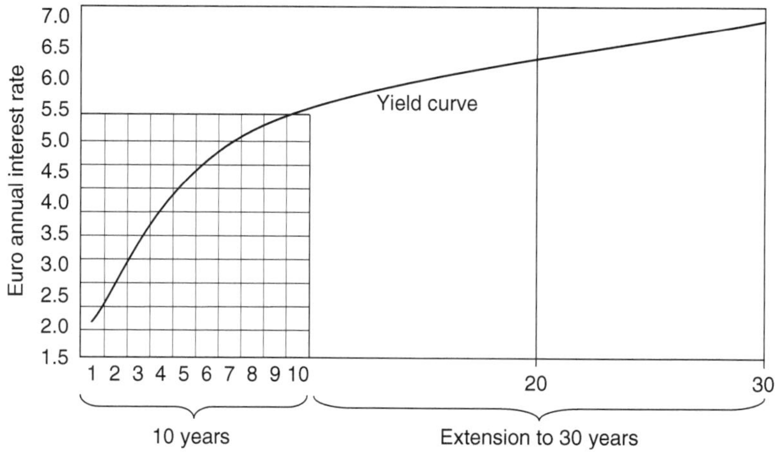

Figure 4.2 Implied overnight interest rates, based on 10-year projection and an up to 30 years extension.

Central banks don't set the yield curve's shape; they suffer it, though they may also try to influence it through statements, interpretations, and projections. Not infrequently, monetary policymakers are willing to let the yield curve invert *if* that is what it takes to dampen speculation in some important asset classes, like real estate.[13] An inversion is possible, but when the curve inverts it may do so in a way that would be different from a similar behavior in the past. Generally, but not always:

- The more long-term interest rates rise,
- The less the central bank has to raise short term rates.

Precisely because interest rates change over time, fixed-income investments face interest rate risk, which can adversely affect a bank's or an investor's financial condition. As a rule, credit institutions and investors are exposed to interest rate risk whenever the interest-related sensitivity of their assets does not match the sensitivity of their liabilities and off-balance-sheet positions (see also section 6).

Changes in interest rates may affect not only an institution's current earnings but also its future earnings and the economic value of its capital. For instance, for an institution or investor whose liabilities reprice faster than its assets, a rise in interest rates reduces net interest income by increasing the cost of funds relative to its yield on assets:

- *If* a bank has liabilities carrying interest rates which change faster than those on its assets,
- *Then* when interest rates rise its net present value will decline.

Hence the importance of studying the *term structure of interest rates*, which describes the relationship between *yield to maturity* and the maturity of a given fixed-income position. This is best done by taking out of the equation the impact of credit risk, using yields on risk-free securities of one of the Group of Ten governments – with different terms to maturity at a given time. (That's a procedure used by investors, commercial bankers, and central bankers.)

A positive-slope yield curve increases the impact of *compound interest rates*, which, as John Maynard Keynes used to say, represent the creative possibilities of capital multiplication. He characterized the power of compound interest over 200 years as staggering the imagination. In 1930, at the depths of global depression, Keynes wrote an essay entitled "Economic Possibilities for Our Grandchildren," which predicted a golden future for mankind, thanks to the labor-saving inventions of science and the driving force of compound interest[14] – but this forecast has not been fulfilled.

Compound interest over how long? Some experts are using the concept of a *holding period* as a measure of an investor's steadiness and, in certain cases, of performance. Evaluating gains and losses resulting from investment decisions solely on a calendar year basis is arbitrary. What one really wants to know is what the odds are on profitable performance over a holding period of a chosen length, with both risk and return as part of the picture.

The holding period and the investor's *time horizon* correlate. Many things can take place even over a short time horizon. While the bloodbath in bonds from February to April 1994 was due to the fact that the Fed raised interest rates several times in a row, falling rates can be just as deadly for some investments. In mid July 1995, on Wall Street, some observers speculated that Salomon Brothers' proprietary house traders, some of whom were paid a fortune in 1994, had lost money betting in the mortgage-backed bond market.

In conclusion, to make money with interest rates and the yield curve, bankers, traders and investors must be ahead of events. The principle with all investment classes is: "Never forget why you invest." The next crucial questions are: "How?" and "For how long?" One of the important characteristics of institutional investors, for example, is that their activity tends to combine, in the same person, both views inherent in investments: the short-term trader/broker viewpoint and the longer-term view of the assets manager. This combination does not give positive returns on all occasions.

6. Managing interest rate risk

Like any other exposure, that resulting from changes in interest rates must be managed. As an example, interest rate risk from loans and bonds with maturities greater than one year are swapped to the institution's treasury by individual back-to-back transactions. There exist, however, financial products like savings and wealth management accounts that have no contractual maturity date or direct market-linked rate and therefore their interest rate risk cannot be transferred by simple back-to-back transactions.

The strategy employed by asset managers in these cases is known as *replicating portfolios*. A replicated portfolio is a series of loans or deposits at market rates and fixed terms between the originating business unit and the treasury. Typically, this operation is structured to approximate, on average:

- The interest-rate cash flow, and
- The repricing behavior of the pooled client transactions.

Replicating portfolios tends to be a monthly rebalancing act, with the structure and parameters based on long-term market observations and the client's risk appetite – with its frequency increasing in nervous markets. The preferred instrument is interest rate swaps, for which there is in principle – though not necessarily always – a liquid and flexible market.

In terms of financial instruments, more sophisticated approaches use interest rate *swaptions*[15] to hedge adverse movements in interest rates. Interest rate swaptions are quoted in terms of the implied volatilities of the forward swap or Libor rates, which are their underlying. Implied volatilities express the market's expectations about future volatility in these forward rates over the life of the option, and are thus useful indicators for gauging market participants' degree of uncertainty. (Swaptions are available over a wide range of both interest rate maturities and times to expiration.)

Swaptions are both a trading and an analytical tool, because of enabling the development of a family of term structures of implied volatilities which provide indications of the market's near- and long-term uncertainty about future interest rates. Usually, but by no means always, swaptions refer to swap rates denominated in dollars, euros, or pounds:

- With maturities between 1 and 10 years, and
- Options on such rates expiring in between 1 month and 10 years.

A sophisticated approach will also consider globalization's impact on rebalancing. An important variable to account for is the main macro risks to the global economy, such as unexpected curtailment in financing from global capital providers – China, the Middle East, and Russia – as inflationary and liquidity pressures continue to intensify. Practically no portfolio can be considered immune to what happens in the global economy.

Not only are nominal interest rate changes by central banks a crucial factor in rebalancing studies but so also is projected inflation (Chapter 3). Long-term nominal interest rates can be decomposed into an expected real interest rate and the premium that investors require to compensate for expected inflation over the life of the bond:

- The real interest rate component can be linked to the economy's average growth prospects, over the maturity of the debt instrument.
- But an economic downturn dampens the short-to-medium-term growth prospects of nominal interest rates, while inflation may still rise.

On the other hand, inflation and inflation expectations may offset downward pressures on real rates. Nothing is carved in stone. No matter what the books may say, most cases in economics and finance have their own characteristics. There are no a priori rules applicable to all cases, hence the need for deeper analysis, particularly in a global environment:

- The degree to which domestic bond yields depend on developments abroad affects the monetary policy transmission process, and
- A time-varying response of international factors can be observed in domestic yield curve developments, often with a different percentage contribution over a given timeframe.

Some economists have criticized the policy of a multivariable analysis, essentially because they regard it as too complex and therefore insufficiently transparent. It should be pointed out, however, that the underlying rationale for comprehensively studying interest rate risks within the aforementioned framework is the lack of a generally accepted theory that can supply a consistent link between the real economic and monetary determinants of interest rates.

Neither is the rebalancing of a portfolio the only reason for analytical studies of the type discussed in this section. A significant amount of interest rate risk also arises from non-business-related balance sheet items like the financing of bank property and equity investments in associated firms. These risks are generally transferred to the company's treasury through replicating portfolios designed to approximate the funding profile mandated by the bank's senior management.

To measure and manage the treasury's market risk position, the entity's consolidated equity can be represented in the books by replicating portfolios of liabilities targeting currency and interest rate profiles. (See also sections 7 and 8 on interest rate and currency exchange rate correlations, which are important to international companies and globally exposed investors.)

No matter what sort of analytical studies they may be making, however, some companies have proved to be masters in the art of wounding themselves financially. Not long ago Tata Motors bought from Ford Land Rover in Gaydon, and Jaguar in Coventry, in a $2.3 billion deal. Ford, which purchased Jaguar in 1989 and Land Rover in 2000, has not been an exceptional owner. Neither company was starved of development funds but return on investment was dismal. Ford:

- Invested around $10 billion in Jaguar and Land Rover, and
- This came on top of the more than $5 billion spent on acquiring them in the first place.

Spending $15 billion and selling out for $2.3 billion is a fire sale which comments very poorly on Ford's quality of management. That's why I never accept blanket statements about strong management and the ingenuity of "this" or "that" highly paid CEO.

It is a good policy to think of Jonathan Swift's Gulliver when analyzing management's performance. Gulliver thought the professors, or *projectors* as he called them, were out of their senses when he visited the Grand Academy of Lagado on the Isle of Balnibarbi. The many improbably schemes like constructing houses from the roof down, and training pigs to plow with their snouts, amused him. But however bold and inventive the various "projects" were, there remained something incomprehensible about his visit to the academy, hinting at a fundamental deficiency in the experts' ideas. And so it is in business.

7. Currency rates, interest rates, and political factors

Financial theory says that relative interest rates and relative growth rates tend to be the main drivers behind currency movements. Practical reasons see to it that this is not always the case. Forecasts on growth rates are often too optimistic, the inflation rate may cut sharply into the current real interest rate of a given currency, or the market may act as a discounting mechanism on a currency's future:

- After the repeal by Richard Nixon of the Bretton Woods agreement, in the early 1970s, currency exchange rates became volatile, and
- Volatility in currency exchange joined interest rates, inflation, and other factors as part of the cost of money in investments and generally in wealth management.[16]

Many factors might work against a currency, like an ongoing credit bubble; a stockmarket crash that discourages foreign investments; a crash in commodities of which a given country is major exporter; or a huge current-account deficit which risks destabilizing the currency. Because it underpins a specific trend in capital flows, the carry trade, too, exercises considerably influence on currency exchange rates, as was the case with the yen and the Swiss franc as long as the carry trade was going strong.

The reader should appreciate however that neither of the aforementioned factors underpinning a currency's value is stand-alone. Economic textbooks say that currencies of economies with large current-account deficits should depreciate relative to those of currencies with surpluses. A case in point is given by the US dollar, which was falling almost steadily between 2002 and August 2008. But over that same period the currencies of other countries with large current-account deficits were appreciating, the Australian and New Zealand dollars being examples. And after July 2008 the dollar appreciated significantly against the euro and the British pound while the current-account deficit continued (section 8).

By the same token, currencies benefiting from foreign direct investments (FDIs), or in which important commodities are denominated, have an advantage over the others. The best example here is the US dollar. A global European-based bank has mentioned that, on a percentage basis in its portfolio, invested assets by currency have been:

- Dollars, 36 percent;
- Euros, 33 percent;
- Swiss francs, 17 percent;
- British pounds, 7 percent;
- Others, 7 percent.

The message the reader should retain from these references is that in terms of currency exchange rates there is much more synergy with interest rates, than journalists thought.

Political factors too make a difference in a currency's appreciation or depreciation. In the mid-1990s, for example, Italian bonds rose to new highs on expectations that Italy would be in on the first wave of single-currency participants in the euro. This significantly narrowed the yield spread between German and Italian bonds, which at the start was a rather surprising development given that at that time the prospects of monetary union were far from being certain.

Yield convergence is not a one-way road, said the president of one of Europe's leading banks, pointing out that if the single-currency agreements cracked the German bonds would shoot up while the Italian and French would plummet. His particular concern was that France's then socialist government would seize the opportunity to devalue.

For an international investor, currency rates, interest rates, and political factors work sometimes in unison and in other cases against one another. Therefore, a main issue in connection to a portfolio's composition is whether opposing interest rate positions in different currencies could be regarded as hedging one another – or whether the opposite is true.

Table 4.1 The policy of maturities on interest rate and currency exchange hedging followed by a global food company

	With maturity
Interest rate swaps for assets	5 years
Interest rate swaps for liabilities	5 years
Currency exchange forward/assets	1 year
Currency exchange forward/liabilities	2 years
Purchased options/assets	1 year

Such studies focus usually on two opposing currencies and corresponding interest rates because exact measurements based on correlations of all rates in all currencies would be very complex and difficult to incorporate into a dependable modeling and measurement system. The most conservative solution is to permit no offsetting between positions in different currencies, even if this constitutes a worst-case approach.

A crucial factor is, most evidently, the time horizon. Some experts suggest that when it comes to hedging prudent management enters into derivative contracts *maturing within 5 years*. Specifically for currency exchange, however, conservative companies see to it that *maturity does not exceed 1 year*. Table 4.1 presents the policy on maturities established by the one of the better-known global firms in the food industry:

- *Interest rate contracts* include: single-currency interest rate swaps, basis swaps, forward rate agreements and products with similar characteristics, interest rate futures, and interest rate options purchased.
- *Currency exchange rate contracts* include: cross-currency swaps, cross-currency interest rate swaps, outright forward exchange contracts, currency futures, and currency options purchased.

A prudent policy in calculating the credit equivalent amount of these instruments is to add together the total replacement cost, obtained by marking to market of all outstanding contracts with a positive value – and an amount for potential future credit exposure which reflects the residual maturity of the contract, calculated as a percentage of notional principal amount according to a matrix. One of the matrices being used is presented in Table 4.2.

Even this more prudent approach to hedging is not devoid of risks, as nobody can really foretell the changing whims and swings of the foreign exchange market. October 2008 saw a tandem sell-off of Brazilian shares and the real (Brazil's currency) as foreign investors rushed to cover losses elsewhere, or just took their money and ran.

Table 4.2 A matrix of residual maturity of interest rate and currency rate contracts

	Interest rate contracts	*Currency rate contracts*
Less than 1 year	Nil	1.0%
One year and over	0.5%	5.0%

In great contrast to a rising Brazilian economy, the sell-off triggered unexpected losses on foreign exchange derivatives that were meant to limit the exposure of local companies to currency moves but have exacerbated it instead. "While the real was appreciating these contracts looked like a fairly safe one-way bet. Companies got Lula-ed into a false sense of security," said Marcelo Carvalho of Morgan Stanley.[17]

An estimated 200 companies held such contracts. For many, such instruments were at best peripheral to their business, but still they represented big losses. In other countries, too, there have been similar stories. To ease the pain, on 29 October 2008 the Federal Reserve announced a deal with Brazil, Singapore, South Korea, and Mexico under which it provided up to $30 billion to each of them, aimed at bringing some stability to currency exchange rates.

8. The US dollar: a case study of the cost of money

The statement was made in section 7 that for an international investor, global bank, or multinational manufacturing and merchandising company, currency exchange rates are part of the cost of money. Whether or not this is appreciated, financial history suggests that a major currency's periods of appreciation or depreciation impact on trade and tend to persist for longer than most experts expect. For instance:

- Since 1973 the average trend of US dollar appreciation has lasted more than 8 years.
- In the first decade of the twenty-first century the dollar has been under pressure for nearly 3 years, and
- In July 2008 the dollar started a period of appreciation versus a broad basket of global currencies, expected to last for several years.[18]

Among the reasons given for the most recent dollar appreciation have been a change in reserve accumulation trends in non-US regions (away from local currencies); improvement in the American current-account deficit; and a better dollar valuation, which is seen as undervalued, especially versus the euro.[19] That's Merrill Lynch's opinion. To the contrary, Crédit Suisse believes that the dollar's gains are not related to any particularly positive outlook for the US economy, but rather reflect:

- Deteriorating confidence in currencies elsewhere, and
- Financial flows tied to the problems of the banking system.[20]

For its part, in 2008 the British pound has been anything but stable as it has lurched down against the dollar, a fall which followed and overtook an earlier fall against the euro in late 2007. Together they drove down sterling's trade-weighted index in a 12-month period.

As for the euro, for a couple of years the single currency looked like an attractive shelter. At least in some eyes joining the euro meant prestige, but it also meant constraints. For instance, governments joining euroland cannot devalue or change interest rates to suit their economic needs. This is something which few of euroland's member countries are willing to accept. Therefore, they pay lip service to it while:

- Gaming the system, and
- Breaking the rules of the Growth and Stability Pact.

Let's face it. The euro is a currency without a country and the European Central Bank has to worry about much more than Italy and Greece with their national debt of about 100 percent of GDP, or the runaway inflation of Slovenia and Slovakia (euroland's newest members). When in September 2008 Ireland provided a blanket coverage of *all* deposits in its banks (and some British banks too) it flooded the eurosystem with money and created budget deficits of up to 10 percent. (Ireland is not expected to balance its budget before 2013.)

One of the ironies with exchange rates is how quickly arguments about the reasons for a currency's strengths or weaknesses drop by the wayside and are altogether forgotten. Over the first two quarters of 2008, the conventional theory has emphasized reasons for the dollar's slide: budget deficits, current-account deficits, rising food and energy costs, as well as an inflation spike. Some economists doubted whether the rising price level was just a temporary blip. Rather, they believed that it was the visible end of a shift toward a higher international inflationary regime as a result of:

- Unfavorable structural forces,
- Loose global monetary policy, and
- Continuing weakness of the currency in which international commodity prices are labeled.

Beyond these considerations has been the fact that, in early September 2008, the integration of Freddie Mac and Fannie Mae into the US government's balance sheet posed a long-term risk to the dollar. The markets had difficulty in digesting the fact that Fannie's and Freddie's $30 billion equity was worth 6 cents to the dollar on 11 September 2008, less than a week after they were taken over by the Treasury – and the nationalization of the giant AIG did nothing to reassure them.

Yet beneath the surface there has been a dollar resurgence, not just a spike in its value that quickly passed over. Statements made by Paulson and Bernanke, respectively the Fed secretary and chairman, left a footprint, aided by downward revisions to global growth forecasts.

From mid July 2008 to mid September 2008, for nearly two months the currency exchange market had voted for this thesis. The British pound was down against the US dollar by 12 percent, the euro by 10 percent, the already weak Korean won by 9 percent, the Brazilian real by 7 percent, and the Canadian and Singapore dollars by 6 percent.

According to this interpretation of facts and figures, the global downward trend in growth forecasts may have caught many market participants by surprise, so they were reacting to an unexpected event by beefing up the dollar. In other words, the US dollar rallied as global economic forecasts were revised down and as markets sensed increasingly that growth is the important issue.

As the dollar took on weight, some of the European Union's economies were in for surprises. Not unexpectedly, these were the previous beneficiaries of the euro's strength against the dollar. As the common currency strengthened to a peak of $1.60 against the dollar from a low of $1.44 in January 2008, the currencies of central European countries rose even faster, because traders bought them to take advantage of higher interest rates. But with signs that the dollar had strengthened, bankers were becoming increasingly nervous about the outlook for: Poland, Hungary, and the Czech Republic.

Worse yet, currency weaknesses were putting further pressure on the already high levels of inflation of these economies, hitting the value of their exports. The double blow of a falling euro and a weakening EU economy was expected to hit eastern Europe hard while its economies were also suffering from financial imbalances that built up in the aftermath of a big expansion of the banking sector, which has tripled after 2000 as domestic and corporate loan books have grown.[21]

For the dollar, this was a positive development. "The phrase 'the US dollar is becoming the US peso' was useful shorthand a while ago," stated a Merrill Lynch study. "But the dollar has staged a nice reversal in recent months... whether the dollar's strength is cyclical or secular..."[22]

Part Two
Debt

5
Leverage Can Be Highly Counterproductive

1. The policy of more leverage led to disaster

Leverage, or gearing, was originally a term describing the use of ownership as a basis for borrowing. In addition, the term refers to the pyramiding of debt so that earnings (but also losses) increase in greater proportion than those based on equity alone. Shakespeare's Polonius advised his son: "Neither a borrower nor a lender be," let alone a leveraged borrower or lender to geared people and companies.

Leveraging has been one of the crucial factors blamed by the 15 November 2008 G20 Washington economic conference for having wrecked the American and the global economy. The third paragraph of the communiqué reads: "[W]eak underwriting standards, unsound risk management practices, increasingly complex and opaque financial products, and consequent *excessive leverage*[1] combined to create vulnerabilities in the system."

In years past, leverage has been more frequently associated with the activities of speculators than with financial management.[2] Times however have changed. Many CEOs and CFOs are bent on high leverage and don't think of themselves as reckless but as clever and skilful enough to exploit the system and multiply their power (till the day of reckoning). Even teachers teach that "using leverage leaves the rest of our identity intact" – which is utterly untrue.

Gearing has been lionized by the media. As Figure 5.1 shows, in the 2003 to 2007 timeframe the investment banks' leverage rose from an already high average of 21 percent to nearly 31 percent, with much more than that in some companies. Big manufacturing corporations too became major unregulated leveraged players in financial markets: Porsche, I have been told, has a finance director who runs the firm like a hedge fund, making far more from financial trading than from trading cars.

When in March 2008 Bear Stearns crashed, Wall Street insiders said it was geared 33 times up, while when Lehman Brothers went down the tubes (6 months later) it was geared 40 times up. Shortly after Lehman's

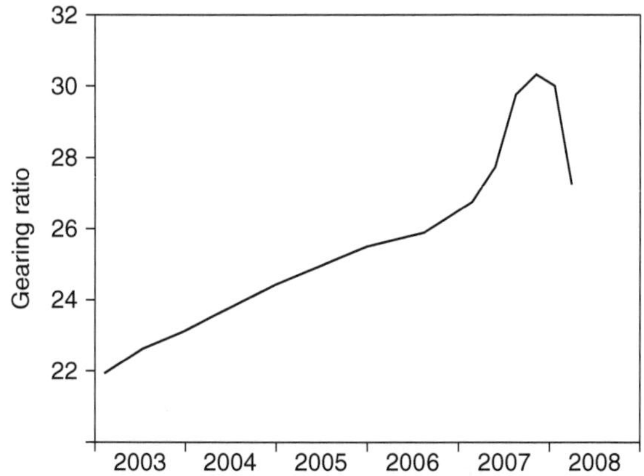

Figure 5.1 Average leverage ratio of US investment banks, 2003–8.

bankruptcy, when Fortis was saved from default by taxpayer's money, an Italian banker told me he had unearthed the following gearing ratios for a bunch of European banks (which I present with the benefit of the doubt):

- Barclays, 63 times.
- Royal Bank of Scotland, 45 times.
- Fortis, 40 times.
- Dexia, 28 times.
- Unicredit, 20 times.

All of them and many more faced further challenges from weak macroeconomics, tougher funding, negative earning momentum, toxic waste in their portfolio, write-downs, loan losses, and balance sheet deleveraging. Past mismanagement led the majority of them to the need of begging the government for money to avoid outright bankruptcy.

High leverage and default probability correlate. That's the way to interpret the dubious substance of the Modigliani–Miller hypothesis which states that the value of a firm is the same whether it finances itself with equity or with debt; and equity is expensive while debt can be cheap. To critics, this is a good theory for getting a Nobel prize, but not for running a company or a nation. Franco Modigliani and Merton Miller saw debt as the best possible solution because:

- Dividends are taxed twice, while
- Interest paid on debt is tax-deductible.

There is a tax loophole, but what's the cost of exploiting it? Both the Fed and the ECB define the default point as that of equality of market value of assets (essentially using as proxy market capitalization) and total liabilities. As equity price drops, total liabilities may exceed capitalization because:

- Debt financing has inflated leveraging, and
- It has created financial instability in a downturn.

Economists now point out that beyond a certain level in gearing (which is not fixed in advance), bondholders act in a way that the cost of a company's debt rises sharply. This obliges management to reduce the entity's debt, as independent rating agencies are watching out for market signals, and banks become wary of giving loans or extending lines of credit – particularly in a downbeat financial environment.

The disaster that follows management reliance on more gearing, and inability to hold both capital and liquidity to face adversity, is exemplified by Taylor Wimpey's fate. This company had been Britain's biggest homebuilder, whose market capitalization approached £400 billion ($700 billion) in 2007. The firm, however, was light on equity and heavy on debt. It also spent freely, handing to its shareholders:

- £117 million in dividends, and
- £252 million in share buybacks.

A year later, in June 2008, Taylor Wimpey went hat-in-hand to its shareholders for £500 million to shore up its balance sheet. Banks would not extend credit to a highly leveraged firm and shareholders would not oblige. Top management therefore returned without a single extra pound to the company's name and its already weak share price collapsed, bringing the homebuilder's capitalization below £40 billion – or 10 percent of where it stood a year earlier. Let this be a lesson.

Geared companies which depend for their survival on continued bank lending or shareholders' benevolence are in for rude surprises. Figure 5.2 suggests that the grand leverage ball attended by the banking industry is over. In mid August 2008 the Fed released its Senior Loan Officer Survey and the results were a disaster. The supply and demand for credit were found to be in a severe downturn, even if in the preceding 12 months:

- The US central bank cut rates 325 basis points, and
- It added a list of non-conventional measures to beef up the credit system.

Worried about their own financial staying power and their clients' creditworthiness, in 2008 lenders have been seriously clamping down on both

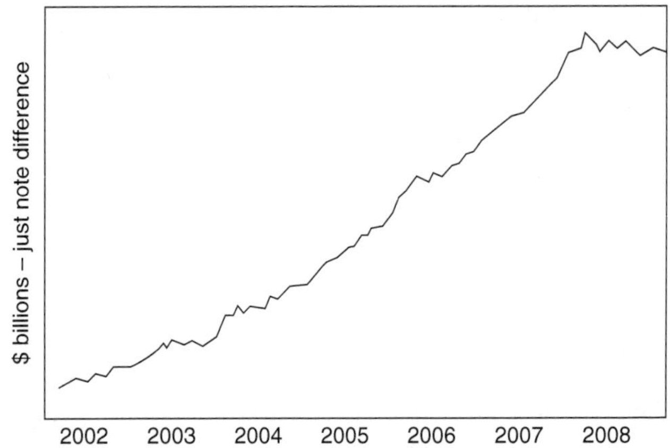

Figure 5.2 Bank credit by all US commercial banks: the great leverage party.

company and household credit. The share of the banks that tightened credit card standards surged to 66 percent in the third quarter of the year, more than double the share in the second quarter and a huge change from 2007 when damage looked contained and the banks were rather easing their guidelines.

Tightening came at a time when households had stepped up their credit card reliance as a source of cash flow. Therefore, the sharp change in the banks' lending policy exerted a dampening squeeze on the consumer (Chapter 7). Critics suggest this was the fault of the banking industry, which overplayed its hand:

- In 1980 financial sector debt was only 10 percent of non-financial debt.
- In 2008 it stood at 50 percent, turning investment banks into debt machines that trade heavily with each other.

Leverage ratios in the banking industry compete with those of hedge funds. In terms of bank-to-bank financial transactions and of toxic waste, collateralized debt obligations (CDOs) and credit default swaps (CDSs) generated concerns, given that the leverage embedded in them does not appear on banks' balance sheets. Some regulators drew attention to the way banks value deeply subordinated portions of CDOs:

- Offering very attractive returns,
- But being at risk of falling off a cliff if something goes wrong.

Neither are the governments themselves, and for that matter the national economy, free of leverage. Summing up federal, state, company and household liabilities (Chapter 7), for every productive $1 there are $3.7 of debt.

To the contrary, it takes $4 of investment to create $1 of productive activities – which means that the west only puts on the table one-fifteenth of the capital it needs to keep going. It would be difficult to find a better example of capitalism without capital.

2. Market players must sort out their nonsense

It is not easy to weed high leverage out of the system because it has taken root in the political establishment. An example is provided by Phil Gramm, a former US senator turned investment banker, who in the late 1990s was a leading architect of legislation to loosen the regulation of Wall Street and, among other accomplishments, killed the Glass–Steagall Act with the help of then President Bill Clinton. Gramm has been financial industry advisor to (and a close friend of) John McCain who, in July 2008, had to step down from his official role in McCain's campaign after:

- Describing the US as a "nation of whiners", and
- Dismissing the severe economic downturn as a "mental recession."[3]

Gramm and his brand of investment bankers/politicians did however leave their footprint on McCain's campaign. The Republican presidential candidate of 2008 said he was opposed to "excessive and unnecessary government regulation," though he promised reform of the "patchwork" of regulatory agencies that oversee Wall Street, around a policy of reducing rather than strengthening financial regulation.

That's not what the US economy needs or investors want in order to regain confidence in the market and turn them positive towards banks. The silver lining of a long series of write-downs and recaps has been the message that the business of most financial intermediaries grew within a shadow banking system whose members are investment banks, hedge funds, money market funds, private equity groups, structured investment vehicles (SIVs), conduits, and other lenders. What these have in common is that:

- They borrowed very short-term,
- Used very high leverage, and
- Invested into illiquid long-term instruments.

In a liquidation, what remains of the thin assets owned by banks could only fetch no more than 20 cents to the dollar. An example is a structured investment vehicle (SIV) known as Mainsail II, which fell into receivership after the credit crunch led to a fall in the value of the Mainsail II assets portfolio. The sale of some $630 million of its assets highlighted what mortgage-backed debt might be worth. Investors faced losses of more than 80 percent of the value of the once top-rated debt they had bought.

After receiving indicative bids of about 20 percent of face value for the securities, 12 banks bid 16.35 percent on the day of the auction. Investors holding senior debt hoped to recover just over 25 percent of the original investment by cashing out of the vehicle whose original value was $1.4 billion (The auction was made by KPMG as receivers; the SIV originally belonged to Solent Capital of London.) Other investors in liquidated SIVs and portfolios full of toxic waste fared even worse.

Banks have been too slow in sorting out their nonsense. A day after the late October 2008 coordinated move by central banks aimed at appeasing the market,[4] shares of Morgan Stanley and Goldman Sachs – the No. 2 and No. 1 American investment banks – tumbled. The news of a sharp cut in interest rates was overshadowed by the fact that Moody's Investors Service put a negative outlook on both companies' credit ratings.

Morgan Stanley's equity was down 38.7 percent in one day, on doubts whether a planned $9 billion cash injection from Mitsubishi UFJ Financial Group of Japan would be enough to enable the company to ride out the current crisis (its shares had lost about 68 percent in just one week). Rumor also had it that, unsure about the safety of its money, Mitsubishi had asked for guarantees by the US government on the safety of its capital injection in Morgan Stanley.[5]

Goldman Sachs shares were down 16.8 percent also in one day, on worries about Morgan Stanley and the broader financial turmoil. Stating that its review was based upon its expectation of an extended downturn in global capital market activity, Moody's warned that it might cut the long-term debt ratings of Goldman, which would increase its cost of borrowing.

Investors had good reason to be worried. As shown in Figure 5.3, all three indices – S&P 500 in America, DJ Stoxx 50 in Europe, and Nikkei 225 in Japan – dived, breaking previous records. Let this massive destruction of capitalization, and therefore of wealth, be a lesson to all who think and profess that high leverage is "the solution." The market had good reasons to be nervous, because in notional principal amounts the banks' exposure was at the level of hundreds of trillions in just two instruments:

- Exposure to credit default swaps (CDSs, section 7) reached $62 trillion in early 2008 (though by October it fell to about $58 trillion), a dangerous level as bankruptcies increased significantly, and
- This has been largely surpassed by exposure to interest rate swaps (IRSs), which stood at nearly $400 trillion in January 2008, with many long-term contracts probably under water in portfolios of counterparties who bet wrongly – as interest rates were cut sharply by central banks.

With so much blood in equities and derivatives, it is no wonder that year-on-year up to 30 September 2008 the "best" investment has been global

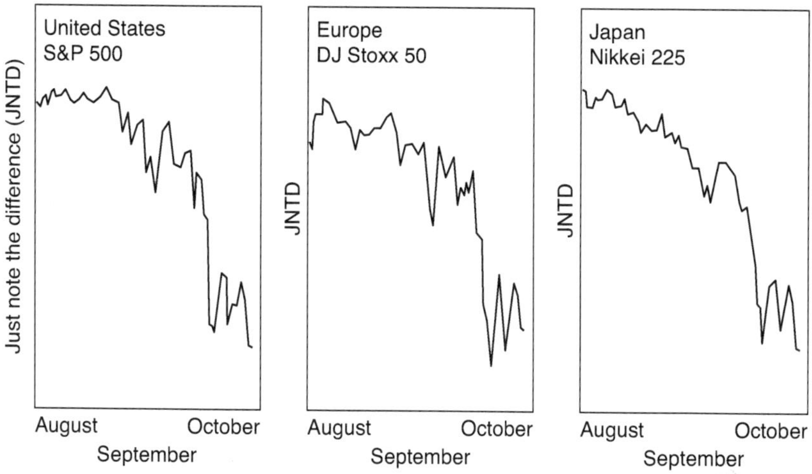

Figure 5.3 As investors woke up to the disastrous effects of high leverage, stock exchange indices dived and fortunes shrank by half.

fixed-income, with return ranging from +4.4 percent for 10-year Treasury Note references to +1.8 percent for cash but with negative figures at −4.1 percent for emerging markets sovereign debt and −10.6 percent for junk bonds. Over the same period the results from equity investments were:

- −19.3 percent for S&P 500;
- −20.6 percent for Nasdaq;
- −35.6 percent for emerging market equities;
- −42.7 percent equities from Brazil, Russia, India, and China (BRIC).[6]

Even seasoned investors, like Warren Buffett, were feeling the punch. The stakes Berkshire took in GE ($3 billion) and in Goldman Sachs ($5 billion) were noteworthy for the terms that it was able to negotiate. The deals have been for preferred stock paying 10 percent interest, which seems extremely generous. But stockmarket blues saw to it that these carefully negotiated deals, too, were going under water.

Volatility has been king with VIX, the volatility index, rising to 70 in October 2008,[7] in spite of the fact that globally central banks and governments took unprecedented steps to counter the financial crisis. A growing number of investors believed that deleveraging and systemic risks within the markets are likely to keep volatility in equities at high levels – notwithstanding the passage of the Troubled Assets Relief Act (TARA, Chapter 10) and ongoing intervention by the British and euroland governments to support European banks.

3. Gaming the capital requirements for banks

Regulatory capital requirements for the banking industry were first fixed on a cross-border basis with the Basel I agreement engineered in 1988 by the Basel Committee on Banking Supervision (see also Chapter 9). The 8 percent capital ratio for international banks has been an improvement over the 6-percent-or-less ratio of previous years. In a short period of time, however, the 8 percent became highly questionable, as in most jurisdictions:

- Central banks and regulators bent over to please the banking industry, by reducing their watch;
- The quality of capital eroded through hybrid deferred tax assets (DTAs), misrated AAAs, and different other bypasses;
- Neither Basel I not Basel II[8] made any provisions for mandatory liquidity; and
- The huge write-downs that followed the subprimes crisis depleted the banks' capital base, and sent them running left, right, and center to get capital.

In addition, debt-based assets and structured instruments assumed to be "safe" turned out to be toxic waste – which came over and above the fact that many banks gamed the rules by shunting assets into off-balance-sheet vehicles, where capital charges have been lower or nil.

As core capital as a share of assets hit bottom, on 13 October 2008 governments obliged the taxpayer to recapitalize wounded banks. The US Treasury did so to the tune of $25 billion to each of Citigroup, JPMorgan Chase, Bank of America, Bank of New York Mellon, and Wells Fargo; $10 billion to each of Goldman Sachs, Morgan Stanley, and others – all of them unwarranted handouts from the $700 billion appropriated by Congress (Chapter 10).

The British government recapitalized the Royal Bank of Scotland, taking a stake of 60 percent in its equity; as well as HBOS and Lloyds TSB, which gave it a 40 percent equity stake. In continental Europe governments were quick to appropriate billions for similar interventions as Herbert Hoover's ghost haunted them with nightmarish memories of the 1929 Great Depression.

Done as an emergency, this recapitalization provided proof that Basel I, Basel II, and the way they have been applied and supervised failed in their objectives. In the background of globalized rules for capital requirements was the fact that to provide a level playing field, regulatory capital must be:

- Comparable throughout internationally active credit institutions, and
- Able to satisfy prudential minimum requirements.

For starters, a standard recognition of own funds which fits all legislations, regulations, and commercial banks is by no means an easy matter

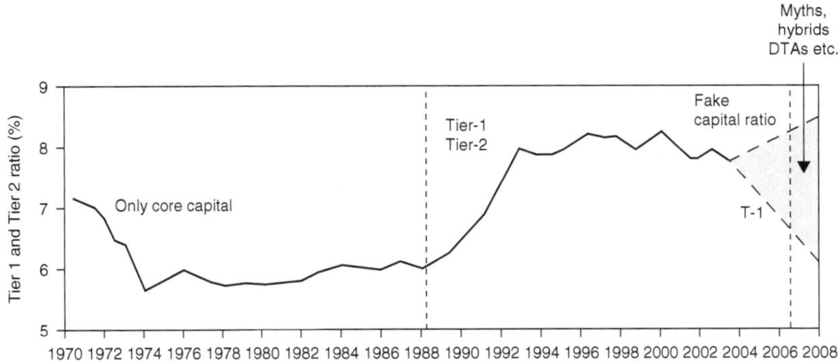

Figure 5.4 The aftermath of gaming the Basel rules on capital reserves in the banking industry.

to determine because it calls for convergence between laws and rules. Such convergence is impeded by limitations arising from legal differences, divergent goals of national banking regulators, and the definition of commercial business of credit institutions. To be meaningful, regulatory capital requirements have to be:

- Coherently established,
- Generally objective,
- Verifiable at any time, and
- With iron-clad clauses which have severe legal penalties associated with them.

That sort of clarity and detail has never been the case. Theoretically, Basel I has applied a capital ratio higher than that preceding it, as can be seen superficially in Figure 5.4. Practically, this is questionable because Basel I was a compromise where – to protect their banks – the Japanese and French pressed for (and obtained) a Tier-2 definition which weakened the capital ratio.

The better way to appreciate the difference between these two main components of regulatory capital, T-1 and T-2, is to understand the philosophy behind them and the criteria used to distinguish between them. Tier-1 was supposed to represent *equity* or *core capital* – a supposition that ceased being relevant a short time after Basel I went into effect. To understand why, the reader should note that equity's A, B, and C is:

A. Performance. Shares are permanent; subordinated debt is not.
B. Possibility of write-offs. A company can write down equity without being sued in court.
C. Possibility of stopping payment. Dividends can be stopped; interest to bonds and loans cannot.

The board cannot write down debt without a court decision, bankruptcy, or filing for protection from creditors under Chapter 11 or a similar law. Between them, the A, B, and C document the fact that Tier 1 can include only what is generally known as paid-up capital:

- Equity proper,
- Endowment(s),
- Published reserves,
- Profits for the year,
- Paid-up cooperative society shares,
- Contributions from silent partners.

Tier-1 capital, however, excludes preferred shares – and this is only one of the reasons why Hybrid Tier-1 capital (HT-1), with interest paid up front, and plenty of other tricks, is fake core capital (more precisely, one of several fakes).

One of the most ridiculous kinds of "capital" invented by the Japanese banks and generalized is so-called *deferred tax assets* (DTAs, Chapter 1). They work like this. A company has a torrent of red ink but the law allows it to recover taxes paid in past years when it was profitable. By a miracle, current losses become an "asset." In reality, it is a pure myth. As an example, take the 1988 Capital Accord, the broadly defined asset categories created opportunities for banks to game the system, thus:

- Reducing their burden of regulatory capital for any given level of risk, or
- Increasing their exposure to risk for any given level of capital.

Plenty of gimmicks became possible, as managing a portfolio to reduce one's exposure involves combining assets with different risks in such a way that, at least in theory, the hazards offset each other. In practice, that's a myth which produced a great number of scandals. (One of the DTA scandals concerned Resona, the fifth-largest Japanese bank. When the DTAs were excluded, its capital reserves fell from 6 percent to 2 percent.) Precisely because there are so many opportunities for fraudulent financial reporting, one of the regulators suggested during our meeting that:

- All potential expected losses should be covered by equity, and
- Only core capital should be the definition of T-1; not Hybrid T-1.

It is also necessary to take a close look at Tier 2 capital, which was a compromise among central bankers at the time of the 1988 Capital Accord. T-2 is "supplementary capital," including some kinds of debt, loan-loss reserves, and up to 45 percent of unrealized gains on securities (paper profits). Paper profits are extremely volatile and T-2 has been further weakened by dividing into two parts:

- "Upper Tier 2", which is perpetual subordinated debt and can be up to 100 percent of Tier 2.
- "Lower Tier 2", which is dated subordinated debt and can go up only to 50 percent of Tier 2.

All this is of course monkey business and it is highly disquieting that governments, legislators, and regulators have allowed banks to keep Mickey Mouse money in their vaults – a situation that has been aggravated over time by the securitized subprimes, SIVs, conduits, collateralized debt obligations, credit default swaps, and so on.[9]

Beyond this, there have been accounting scandals. As Bloomberg news had it on 12 October 2008, AIG's chief auditors had warned in 2007 that derivatives valuation may be flawed – but top management chose to look the other way.

In fact, not only are derivatives valuations flawed because *creative accounting* has become generalized practice, but also the metrics used by regulators are near-sighted and incapable of conveying the true level of a bank's exposure. A case in point is value at risk (VAR), which came along with the 1996 Market Risk Amendment by the Basel Committee.[10]

4. The bubbles of the 1920s and the early years of this century are twins

The superleverage of the banking industry has been helped by the fact that through 2005 and part of 2006 there was available cheap, plentiful debt that companies were able to use for a swarm of deals. With regard to US dollars, the cost of money was the lowest in half a century, allowing firms to lower the cost of capital, increase earnings per share, and reward their top brass and their traders with huge bonuses. Helped by cheap credits, there was a rapid appreciation of real estate:

- Because it was an accomplice to the profits generation through creative accounting, and
- None, including regulators, bothered to notice that all this flood of "profits" was deprived of real substance.

There is a close and disturbing similitude between the real estate bubbles of the mid to late 1920s and that of the last few years. To quote a 1924 reference in the *New York Evening Post*:

> Of late years [those immediately preceding 1924] real estate bonds have been sold perhaps more widely than any other type of bond; they have

> been placed with the *small investor* [emphasis added] so well in cases that many have come to regard them as the personification of safe investing.[11]

It sounds like the typical fraudulent sort of "alternative investments" (read: illiquid, leveraged derivatives) pushed down the throat of small investors who understood nothing of them.[12]

In the 1920s as in 2003 to 2007, financial institutions not only practiced reckless very short-term behavior themselves but also encouraged their clients in it. Neither in the 1920s nor in the first years of this century were there curbs on the pay of the bosses of banks that benefited from the proliferation of dubious credits and the hard sales of a wide range of shaky debt instruments (see also Chapter 8).

If anything, firms with compensation systems that encouraged their managers to lend carefully got into trouble, while institutions that exploited the gap in legislation and supervision reaped rewards. A relatively recent example is the funds-of-hedge-funds which flourished in the years immediately after the stockmarket crash of 2000.

Practically all big banks (and some smaller ones) ran hugely leveraged funds-of-hedge-funds "at home," whose paper they sold aggressively to their clients. Their strategy was that 20 percent of each of their retail clients' net worth should be put in this shaky, risk-prone "investment".[13] Some clients resisted; others however went along, lured by imaginary promises of high returns.

The crisis that started in July/August 2007 revealed that the track record of such "investments" has been dismal. (From 1 January 2008 to 30 September, in the first three-quarters of the year, the hedge fund industry's performance was −11 percent, of which −5 percent was in the month of September 2008 alone. Neither were the P&L results brilliant in the previous years. In 2004 they stood at +6.9 percent; 2005, +7.5 percent; 2006, +10.4 percent; and 2007, +10.3 percent – hardly the stuff justifying colossal fees and premiums.)

It is therefore not surprising that as Citigroup credit analyst Matt King said, anecdotal evidence suggested at least 20 percent of the hedge funds industry's assets could be pulled out in the December 2008 redemption window. If accurate, this figure would reverse 3½ years of inflows, depleting hedge funds as well as funds-of-funds.[14]

Part of the hedge funds problem in terms of assumed risks, unwarranted sales, and high fees is that they are not regulated. Yet it has been a long-standing thesis of George Soros, himself a hedge fund manager, that hedge funds should be regulated like anything else; and that their leverage can be best checked through the banks:

- Reserves for lending by credit institutions should reflect the gearing and riskiness of the borrower, and

- They must be higher when lending to hedge funds and other vehicles with significant risk appetite.

In an interview he gave on 26 May 2008 on Bloomberg news, Soros pressed the point that *if* future crises are to be avoided, *then* leveraging should not be allowed to reach the levels it did in recent years. When this happens it is followed by a period of rapid deleveraging, which we are in and for which everybody pays.

To avoid repetition of the same mistakes regulation should be tightened and new rules must reflect limitations proper to human nature. The regulators, Soros said, are imperfect and they are moreover bureaucratic. He could have added that regulators are also pressured by the government and politicians who tend to count the wrong way,[15] the result being a watered-down supervisory zeal.

Lobbies and government pressure (up to a point the two are synonymous) also see to it that urgent new rules are delayed and in many cases scrapped. Keeping some accounts *off-balance-sheet* (OBS) was permitted by central banks in the early 1980s when these amounts were trivial because it was not quite clear where to write them: on the left or the right of the B/S. But by the mid 1990s the OBS accounts had zoomed and banks were required to reintegrate them into their balance sheets.

Commercial and investment banks, however, are inventive. The SIVs and other vehicles (as well as many novel instruments) of the twenty-first century were developed and kept off-balance-sheet. Finally, after the deluge in credit risk, in April 2008 the Financial Accounting Standards Board (FASB, which regulates accounting practices) required that banks consolidate off-balance-sheet vehicles used to package assets into securities – which is right.

Then, under government pressure, by the same Bush Administration which created the Big Bubble in the first place, on 30 July 2008 the FASB voted to move the date for the rule change back one year to fiscal years beginning after 15 November 2009:

- *If* the rules were to be implemented in 2008,
- *Then* banks would have to raise more capital to carry their off-balance-sheet liabilities.

In the prevailing market environment this would of course have been difficult to achieve for those banks whose creditworthiness was wanting[16] – but the delay also provided irrefutable evidence that the banks had taken big OBS risks for which they had no capital coverages. Several members of the FASB said that they were delaying the rule's effective date reluctantly, because investors would benefit from clearer information about the risks banks face from off-balance-sheet assets and liabilities.

5. Leveraged lending and borrowing

When on 5 September 2008 Nevada's Silver State Bank became the eleventh credit institution to be taken over by the Fed, it dawned on financial analysts that derivative financial instruments and off-balance-sheet vehicles were not alone in undermining the banking industry. Leveraged lending was still another factor. This feeling was reinforced when five American banks failed within an equal number of weeks, up to 10 October.

Both Washington Mutual and Wachovia provide convincing examples of the destructive power of leveraged lending. They were undone not by marking-to-market losses, but by the curiously low quality of their loan books. (The same is true with commercial banks in Britain and many European Union countries.) Bad loans that in the current environment cannot be sold at any price exercise great pressure on the balance sheet, and banks are having trouble raising long-term debt:

- As their debt matures, they are having to refinance with shorter-term debt.
- But the market does not take it kindly, thereby raising significantly their costs and their vulnerability.

Added to this is a story of falling dominoes where lenders, guarantors, and regulators try to guess which institutions, and which of their "dear clients," might next be hit by write-offs. Theoretically, up to mid 2008 the damage to banks from loans gone sour was contained. Practically, it is not, and there exist second-order effects which will not go away, if for no reason other than that they are sustained by the presence of deep structural flaws which are still present:

- Leveraged lending,
- Complex derivatives,
- Dubious creditworthiness,
- The shadow banking system, and
- Bizarre events of dealings made to create bogus bonuses.

Beyond that, the fact that regulators did not sanction the bank's manipulation of different asset categories, including the masquerading of their creditworthiness, has opened the doors to more regulatory arbitrage. Capital requirements proved to be elastic, and therefore ineffective in holding banks in line (section 3), and this discussion about tougher regulations went nowhere because of political interference.

The problem with leveraged loans is multi-fold. On the one hand, a bank that doesn't have enough funding through deposits and tries to replenish its treasury encounters problems in the wholesale markets. On the other hand, its attempts to shore up liquidity do not necessarily address its capital shortfall or quell concerns about rising impairments on its portfolio. A third factor, one that's part of an ongoing irony, is that even if necessary:

- Government interventions make it even harder for private investors to come forward with funds.
- Yet, had private funding been left to its own devices it might have been able to heal the system.

Cash is king. No wonder therefore that the credit institutions themselves have reverted from a state of leveraged lending to becoming lending-thrifty. Lenders have raised rates while the central bank was hoping that they would follow its policy and reduce them:

- Tight liquidity has been responsible for that, and
- Lenders also recognized the damage done to their portfolios by subprime mortgages.

In parallel with this development the commercial paper market, already hurt since the beginning of the banking and credit crisis, faded. The volume of commercial paper outstanding fell further in late September 2008 while investors became more unwilling to lend for long. On 30 September 2008, AT&T said that the previous week it had been unable to sell any commercial paper with a maturity longer than overnight:

- The volume of asset-backed commercial paper maturing in four days or less ballooned from $32 billion a day to $104 billion, and
- In parallel with this the amount maturing in 31 to 40 days fell by an impressive 63 percent.[17]

Confronted with a crash of the commercial paper market, in the first week of November 2008 the Federal Reserve Bank of New York said it would begin buying "eligible" money market securities as part of a new funding drive. Such purchases are part of the Money Market Investor Funding Facility (MMIFF), designed to improve liquidity in short-term funding markets and open to a certain type of money market mutual funds:[18]

- MMIFF is the third Fed program aimed at supporting the commercial paper market,
- The other programs are the Fed's commercial paper funding and direct purchases of asset-backed commercial paper.

The reason given for these handouts has been that the $3.4 trillion money market fund industry is the largest provider in the US commercial paper market. After Lehman's bankruptcy, in mid September 2008, money market funds were hit by a wave of redemptions that caused them to sharply rein in lending. In turn, this created problems for companies looking to raise short-term capital.

As this continuous rip-off of the American taxpayer demonstrates, the business model of companies which depended on leveraged credit for their profits got unstuck. Another example is that of infrastructure investments like power plants, transmission cables, and ports made with other people's and companies' money (sometimes even money from central banks) pioneered by Macquarie, Australia's investment bank, which briefly prospered at the heart of a highly leveraged global business:

- Critics said that there has been a flaw in the highly leveraged investment line adopted by infrastructure funds.
- The pros answered that they held assets which were dull but stable and this could support high leverage.

The market's verdict supported the doubters' viewpoint. On 27 August 2008, Macquarie's shares tumbled nearly 10 percent following the words of a UBS analyst who said that the global credit squeeze was hurting its business.[19]

This came 5 days after they were hit by another brick when Morgan Stanley issued a very bearish report on Macquarie's main listed fund, Macquarie Investment Group (MIG). In the background were numerous negatives, like MIG's long-standing practice of paying out more in distributions to shareholders than it received from underlying investments.

Another debt-happy Australian investment bank has been Babcock & Brown. Its shares tumbled in August 2008 and it was selling assets and having problems rolling over short-term liabilities. As brief reminder, in 2004 Babcock & Brown had gone public at \$A5 a share,[20] only to see its value peak at \$A35 in mid-2007 before collapsing to \$A0.76. According to the pros, the main reason was liquidity, which had been no problem when it was easy to sell assets and refinance debt – but nobody liked Babcock's debt structure any more.

In August 2008 Babcock had admitted it would receive \$A100 million for a power plant in which it had invested \$A220 million – a 55 percent loss, yet even that was a favorable transaction. The buyer was the Tasmanian government, keen to avoid power shortages. There goes all that blah, blah that a leveraged assortment of toll roads, ports, and buildings is better than having liquid money.

6. The swarm of self-inflicted wounds

Through the 1990s the rise of complex derivatives trades saw to it that bank failures became minimal, and this remained true even during the Asian and

Russian debt crises of 1997 and 1998 as well as the dotcom collapse of 2000. By securitizing their loans and keeping fewer of them on their balance sheets, banks found their life's elixir:

- Reporting strong returns on their assets,
- Generating bumper earnings, and
- Paying inordinate salaries and commissions along with colossal bonuses.

In essence, however, credit institutions simply replaced the risk of lending which resided classically in their own courtyard with exposures from outside their sphere of expertise. There, they navigated in uncharted territories with scant attention paid to warehoused current and potential risks.

To further inflate jumbo profits and bonuses, several lenders railroaded naive borrowers into taking on mortgages they could not afford, knowing they would sell these unsound loans into the market with few questions asked. Additionally, many banks made themselves vulnerable by financing long-term loans through vehicles operating in the short-term money market,[21] rather than from depositors or through issuance of bonds.

With all these ingredients which represented a very bad practice, it is not surprising that banks were strangled when the money markets seized up. Their vulnerability increased as stresses in mature financial systems, like those of the American, British and euroland economies, became deeper and more drawn out:

- The initial liquidity problems encountered in mid 2007, in the early phases of the turmoil, gave way to more fundamental concerns about capital positions and creditworthiness, and
- Some original optimism that the extent, size and spread of the credit crisis and banking crisis would be largely known by the end of 2007 was replaced by continuous write-downs in 2008 by big financial institutions, as they preceded with asset valuations.

Under both US GAAP and IFRS accounting rules, marking-to-market losses on structured instruments like collateralized debt obligations (CDOs) are mapped directly into the income of audited full-year financial statements and quarterly reports. Little by little, financial statements have shown that many big banks were hit hard by the unprecedented market turmoil which they themselves had created.

While the agent was said to be the surging delinquencies on American subprime and Alt-A mortgages, in reality equally potent reasons for continuing heavy losses have been (and continue to be) the unprecedented amount of leverage (section 1). There has also been the fact that credit derivatives did not perform the major miracle that commercial bankers, investment bankers, and several central bankers expected them to do – that of returning credit institutions to a pristine state of capital adequacy.

As a matter of fact, the explosive growth of credit derivatives markets over the past 10 years has not been nearly as effective as experts thought in taking the credit risk from the balance sheets of commercial banks and transferring it to other investors. Most of the exposures thought to have been mitigated remained within the banking system, even if they were redistributed within and between different financial industries.

At the end of the day, therefore, banks had to acknowledge that they were bearing the full impact of credit risks – even though many of them had taken care to buy insurance offered by other credit institutions (section 7). Taking huge risks, structuring them and swapping them was a sort of selling hot cakes as long as this business was novel, but it became harder to do so as years passed by. Moreover, the fact that banks failed to reassure every one of their counterparties provided one more piece of evidence that complex financial instruments can become lethal. In the longer term, novelty does not relieve an institution of the time-honored principles of:

- Liquidity,
- Capital adequacy.

When the capital markets dried up, banks found themselves obliged to court shareholders (through capital increases), depositors, and other bankers for urgently needed cash. In parallel to this, sovereign wealth funds were taken to the cleaners – and after they said "no more, thank you," the taxpayer was asked to pay the bill for 5 years of mismanagement.

Self-wounded banks also had to face the fact that all market participants who count have grown increasingly fearful that their counterparties can face significant losses on leveraged instruments, commercial paper, and subprime-related securities – hence the greatest care was good enough no more. Neither did the housing industry recover (Chapter 7), and in the opinion of many experts one of the great puzzles in the current crisis is which one will blink first:

- The credit squeeze, or
- The severe housing crisis.

People of experience wonder how far the two correlate between each other, and with the likelihood of bank failures. Studies show that estimates of asset correlations based on equity prices tend to be considerably higher than estimates based on default rates – and asset correlations are a key driver of credit risk.[22] Bankers who know how to look ahead with regard to the effect of severe shocks on financial stability appreciate that the future trajectory of American house prices will be one of the key determinants of economic outlook for the coming years. Market expectations are increasingly influenced by guestimates about the ultimate amount of credit losses that will be incurred on underlying mortgages with the final cost depending on:

- Default rates, and
- Loss given default (LGD) rates.[23]

Both are a function of house price dynamics which at the present time are negative, and for which nothing has been done in spite of the lavish money thrown at the bad money pool of big banks by western governments. Some market-based estimates are even implying loss given default rates nearing 100 percent in markets where house prices may fall by 20 percent to 30 percent off their peak, as in the US and in Britain – which pretells a likely swarm of bank failures.

Closely connected to these fears is the fact discussed briefly in the opening paragraphs of this section, namely that according to expert opinions default rates have been held artificially low over the past 6 or 7 years. Not only derivatives but also easy credit conditions, the abundance of liquidity in markets, and very low spreads on junk bonds have given market players a distorted perspective which contributed to the initial success of the *originate-to-distribute* model of banking loans:

- With artificially low interest rates, banks made poor decisions with long-term effects, and
- This led to risk distributions with long tails where leveraged institutions are now facing high refinancing costs, and formerly creditworthy banks have turned into speculators.

Experts suggest that an additional source of anxiety is supply-and-demand imbalances, expected to deteriorate further in the course of 2008 and 2009, with the majority of outstanding stock of adjustable rate mortgages (ARMs) scheduled to reset in the course of these two years. As if this were not enough the credit quality of such mortgages is known to be inferior to the ARMs which reset in 2007, risking pulling down weaker banks and hence igniting an even bigger fire at the side of credit default swaps.

7. Can credit default swaps be the nemesis of the banking industry?

On 23 September 2008, Christopher Cox, chairman of the Securities and Exchange Commission, said that the credit default swaps (CDS)[24] market must be regulated immediately.[25] Years earlier several economists and financial experts had made the same request, but the Bush Administration was against it. Cox was waking up too late to the pending disaster, but better late than never.

The risk embedded in credit default swaps and the probability of default on a loan by a borrower correlate. We have gone a long way down the road of exposure to creditworthiness since 1864 when the directors of the First National Bank of New York resolved never to lend except against collateral of US government bonds. In fact:

- They would not lend to anyone who did not have unimpeachable collateral, and
- They looked at risk as commensurate with reward, a policy which is tantamount to prudent and profitable lending.

This is not the policy which has guided the hands of loan officers, credit departments, loans committees, and boards 140 years later. Instead, as we saw in section 5, leveraged lending and borrowing held the upper ground with total disregard to what would happen to the bank in the case of exceptional circumstances like:

- The disappearance of market liquidity,
- A rise in the number of bankruptcies, or
- Even worse, both events happening at the same time.

Many banks loosened up their lending standards and disregarded the fundamentals of borrower creditworthiness because they thought they were protected by buying a CDS – without duly examining critically whether in reality they were exchanging one credit risk for another, while over and above that they were paying a fee. The rude awakening came in June 2008 when company bankruptcy filings in the US outpaced individual bankruptcy filings. No wonder that the G-20 15 November 2008 Washington economic conference was preoccupied by the huge exposure to CDSs:

- Advising on the need for strengthening the resilience and transparency of credit derivatives markets, and
- Taking account of "the imminent launch of central counterparty services for credit default swaps (CDS) in some countries."[26]

According to an article in *The Economist*, when in March 2008 the Fed helped JPMorgan Chase to rescue Bear Stearns,

> it sent a signal to the markets – a kind of "No Bank Left Behind" Act. If the Fed was willing to save an investment bank, without any retail depositors,

then the system would not be brought down by a "plumbing problem", such as the collapse of a counterparty in the derivatives market.[27]

Yes, but in September 2008 the Fed left Lehman Brothers, a bigger investment bank than Bear Stearns, go down the tubes.

One of the key problems with CDSs is that market's huge size. While, as we saw in section 2, this is itself dwarfed by the market of interest rate swaps (IRS), the IRS are a different Ponzi game, both in fundamentals and because of the fact that (at least so far) it has not come up as a potential catastrophic enabler. Up to a certain time, that was also the CDSs story:

- Until 2007, they were hailed by luminaries – including Alan Greenspan – as a wonder of modern finance.
- But since September 2008 a wave of large defaults and near-misses involving banks, brokers, insurers and government-sponsored agencies has sent the CDS market reeling.

Already by the second quarter of 2008 corporate defaults were trending higher, and this put under stress the protection sellers of CDSs. The combination of deteriorating credit quality and downturn in credit markets led to a rise in corporate defaults which contrasted darkly with speculative global default rates. (For a few years, the latter have been running at historically low levels.) According to Moody's, the rating agency, trailing 12-month defaults moved to 2 percent in June 2008, up from levels near 1 percent at the start of the year.

Moody's anticipated that defaults would more than double by year-end 2008, with a further increase to over 6 percent within 12 months:[28]

- The course of defaults will be determined by the course of the economy and the turn of the credit cycle characterized by the diminishing availability of capital and tightening lending standards.

As was to be expected, in the aftermath the bond market has had a beating. Following a long period with scarcely any bond defaults by companies, there have been plenty of failures, particularly of junk bond issuers, with debt of over $100 billion deemed vulnerable to default. The most scary is that corporate debt rests on shaky foundations for trillions of dollars of derivative contracts.

(By early October 2008 the face value of distressed American corporate junk bonds debt hit $328 billion, up from $59 billion in January of the same year.[29] Statistics show that once a bond becomes more distressed it has nearly twenty times more chance of defaulting in the following 12 months than a non-distressed high-yield bond. According to same forecasts, between

5 percent and 6 percent of American "high-yield" bond issuers would default in 2008, up from 0.9 percent the previous year, with the number of large bankruptcies[30] rising to between 50 and 75, from 13 in 2007.)

The hurricane hiding behind these statistics derives its force from the fact that an estimated $62 trillion of CDSs (in notional principal amounts) were outstanding in early 2008 – which far exceeds the $7.1 trillion mortgage market and $4.4 trillion Treasuries market. The fact that by late 2008 the CDSs hangover had been reduced to about $58 trillion will do nothing to reduce the strength of the winds. To the contrary, what is important is that:

- Banks and insurance companies are (at least supposedly) regulated.
- The credit default swaps market is not – hence the call Cox made that it must be regulated immediately.

It also remains to be seen what is meant by regulating CDSs. The way market rumors go, this will start with quasi-voluntary efforts which will do nothing to reassure investors who have been calling for more dramatic intervention. Buyers and sellers of swaps will probably be required to disclose "more information." In all likelihood they will also have to put up more capital to trade.

The evidence is provided by no lesser an authority than AIG, infamous for its torrent of red ink with derivative financial products its bankruptcy and nationalization. From September 16 to December 31, 2008, the big stakes gambler made $49.5 billion in payments to counterparties connected to credit default swaps: The lion's share or nearly $13 billion went to Goldman Sachs who had "guessed right" while playing in the Grand Casino; each of Société Générale and Deutsche Bank got $12 billion; to Barclays went $8.5 billion; Merrill Lynch, Bank of America, UBS, BNP Paribas had to do with a little less.[31]

All this was taxpayers money, since the US Treasury had taken over the obligations of AIG. JPMorgan Chase should have thought of it before its self-congratulations for having made $5 billion in derivative "profits" in the 4th quarter 2008. To these $5 billion of gains might well correspond another $50 billion of losses to be paid by the sweat and tears of American taxpayers, *if* the Treasury decides to take over the only Grand Casino bank still standing on its feet.

Bankers who oppose even a light regulation of CDSs already say that the market will be a bit duller, a lot less lucrative, and not necessarily much safer. For their part, investors see these likely first moves as being utterly inadequate and unconvincing. They also point out that interest rate swaps should not be left out of a holistic, more rigorous regulatory framework, because they stand at $400 trillion – and if they are hidden from view this may well be the worst single decision governments have made during the last years.

6
Asset Allocation, Credit Regulation, and Banking Supervision

1. Too much money has gone down dry holes

Chapter 3 brought to the reader's attention two of the basic functions of central banks: monetary policy, which aims at establishing the right money supply for the economy, and the fight against inflation to safeguard the value of money earned and saved by people and companies. Chapter 4 pressed the point that money has a cost which in nominal terms is expressed by the interest rate established by the central monetary institution. It also explained why currency exchange risks and other factors impact on the cost of money.

An added function of central banks is the regulation of the financial industry, which they often share with specialized entities generally (but not always) known as financial services commissions or authorities. Examples are the Financial Services Authority (FSA) of Britain; the Commission Bancaire of France; and the Office of the Controller of the Currency (OCC), the Federal Deposit Insurance Corporation (FDIC), and the Securities and Exchange Commission (SEC) of the United States.

One of the problems with specialized supervisory entities, which are supposed to watch over risks in the financial industry, is that they are under the boot of politicians. This means that they are prone to bending supervisory standards.

As we have seen in Chapter 2, George W. Bush fired William Donaldson, the boss of the SEC, because the latter wanted to register and control the hedge funds. Christopher Cox, Donaldson's successor, got the message that to survive he had to look the other way no matter what was happening. For several years Lehman Brothers, the investment bank, was not subjected to any supervision till it went into bankruptcy in mid September 2008 – as Dick Fuld, its CEO, said in his deposition to the US House Committee on Oversight and Government Reform on 6 October 2008.

Financial services authorities also mellow their duties and cut their punch by turning themselves into old chaps' clubs,[1] which meet periodically over coffee to talk about the birds and the bees. *If* this was not the case, *then*

Northern Rock would not have gone to the wall in August 2007 at the very start of the banking and credit crisis and two other British banks would not have followed it (Chapter 2) – Royal Bank of Scotland would not have drained itself of resources with its equity losing 39.5 percent of its market value in just one day (7 October 2008) and HBOS would not have lost its capital and had to fall into the arms of Lloyds TSB at the twelfth hour. And so on and so forth.

Inadequacy in banking supervision cost the British taxpayer £100 billion with Northern Rock alone, and another £250 billion on 8 October 2008 through two salvage plans put together by the Labour government without any thorough study of costs, benefits, or aftermath. To appreciate what the regulators are supposed to do – but they don't often accomplish – we should review briefly what functions commercial and other banks are expected to perform for society.

In the national as well as in the global economy, the main function of the banking sector is to take deposits and savings and then – together with investment capital – channel them into the most productive and enterprising sectors of the real economy. This, and *not* speculation, is the banking system's reason of existence, and it presupposes two things, namely that:

- The productive sectors are free markets open to investment, and
- The banking sector is not pushing too much of the world's capital into trades which have a history of bubbles.

Economic history also shows that massive government-led bank bailouts and other covert State Supermarket policies and practices, like those experienced in 2008, do not help reignite the economy. Bank supervisors should also have known that globalization has changed several of the regulatory duties – and this not only because of daily cross-border supervisory challenges.

For instance, massive current-account deficits and the rapid accumulation of savings in emerging markets have created important transborder flows, with some institutions gaining the lion's share in the deployment of capital.[2] The G-20 15 November 2008 Washington economic conference decided that among its priorities are:

- Defining the scope of systemically important institutions and determining their appropriate oversight.
- Encouraging financial firms to re-examine their internal controls and implement strengthened policies for sound risk management.
- "Strengthening cross-border crisis management" and requiring supervisors to "collaborate to establish supervisory colleges for all major cross-border financial institutions."

Effective cross-border solutions are at a premium. With capital continuing to go out of Asia and into western economies, US and European financial institutions found themselves at the receiving end of a large transfer of money. As a result, bank liabilities and leverage soared, prompting a great surge on lending and making the US financial system inordinately geared in terms of loans-to-deposits ratios:

- In principle, capital formation is capitalism's first most important function.
- The flow of accumulated savings into new *productive* facilities is capitalism's second vital business.
- But when the flow of money sinks into non-productive trades like CDOs and other toxic waste, the net result is capital destruction.

Capitalism works best when money is invested in great productive opportunities at carefully controlled risk levels. This has not been the case since the 1970s and 1980s. Hard pressed because of a soaring current-account deficit, the American government welcomed foreign financing without any questions being asked.

For their part, however, bank supervisors and central bankers should nevertheless have seen that this meant trouble for the future. Moreover as the US construction sector became saturated, including housing and the commercial real estate market, a significant amount of capital started to flow into real estate markets in other parts of the world, leading to a global but unsustainable boom in property values.

What these references suggest is that globalization's colossal capital flows have radically altered the requirements of banking supervision. It is not just small-time fraud that the supervisors should be going after. While the small game is still on, the new need is for big game controls established at a global scale to:

- Save the economy from boom and bust cycles, and
- Even save go-go bank CEOs from themselves.

"Dick Fuld [of Lehman] and Jimmy Cayne [of Bear Stearns] took reckless gambles," said a feature article in *The Economist*.[3] Quite so. They took reckless gambles because they found themselves in Ali Baba's cave, which was chockablock with an unthinkable amount of money, and supervisory authorities allowed them to do as they pleased, with a nearsighted, get-rich-quick policy as their guide.

As of 30 August 2008, write-downs reached an estimated total of $500 billion; by contrast, the wounded big banks raised "only" about $200 billion of Tier-1 capital (core capital)[4] out of some $285 billion collected (till then) through loans, preferred stock and other deals. Many economists lamented this imbalance, but nobody really thought that within a fortnight Fannie Mae and Freddie Mac would be virtually nationalized, Lehman Brothers would go bust, and AIG would be taken over by the US government.

Neither was a thought given to the fact that America's government would rush to unveil a plan aimed to end the credit crunch by spending $700 billion to buy troubled assets from financial institutions. Yet that's exactly what happened as Hank Paulson, Treasury secretary, and Ben Bernanke, chairman of the Federal Reserve, argued that swift and forceful action was needed to stem growing panic about the soundness of the financial system.

With good reason, members of Congress, which had to approve the plan, complained that the government was seizing too much power, letting reckless bankers off too lightly and failing to help struggling homeowners. They were right in saying so, but what should be appreciated is that the unmitigated disaster did not happen overnight. It was created over years of bad management and of pitiful or altogether absent bank supervision – raising the question which is posed in section 2.

2. Should central banks be involved in asset allocation?

In 1913, the US Federal Reserve was created with authority over monetary policy like that of other central banks. Like the German Reichsbank (after which it was modeled) but unlike other central banks that have acquired independence from political interference later on in their lives, the Fed's status gave it that freedom from the start.[5] Now several cognizant people worry that it may be in the process of losing its independence from politicians, and the reason is its involvement in *asset allocation*. To put it bluntly, not only the Fed's but:

- Every central bank's dilemma has recently become one of mandate versus markets, and
- The answer is in no way self-evident because what has happened during and as a sequel to the 2008/2009 crisis constitutes a troublesome precedence.

As preceding chapters have brought to the reader's attention, good governance of monetary policy commands that central banks be independent from government and parliamentary interference because the power to print money must be separate from the power to spend it. Partly for this reason several (albeit not all) central banks have given up non-monetary tasks like bank supervision, since they often involve political judgments that easily interfere with monetary policy. What happened with the Fed in March, September, and October 2008 poses two questions:

- Is this about to change, and
- What are the implications of the salvage of bankrupt investment banks, mortgage giants, and insurance conglomerates?

Precisely in order to preserve its independence for six long decades, starting with its inception in 1913,[6] the Fed avoided any act which might be interpreted as an asset allocation decision, but in the 1970s at the request of Congress it bought Fannie Mae and Freddie Mac debt.[7] Some years down the line, an internal Fed study concluded that there are risks in favoring particular assets or borrowers due to the fact that this could:

- Result in too much investment in preferred sectors as well as too little in others, and
- Bring the Federal Reserve into arguments about fiscal policy or even lead to compromises in its monetary policy.

This issue came up the big way in 2007 and 2008 when Ben Bernanke's first step was to lower the interest rate and lengthen the term on direct loans to banks from the Fed's discount window. As commercial banks were slow to respond, and the liquidity situation worsened, the US central bank announced the creation of the *Term Auction Facility* (TAF, Chapter 9) to make loans at its discount window cheaper and more anonymous – a rather controversial move, which critics said was likely to become a permanent feature.

In March 2008 came the Fed's new policy of swapping up to $200 billion of Treasuries for investment banks' holdings of mortgage-backed securities, followed by the guaranty to JPMorgan of $29 billion of Bear Stearns's obligations. Four months later, in July 2008, the Fed agreed to lend to Fannie Mae and Freddie Mac from the window should this be necessary. It also said it would accept any AAA-rated securities as collateral, including those backed by student loans.

True enough, as the 2008/2009 credit and banking crisis unfolded the Fed (and all other central banks) have been confronted with a diversity of systemic risk, which cut across historic functional boundaries. Institutions that posed potential systemic threats included not only commercial banks but also, if not primarily, investment banks as well as mortgage and insurance groups desperately short of capital. Part of what made the 2008/2009 upheaval so dangerous was the very large role investment banks played in the financial system:

- Without access to retail deposits, their funding base has been most volatile, and
- Their assets tended to be very risky while engaging in a huge volume of transactions among themselves, with hedge funds, and with commercial banks.

Fluctuations in the investments banks' balance sheets contributed greatly to the pro-cyclicality of financial markets. To many experts it seemed inconceivable that regulators permitted investment banks to operate with such a narrow capital cushion. But they did do so. The collapse of Bear Stearns, the bankruptcy of Lehman, and the takeover of Merrill Lynch by Bank of America provided evidence that the investment banks' business model is no longer viable, but:

- Should the Federal Reserve alter its status single-handed? And
- If yes, where should the limits be?

Some senior Fed executives admit that some recent initiatives have moved the central bank closer to credit allocation. That is why they were designed to be self-liquidating as markets improve, suggested Donald Kohn, the Fed's vice-chairman, in a recent speech. Where however is the proof that these were only one-tantum decisions taken in the heat of the moment?

Economists concerned by the implications of such moves were alarmed when the Fed extended some of its programs, such as granting investment banks access to the discount window until September 2008 and then extending it again to the end of January 2009. Critics added that, most likely, regardless of whether that window is officially opened or closed it will be opened on an ad hoc basis if there is an emergency:

- Expanding the Fed's non-monetary duties, and
- Bringing the central bank squarely into credit and asset allocation.

The risk is that such decisions would politicize the Federal Reserve (and any other central bank following a similar policy) by identifying it too closely with the firms it regulates, and by setting a policy favoring financial stability at the expense of price stability. The central bank could also be drawn into contentious debates about how financial institutions should run themselves, and be blamed when the next crisis comes.

Some advice on how to deal with that particular challenge came from the man whose policies (when he was Fed chairman) were instrumental in creating the 2007 subprimes bubble and subsequent banking crisis. Alan Greenspan suggested the institution of a high-level panel of American financial officials to be given broad power to seize any bank whose failure threatens the entire economy and close it down.[8] And he asked for laws that specify and limit the conditions for bailouts rather than having ad hoc central bank intervention.

Part and parcel of this proposal is to have a blue-ribbon standby panel empowered by Congress to determine whether a financial institution's failure is dangerous enough to require taxpayer money. *If* so, *they* (presumably the panel) should form a vehicle to take that company under *conservatorship*,

- Wipe out its equity,
- Impose a haircut on its debts, before guaranteeing them, and
- Then sell its assets.

Greenspan's suggestions about the resolution of a banking crisis by putting risky players under quarantine are too committee-based to be appealing. As an old adage has it: "A committee has neither a soul to blame nor a body to kick." Besides, what the former Fed chairman proposes is the opposite road to that promoted by Hank Paulson, the Treasury secretary, which would give the Fed broad responsibility:

- Over all sorts of bank supervision, and
- Over general market stability.

One can detect behind Greenspan's suggestion some thinly veiled personal rancor, and it needs no explaining that the last thing the American economy needs at this moment of crisis is a tug-of-war between big egos. It is enough that regulators and supervisors are always a step behind practitioners in understanding the risk being posed by a rapid financial innovation coupled with opacity.

3. Confronting the deregulation of credit

Financial history books suggest that the market for trading securities developed in London in the late seventeenth century. The concept underpinning it, however, is much older, because securities have been similar to other forms of asset titles, ranging from food to land, with asset quality playing a key role.

In different terms, from ancient times to seventeenth-century England and today, damaged assets create particular concerns, like those that nowadays surround US mortgages and mortgage-related securities, other consumer lending exposures, and novel inventions of dubious quality like deferred tax assets (DTAs). Uncertainty about asset quality puts under pressure lending commitments and cash calls, pressuring balance sheets and liquidity. Other contingencies also exist, such as:

- The likelihood of adverse effects from probes and litigation surrounding the securities industry, and
- The evolving complexity and expansion of derivatives which have led to ever-increasing levels of interdependency within the financial industry.

Doubts about creditworthiness, economic weakness, and market dislocations add risks of volatile earnings, as well as inviting speculation. Prior to the development of securities markets, speculation in money and in real assets was largely frowned upon, because a lot of speculative activity was either illegal or tightly regulated.[9] In the beginning that applied to securities too, even if early securities markets were regulated much more heavily than they are today.

Precisely because novel financial instruments have made small game of creditworthiness by means of credit risk transfer (CRT), with credit default swaps (CDSs) being the best example, the links between the global credit crisis and a wide economic recession are not that difficult to understand. Credit is the lubricant that keeps the economy's engine working. When creditworthiness becomes an unknown or doubtful entity, the capital markets tighten and restrict the capital flow with the result that:

- Liquidity disappears from the market,
- Economic activity slows, and
- The credit crunch is intensifying, spreading in the global economy.

Two examples from mid to late 2008 provide eye-opening evidence of how much and how deeply the aftereffects of credit deregulation can hurt the economy. In September, during the so-called "historic week" on Wall Street, when the American investment banks disappeared from the radar screen, gold would have hit for the stars *if* there was a sound credit environment – and therefore liquidity in the market. It did not (only moving modestly), because investors and speculators did not have the money for a big play.

A little over a fortnight later, when on 8 October in an unprecedented concerted action a bunch of central banks (the Fed, the Bank of England, the ECB, and the monetary institutions of China, Switzerland, and Canada) cut interest rates by 50 basis points, the price of bonds – particularly credit-risk-free Treasuries – would have skyrocketed *if* there had been liquidity. It did not, because money was scarce and the credit crunch had become increasingly global in nature.

Where essentially this points is to the fact that the regulation of creditworthiness,[10] liquidity and monetary policy correlate. Therefore, central banks have a direct interest in credit regulation as an adjunct to their core task of safeguarding economic power and financial stability as well as for:

- Investor protection,
- Safeguarding a functioning liquidity framework, and
- Preventing potential systemic risks due to credit excesses.

Widely perceived and generally appreciated creditworthiness promotes liquid markets, and liquidity presents the opportunity of finding at reasonable cost a trading partner at any time, while increasing the willingness to invest in the first place. Therefore, a basic objective of regulatory efforts should be to lend support to a structural framework of creditworthiness that can assure deep, broad, robust, and dependable market activity.[11]

As we will see in subsequent sections, like any other object of regulation, creditworthiness is obviously not an end in itself; but in spite of that the regulatory framework has to be assessed in terms of its effectiveness. It must fulfill the desired functions while remaining competitively neutral – which means without giving preferential treatment to, or discriminating against, any given player.

Transborder coordination and collaboration of supervisory authorities is vital because the globalization of financial markets has made it possible for bankers, traders, asset managers, and investors to switch to lightly regulated or completely unregulated market environments, an example being the offshores. Such an opt-out option has led to a practice known as *regulatory arbitrage*.

Potential host countries have an incentive to reduce the depth and intensity of their regulations to attract capital and business activity. There is indeed an ongoing effort by several government and supervisory authorities to outdo each other in reducing regulatory standards. This is a sort of race to the bottom, at the end of which there remain only minimum regulatory standards and practically none of them is enforced. The net result has been the 2008/2009 crisis, as America competed with Britain on who would do *the least* in terms of:

- Credit risk control, and
- Financial supervision.

Prior to financial deregulation *without limits*, which started in the years of the Carter presidency (the late 1970s), there was a time when banks and other market players accepted a strict regime because they appreciated that at the end of the day this was to their advantage. The US presented an example of sound supervision, and companies from other countries wanting to tap into, or keep their foothold in, the American capital market had an incentive to subject themselves to its regulatory standards.

Let me add that a high standard of regulation is also regarded by alert investors as an advantageous sign of quality, which sees to it that weakly regulated markets feel pressure to tighten their own regulatory rules in order to maintain or regain their competitiveness. All this is now past, as an unprecedented deregulation turned the financial markets – and most particularly with regard to creditworthiness – into a global casino.[12] To be in charge once more, governments, central banks, and regulatory authorities must:

- Assure that the same rigorous creditworthiness principles are universally applied,
- See to it that violators are brought to justice without nepotism, *ifs*, and delays, and

- Close loopholes which exist or are created by gaming the system of credit analysis and control.

These loopholes are sometimes created under statutory regulation where the state directly influences the market by prescribing weak rules and by conferring upon a supervisory government authority half-baked powers for monitoring and enforcing compliance. As we have seen in section 1, this turns the supervisory agency into an old chaps' club.

4. Learning from past financial crises

Whatever section 3 stated about the need to keep a close watch over counterparty risk, and the high cost the economy has suffered from the deregulation of credit, is equally valid for market risk, operational risk, and liquidity risk – as well as their supervision. One of the global financial ironies of our time is that up to a point everybody was thought to have benefited from deregulation, but in reality everybody paid for it most dearly in 2008/2009, particularly those who believed they had "benefited" the most.

Therefore it is most instructive to briefly review what has happened with previous financial crises, before we enter into a discussion on what needs to be done to strengthen the watch over the financial system. According to economic history, the first banking crisis on record dates back to AD 33 under the Roman emperor Tiberius. As in 2007/2008, it was created by excessive debt:

- In AD 33 panic followed a credit crunch and a steady rise of interest rates charged by usurers.
- In AD 2008 panic followed the credit crunch and banking crisis which came on the heels of the subprimes debacle.

To stabilize the market, Tiberius injected 100 million sesterces. Unlike what Paulson did in 2008, these were placed not in the pockets of a bankrupt banking system but in new public banks administered by Roman senators. A law made it possible for all Roman citizens to borrow without interest for three years.

Another credit institution set up by Tiberius provided liquidity to landowners, ending the credit crisis in farming. This dual approach was vastly preferable to that followed by the US Treasury, the British government, the Fed, the ECB, and other central banks in 2008, who have followed the (wrong) policy of having good money run after bad money, pouring taxpayer funds into the coffers of virtually bankrupt big banks where it simply evaporates and disappears while:

- The market panic is not lifting, and
- The credit crunch continues to worsen.

Another lesson can be learned by looking back to the last 150 years. Economists identify the long recession which begun in 1873 as the first case of a globalized crisis in modern financial history. This was followed by the US railroads and other nineteenth-century crises, then the crises of 1903/1907 and downturn of the late 1920s which morphed into the Great Depression of 1929/1933. Much more recently, the global economy confronted the Asian crisis of 1997 and the Russian meltdown of 1998 – all of them built on excesses.

What the aforementioned events have in common is that each of them followed a period of strong credit growth, which led to the leverage of the economy and fed a rapid boom of financial markets followed by an extended bust. This general pattern repeated itself time and again even if the specific events which punched the bubbles varied, because nothing was done to right the balances.

In 2007, for example, in an environment where financial supervision was totally absent, the most likely trigger was the decision by a small number of investment funds to freeze redemptions, in the wake of Bear Stearns's intervention to save two of its hedge funds from bankruptcy. The stated reason for the freeze was the inability to value complex assets in the funds' portfolios; but according to experts the real reasons were three:

- A projected oncoming collapse of the market for structured products based on mortgages.
- Massive withdrawal of investors from asset-backed commercial paper deals which had started looking shaky, and
- A sudden drying-up of interbank term money markets in major currencies, as financial institutions no longer trusted each other's valuation of their holdings.

Together these three reasons made a mockery of the September/October 2008 statements by some economists about the "mistake" of new accounting regulations which obliged banks to mark to market their holdings. Holdings like the CDOs of subprimes proved to be the worst toxic waste banks had ever held in their vaults:

- *If* marking to market was tough,
- *Then* accruals accounting would have been the parody of the century (see Chapter 8).

Accruals is a system totally unfit for derivative financial instruments. A better alternative, of course, would have been not to allow banks to develop, trade and warehouse complex derivative products (particularly OTC) that were opaque, of suspicious value, and intended solely for making a quick buck by selling the garbage to others.

Precisely because they had most unwisely accumulated lots of senseless paper, not only banks but also insurance companies kept on announcing sizeable losses related to subprime mortgages and associated structured products. Independent rating agencies which had contributed to the debacle by granting worthless assets a AAA grade found themselves obliged to downgrade, or threaten with downgrades, a lot of instruments and companies.

For their part, hedge funds which depend on prime brokers faced margin calls as asset prices fell. This is precisely the nature of a financial snowball, which is most difficult to stop after it has started gaining momentum. This situation was further exacerbated by:

- A weakening in the real economy,
- High household debt levels (Chapter 7), and
- A superleveraged global financial system which showed clear evidence of stress.

Economists who are paid to worry about future developments have been led to the conclusion that the problems so far encountered may not tell the whole story, and the magnitude of those yet to be faced could be much greater than central bankers, commercial bankers, fund managers, and other experts had conceived up to November 2008, 16 months after the start of the snowball.

Not surprisingly, the result has been nervousness in the market about the size of hidden losses, their distribution, and their impact on the valuation of portfolios that did not stop revealing new rivers of red ink quarter after quarter. Rather than improving risk control, structured finance transformed all sorts of exposure into higher levels, obliging western central banks to:

- Accept a wider range of collateral from a broader set of institutions,
- Engage in operations at longer maturities, and
- Look the other way when evaluating the creditworthiness of the collateral commercial and investment banks presented to them.

Termed *garbage collection* by some experts (Chapter 9), this process had as an objective urgent liquidity injections to help in averting a wide banking crisis. As time progressed, however, there was evidence of weakening economic activity, growing counterparty risk, and increasing inability to value complex and opaque assets and liabilities. Therefore, it became fairly clear that, though necessary, liquidity injection measures were insufficient, and that an effective solution to the crisis would involve difficult tradeoffs – as well as the need to establish a rigorous and effective regulatory regime.

5. The changing perspective of regulatory duties

In the aforementioned interview he gave on 7 August 2008 to Bloomberg Financial Services, Dr Henry Kaufman stressed the point that you cannot only supervise the creation of credit, which is the classical function of central banks. In order to have a well-rounded process of economic development and exposure, you must also supervise and regulate the allocation of credit. In America, Kaufman would give such dual mission to the Federal Reserve.

Closely connected to this approach is the extent which should be reached by credit allocation decisions. Kaufmann's proposal is that the Federal Reserve would need to supervise and regulate the 25 to 30 largest institutions in the country, whether these are commercial banks, investments banks, or other financial entities – because in today's market it is no more possible to trace clear lines between distinct sectors of finance, as was the case in the past.[13]

If the largest and therefore most risky 25 to 30 big American financial entities should come under close scrutiny by regulators, worldwide this number would rise to between 100 and 130. However, an approach which targets the big financial companies' exposure might be effective if, and only if, in the globalized economy the standards, measurements, and measures taken by central banks and regulators are uniform. This is far from being the case today.

Still, a certain change in regulatory perspectives has been note referenced with the twin events of the Russian default and Long-Term Capital Management (LTCM), in August and September 1998 respectively. This was made necessary by mounting concerns about a global credit crunch. The proprietary desks of several hedge funds and banks had reported big losses, mainly as a result of the widening of corporate bond and other risk spreads, leading to widespread concerns that LTCM would be forced to unwind big positions in already tight market conditions. However, the intervention by the NY Fed which brought LTCMs investors into the rescue plan:

- Helped the market to begin functioning normally again, and
- Put thoughts about restructuring and globalizing regulatory processes in the time closet.

Ten years later, in an effort to enlarge the domain of supervisory activities affecting the global economy, the Bank for International Settlements created a peer to the Basel Committee on Banking Supervision: the *Markets Committee*. The latter brings together in bimonthly meetings senior officials from the Group of Ten central banks responsible for market operations. Their objective is to provide an opportunity for participants to exchange views on:

- Recent developments,
- Structural changes in foreign exchange, and
- Events related to financial markets at large.

The Markets Committee also considers the short-run implications of particular current events, and their impact on the way financial markets are functioning. This includes a range of issues like the reasons for recent large movements in major bilateral exchange rates, the implied volatility in exchange rates, the low level of both nominal yields and implied volatility in major bond markets, and so on.

Other responsibilities of the Markets Committee are the study of the aftermath of search for yield on credit spreads, the effects of the presence of hedge funds, the financial market impact of changes in pension fund regulations, the influence on market functioning of the growth of electronic trading platforms, and the financial market impact of foreign exchange reserve accumulation.[14] As these examples document:

- The objective is information-sharing among central banks.
- This is not a supervisory duty, yet each of the above examples cries for global supervision.

In addition, the domain of global supervision should be extended to cover issues that used to fall under commodities trading but have morphed into financial assets. An example is provided by exchange traded funds (ETF) and exchange-traded commodities (ETC), which in reality are financial note references – like paper oil and paper ships.

The need for broadening supervisory duties cannot wait forever to be fulfilled. In mid September 2008, the collapse of Lehman Brothers exacerbated the problem connected to commodities trading, as the 158-year-old Wall Street firm ran an estimated $5 billion commodity index business. Counterparty woes were highlighted by Criterion, a Toronto-based hedge fund, which said it was converting into cash its investment in derivative note references linked to the DJ-AIG commodity index as a result of uncertainty regarding the note references issuer.

In addition, ETF Securities, the London-based issuer of commodity-exchange-traded funds, hit problems when several market makers of its funds stopped trading them amid concerns about AIG, which was its counterparty for about $2 billion in DJ–AIG commodity products. Investors in commodity indices suddenly became aware that they did not own hard assets in wheat, corn, cotton, and other commodities. Instead:

- What they held was a swap on an index of commodity futures, and
- This financial paper was full of market and of counterparty risk.

These and plenty of other cases saw to it that the better-informed and most alert among bankers and analysts, who had looked at the rescue of Bear Stearns as an urgent step necessary to avert the implosion of the global financial system, started to point out that current regulatory rules and procedures would have to be thoroughly revamped. This would include not only a more stringent control of the banks' risk-taking and leverage ratio, but also redefinition of the whole domain of financial activities, including:

- Their meaning,
- Their reach,
- The extent of their work, and
- The types of impact of associated risks.

The question is: "Who is going to do it?" This is a particularly acute issue in America because commercial banks are controlled by the Federal Reserve (as well as by the Office of the Controller of the Currency and the Federal Deposit Insurance Corporation), while investment banks have since the 1930s been under the watch of the Securities and Exchange Commission (SEC). Bringing them under the Fed's wings as bank holding companies has not yet been tested in court in terms of responsibilities.

"We lack appropriate constraints on risk taking at investment banks," said Barney Frank, chairman of the House Financial Services Committee.[15] Frank wanted Wall Street to be subject to capital requirements similar to those for commercial banks, even if investment bankers oppose such a measure tooth and nail.

US regulators are also said to favor an *aged* inventory capital charge, which would penalize banks that hold financial paper for more than (probably) one month. Another congressional proposal in discussion has been to limit the bank's venture capital and hedge fund holdings and financing. (Nothing has come out so far in terms of legislation, because the lobbyists who oppose it got into high gear.)

American legislators and regulators would also like to see a mechanism for winding down a failing investment bank. One suggestion came from Sheila Bair, who heads FDIC. The concept is that of extending a bridge-loan model already existing for commercial banks, which allows the sustaining of key business (with federal money) while selling off the wounded entity's assets. Hank Paulson, the then Treasury secretary, also placed this issue on his agenda, but nothing had transpired in terms of concrete measures when the Bush administration went out of office. (See the discussion in Chapter 10 below of the press conference given by the Obama Administration's Treasury secretary, Timothy Geithner, on 10 February 2009.)

To the contrary, instead of tightening regulation there has been another move towards deregulation. In mid September 2008, in a bid to attract more investment to America's struggling financial sector, the Fed relaxed rules on bank ownership. Private equity firms would now be allowed to own bigger stakes. Critics worry that gaming the system would become both easier and with deeper aftereffects.

In conclusion, what is needed is not only more rigorous regulation but also a revitalizing of the code of ethics. The way William Donaldson, the former chairman of the SEC, puts it, there is ultimately a limit to how much regulation can do. In the final analysis, one could write all the rules one wants, but there has to be a philosophy of ethical behavior that comes from human beings operating in a professional way. Are we really on that path? I would doubt it.

6. Accountability of financial supervision

The banking crisis and credit crash of 2008/2009 has triggered an intensive debate about the role, objective, and accountability of financial market regulation. This is leading to a growing number of suggestions for regulatory reform, including a more standard framework across jurisdictions and financial sectors, able to address the growing interdependence among:

- Markets, and
- Products.

Additionally, to avert the risk of short-sighted and ill-designed measures with unintended consequences, at least some proposals emphasize the need for *accountability* by bankers and regulators. This implies post-mortems and reviews able to assure that regulatory policies have been focused, well-observed, and rooted in the sound economic analysis of underlying market failures.

Steady attention to the regulatory agency's accountability, and that of its personnel, is a "must" because the proper regulation of a market evolves as a result of constant interaction among players, the products they peddle, and associated supervisory measures. To a significant extent, the status quo of a financial system's regulatory framework tends to mirror what has been needed in the past, which is not necessarily in touch with the present and the future.

This is not written only in the sense of the increasing integration of financial markets and its consequences for regulation. The aforementioned reference is also valid in regard to the nearsightedness of numerous national rules and supervisory activities. An example is the £798.5 billion ($1.4 trillion) loss by British municipalities announced on 10 October 2008 because of the crash of the three main Icelandic banks. This torrent of red ink has not come overnight out of the blue; it built up over time, which poses tough questions:

- Why were British municipalities permitted by their regulator to invest such large sums in Icelandic banks?

- How did it happen that Iceland's troubles in early 2007, due to the carry trade, did not lead to disinvestments?
- Were the regulators looking the other way, were they utterly absent, or were they absolutely incapable of performing their duties?

The excuse that the elimination of barriers to the cross-border exchange of financial services was the cause of that failure holds no water. The cross-border watch of the production, distribution, and warehousing of financial products is important for the effectiveness of financial markets and the confidence their users place upon them. The best approach is *ex ante* coordination, which should be ahead of the ever-advancing integration of markets.

Till the deep crisis of 2008/2009, it has not been generally appreciated how important it is to assure the effective monitoring of and response to cross-border financial risks, while providing at the same time a streamlined supervisory interface and a level playing field for market participation. Achieving such an objective requires significant improvements at each step of the supervisory process – with home-host cooperation arrangements for foreign branches deserving particular attention.

The essence of banking and trading has always been taking calculated risks. The difference is that now dealers place bets in more places with more clients, and they are using more sophisticated financial products than ever before. Three major changes characterize financial wheeling and dealing in this century (though lobbyists in Washington and Brussels will not admit it):

- The emergence of a new class of leveraged bank clients: hedge funds and private equity;
- The alchemist's trick of turning debt into fake "assets" through derivatives; and
- The highly opaque global capital markets with dark liquidity, which multiplied with globalization.

By early 2007, roughly half a year from the start of the great financial tornado, hedge funds – a non-regulated industry sector – accounted for more than half of all credit derivatives transactions. Commercial banks sold off loans and bought structured credit products instead, first feeding liquidity into the capital markets, then going to the wall as the commercial paper market dried up, business confidence waned, and liquidity disappeared.

No attention was paid to early warnings. In 2005, two years prior to the great crisis, Gerald Corrigan, a former head of the New York Fed, led some of the world's most senior bankers into a study which crystallized in a comprehensive report on financial stability from a private sector perspective. This report differentiated between:

- *Disturbances*, as isolated problems, and
- *Shocks* of a systemic nature.

The Corrigan team also identified three red zone shocks: the emerging markets debt crisis of the mid 1980s; the stockmarket crash of 1987; and the Asian and Russian crises culminating in the near-collapse of Long-Term Capital Management in 1998. To help prevent further shocks it produced guidelines for regulators which included watch over:

- Unexpected tail risks, and
- The need to "know your counterparty."

Banks were discouraged from doing business with hedge funds that reveal little about their exposures or risk management systems. But nobody listened, including the regulators. Had they done so we might not have been in the mess in which all who were active in the global economy found themselves two years later.

Not only should the regulators pay attention to contrarian opinion and tail events, but they should also be knowledgeable of the tricks of the trade, confidently in charge of their remit as well as believable and inspiring confidence. The worst can be expected when business confidence wanes. People are scared, and already nobody believes what is coming out of the mouths of politicians and chief executives, or is printed in the companies' financial reports.

The legal and market supervision of banks, other financial firms, and exchanges are inseparable from one another. *Legal supervision* means monitoring compliance under the letter of the law. *Market supervision* requires hands-on knowledge of assumed risks, aimed to assure that trading is conducted in accordance with:

- The terms and conditions of sound business practices, and
- Full observance of established rules and regulations.

Behind every requirement described in the preceding paragraphs should lie clear-cut accountability regarding the quality of the work done within each supervisory agency's domain. This includes the understanding, risk assessment, and control of novel and sometimes exotic or mystifying financial products, which are paraded as "sure things" by their clever vendors.

In addition, because modeling has developed into a financial science, regulatory authorities should have the experience to conduct reality tests on the bank's financial artifacts – and not only to observe whether banks are serious or complacent about their financial models. Nowhere is this more important than in pricing.

By definition, the prices of new instruments have short histories, which makes it hard to predict how they will react in a crisis. At the height of a pile of troubles with subprime mortgages has been the price of indices based on tranches of subprime loans which went into free fall. Wrong premises and outright errors with risk modeling:

- Reinforced the downward spiral in prices, and
- It therefore mattered very little that central bankers belatedly became more vocal about the danger.

Critics also add that a major organizational deficiency of current supervision is lack of unity of command. This is particularly true in America. The now virtually bankrupt AIG, a big hedge fund with insurance business on the side, was subject to a mild insurance oversight in New York State, which proved to be awfully inadequate. To the contrary, for commercial and retail banks there are four overlapping regulators:

- The Federal Reserve,
- The Office of the Comptroller of the Currency (OCC),
- The Federal Deposit Insurance Corporation (FDIC), and
- The Office of Thrift Supervision (OTS).

Till September 2008, investment banks were supervised by the Securities and Exchange Commission,[16] but as bank holding companies they now come under the Fed's watch. Today, however, a great many transactions (and particularly in derivatives) are conducted off-exchange, bank to bank. Nobody is watching the over-the-counter (OTC) market, which deals in instruments with a high quotient of potential risk. That's a God-size loophole in bank supervision.

7. Progress in financial affairs is cyclical, not cumulative

"Controlling money [by the central bank] does not control credit," said George Soros in an interview on Bloomberg.[17] "Money and credit don't go hand in hand. You have to influence the banks' ability to lend, which the Fed did not do." Controlling the money supply is the job of the central banks and controlling credit, in the full sense of the word, is an issue engaging the responsibility of both central banks and supervisory authorities. Other common responsibilities include:

- Regular meetings to evaluate macroeconomic factors.
- Research devoted to the monetary policy implications for the banking industry.
- Initiatives to diffuse a developing bubble before it reaches dangerous dimensions.
- Control of the impact on the economy due to the banks' and other financial sectors' leverage (Chapter 5).

- Evaluation of underlying causes and potential economic consequences of turmoil in the making.
- Frequent and detailed reviews with financial market participants on risks which might be in the offing.
- Feedback studies on new regulations aimed to enhance transparency and understanding of central bankers' and regulators' actions.

Past policies by the Basel Committee on Banking Supervision, to help make the banking system more resilient to financial shocks, have called for discussion papers which take years to formalize as new regulations. Basel II, for example, took 8 years. In the meantime a good initiative is watered down, its clauses are weakened by pressure groups and lobbies, regulatory arbitrage is building at drafting board level, or even the financial environment changes so much that the "new" rules become irrelevant.

There is great merit in compressing time scales to, say, 6 months by co-involving bank CEOs in general meetings rather than by pushing paper. A great principle to recall in all legislation and regulation is that *progress in financial affairs is cyclical not cumulative*. Good laws and rules can be undone by too-long discussions and delays, which see to it that:

- Key clauses are manipulated, and
- At the end even the reasons for new laws, rules and regulations are forgotten.

Basel II (see also Chapter 9) provides an example of the cyclical nature of progress in the financial business. By requiring credit rating, identifying which independent agencies are better fit to do it, and introducing mathematical models into the capital requirements cycle for the banking industry, the Basel Committee and national regulators aimed to:

- Provide risk-based capital estimates,
- Reduce market uncertainty, and
- At least on paper, strengthen the credit institutions' capital base.

Eight years of work were devoted to (supposedly) reaching that result and in the end what happened was precisely the opposite of what was wanted, as attested by the 2008/2009 banking and credit crisis. There is no better evidence of this than the crippling impact on market liquidity of skyrocketing uncertainty about the scale of risks and who held them. To work efficiently, markets must be liquid. Central bankers and regulators should have known that:

- Uncertainty breeds illiquidity,
- High leverage leaves the system acutely vulnerable to a panic, and

- Reliance on short-term wholesale funding rather than retail deposits destabilizes the banking industry.

Looked at as saviors by both central bankers and regulators, credit rating agencies found themselves torn between their business model and their use as a regulatory tool. The markets and supervisory authorities used public ratings to determine the riskiness of assets, forgetting that independent credit agencies are paid by the issuers of securities – and so have an inbuilt incentive to tailor their ratings to their clients' requirements.

"Bankers deserve D," said Paul Volcker who gave financiers their "D" rating along with a devastating critique. "For all its talented participants, for all its risk rewards," he stated in April 2008, "the bright new financial system" has "failed the test of the market place. "[18]

A financial system and its agents that end up with the government taking over some of the biggest institutions in serial rescues, and which requires the promise of $700 billion in American public money alone – plus hundreds of billions more of British and euroland taxpayers' money – indeed deserves "F" for failure, the lowest possible grade in college. Volcker was very kind giving it "D," the lowest grade in credit rating.

Here is how the Bank for International Settlements looked at this issue:

> Uncertainty about the size and distribution of losses was exacerbated by the complexity of the new structures used in the securitization process. Retrenchment from risk taking led to illiquidity, exposing weaknesses in the funding arrangements of many financial firms ... the situation was punctuated by the near failure of sizeable financial firms, prompting intervention by the public sector to avert potential systemic repercussions from a disorderly collapse.[19]

The measures that have to be taken to avoid a repetition of the same vices divide into the strategic and the tactical. The strategic ones involve the *personal accountability* of bankers and supervisors, along with the disgorgement of bonuses based on fictitious "profits."[20] The tactical are rather technical, like settlement risk, which arises in transactions involving exchange of value when:

- A bank must honor its obligation to deliver,
- But is not always able to determine in advance that it has the countervalue.

Two rather recent areas of focus by supervisory authorities and the better-managed commercial and investment banks have been *trade settlement* and *novation*, which stands for change of counterparty as buyer or seller of protection. With novation, buyers and sellers need to know promptly when the counterparty to a trade changes, but today they are being swamped with thousands of novation requests every day.

Hence the initiative by a bunch of large dealers to launch a clearing house for credit derivatives. In a way emulating an exchange based clearer, this would act as a central counterparty, backed by a default fund. Hopefully, this approach will reduce the risk of any one party's failure destabilizing the system. Theoretically, by *netting* the trades it handles, the clearer might reduce the overall value of outstanding contracts. Practically, the clearer will assume plenty of netting risk.

By morphing their market into centrally cleared but still privately negotiated deals, big banks and other players hope to make it more robust, while at the same time preserving the fat spreads they earn on OTC transactions. This is, however, like eating one's cake and having it too, because once standardized many financial contracts will inevitably gravitate towards exchanges, even if demand for customized contracts will quite likely remain heavy, in a way defeating the netting concept.

Furthermore, what the market really needs, but does not seem to get, is much greater transparency. Transparency is another example where progress in financial affairs is cyclical, not cumulative. A lack of disclosure on CDS exposures has frequently led the market to miscalculate risks.[21]

Lack of transparency makes the market nervous, and it may well work to the detriment of financial companies. Post-mortem, it has been revealed that settlement payments on Lehman swaps were most likely a "mere" $6 billion, rather than the hundreds of billions feared. Part of the turmoil in debt markets might have been avoided had that valuation been done factually and in time, and had the published results been believable.

Part Three
Case Studies

7
Household Debt and the Housing Market's Debacle

1. The ever-rising household exposure

The portfolio of households which contains their wealth may include bonds, equities in residential property, and money in the bank – essentially in savings accounts and time deposits or some other instruments. But the *pièce de resistence* of their wealth, and at the same time their castle, is their house. As the value of family holdings increases, it induces households to spend more. Curiously enough, a similar effect may be produced through easy-to-get household debt.[1]

The concept of *personal debt*, as contrasted with mortgages and corporate debt, finds its origin in the late 1920s. In May 1928, on opening day at City Bank's personal loan department in New York, 500 applications for personal loans poured in from an equal number of individuals. The next three days brought another 2,500. The way a bank officer related that event: "The men outnumbered the women, and the married men outnumbered the single men. There are policemen and firemen and mail-carriers and clerks and stenographers – mostly office workers."[2]

Till then, contrary to the policy followed with company loans, the working man in search of a *personal loan* was viewed as a case of philanthropy rather than of business. In 1928 a new epoch began, but because of the intervening First Great Depression and World War II which followed, it took another quarter of a century till personal lending became a:

- Respectable, and
- Profitable transaction.

The economic developments that came after the end of World War II saw to it that the reasons for outstanding liabilities multiplied greatly. Personal lending spanned across unsecured personal loans, mortgages, loans for home improvement, credit card usage, auto purchases, appliances and more – while the amounts involved skyrocketed. In addition, these rapidly growing *personal liabilities* have been repackaged and sold to investors as *assets*. This:

- Expanded lending and borrowing, as well as magnifying its aftermath,
- Influenced the direction and behavior of investors, financial institutions, and market players at large, and
- Led to the banking and credit crisis which started in July/August 2007 with the subprimes and then morphed into a credit crunch.

Total personal debt comprises loans granted to households by all institutional sectors. Banks are eager to lend for house purchases, spending on durable consumer goods, leisure activities, consumer staples, discretionary items, and other reasons – and households are ready to borrow, particularly as long as a robust consumer confidence prevails.[3] Few people appreciate however that their balance sheets face three main risks:

- Income risk,
- Equity risk, and
- Interest rate risk (section 2).

Income risk applies to a household's ability to repay its debt out of its income. Therefore, it depends not only on the current level of earnings but also on the sensitivity of such income to the economic environment. The loss of a job can jeopardize the income equation, for even if another job is found it may be at a lower earnings level. Income risk becomes truly biting as the ratio of debt to income increases (more on this later).

Because households have been steadily pushing up their liabilities, loss of employment (and the associated difficulty of finding new employment) by one of the income earners in the family severely affects the debt servicing burden. This is as true of personal debt as it is of mortgages. Unemployment is connected not only with loss of jobs, but also with other causes like major health problems or disability.

A family's financial problem may deteriorate further for reasons such as lawsuits, the need to support additional family members, the children's college fees, or plain macroeconomic events (Chapter 2).

Consumers are not being told all-important facts connected to the debt culture. Today in America:

- Seven million households are plainly in debt, which means that they have less than zero assets.
- An additional 35 million households have practically no net worth, and
- One American household in three is a single "event" (such as loss of job, major illness, or accident) away from bankruptcy – a startling fact.[4]

Equity risk is connected with the market price of an asset bought,[5] relative to what its owner paid for it at time of acquisition. In the housing industry (section 4), equity risk has shown up in a big way following the market's sharp downturn in 2007 after a 3- or 4-year rise in house prices. In a matter of a few months, one-third of US homeowners who had bought their house after 2003 were under water; that is, they had a *negative equity*.[6]

This rises to half for those who bought their house in 2006 or afterwards.

The price of equity is not falling only because of market forces. It may also be subject to trickery, abuse, and speculation. The housing market is not free from such occurrences. Some of the people who bought houses paid way above their real value, or did so to resell them and profit from what seemed to be an unstoppable prize increase. If so, they miscalculated twice because:

- There are always limits to how much prices can grow, and
- Real estate is notoriously slow in converting into liquid money, particularly when demand dwindles and prices start to soften.

Equity risk increases when the housing market contracts. For instance, in April 2008, three-quarters of a year after the beginning of the subprimes debacle, newly built homes in America were down by 42 percent compared with a year earlier; homes sales in Spain, another overheated housing market, had fallen by some 40 percent; and March/April 2008 house prices in Britain dipped by 2.5 percent, month-to-month, the largest monthly fall ever in the Nationwide's index.

Prices nationally could fall an additional 25 percent before hitting bottom, said an article in *Business Week*. And meanwhile, credit agencies were racing to keep up with the changing housing market perspective. Already in February 2008 S&P was cutting and reviewing its ratings on $534 billion in mortgage securities, which increased equity risk.

When the news from the credit market is dismal, mortgage securities are downgraded, and house prices are drifting, people say: "I'm not buying until prices are lower." This affects the owners of real estate who are contemplating selling their house. Typically in such cases nobody can be sure how far prices will decline.

When house prices drop by 20 percent to 25 percent, as they did in the US in 2007 and 2008, it means trouble not only for households but for the economy as well. It blows a hole in the balance sheets of banks and households. Among the families hardest hit by equity risk have been those that used their homes as cash cows during the boom years. With rock-bottom interest rates (section 2):

- They lined up for cash-out refinancing or home-equity loans, to turn housing wealth into spending money.

- When house prices zoomed this practice had started becoming popular, but it became painful when house prices caved in.

A noticeable effect of the decline in house prices on consumers is that equity losses undermine the long-held premise that home ownership is the most reliable way to build wealth and a middle-class life. The real estate crisis of 2008/2009 demonstrated that, like "diamonds are forever," home ownership was oversold.

The selling arguments have been that the rates for 30-year conventional mortgages have been at their lowest level for 50 years; that a fast-growing population, including immigrants, will soon fill up the supply of unsold homes; and that sellers will take their homes off the market rather than sell cheap. Hence even if sales volume falls, prices will not.

Critics of this unreal approach to equity valuation pointed out that eventually sellers would have to capitulate. There was no way to beat the forces of supply and demand. As for baby boomers, they had been big buyers of first and second homes, but that source of demand was fizzling.

The same critics advised anyone who would listen that interest rates were falling because the economy was slowing. If a recession hit, housing would really get whacked. Some went even as far as saying that a housing crash would force families to live within their means, which would enable the US, Britain, and other countries to work off some of their towering debt. In the end, the critics proved right.

2. Interest rate risk and households indebtedness

For households as well as for all other borrowers, *interest rate* risk refers to the possibility of higher repayment burdens – which may be induced by a rise in interest rates if debt is contracted at variable (flexible) rates, or by a drop in the debtor's creditworthiness. In the US and elsewhere, many homeowners discovered to their expense that when the very low "teaser rates" they had been offered at the outset of a mortgage expired:

- They were confronted with high interest payments likely to last many years, and
- This change in the dynamics of interest payments can have very negative consequences on household balance sheets.

Up to a point, the damages created by inflation and interest rate risk correlate. Rising inflation obliges households to direct more of their income towards staple items like food and fuel, leaving much less money for debt servicing. At the same time, by fulfilling their mission to maintain financial stability when confronted with inflation, central banks find themselves obliged to increase interest rates.

Interest rate increases make debt servicing more difficult, when loans have been contracted predominantly at variable interest rates. It is by no means a coincidence that in the banking and credit crisis the class which exhibited much higher delinquencies have been subprime adjustable-rate mortgages (ARMs), registering a delinquency rate of 20 percent in the fourth quarter of 2007 compared with 6 percent 2 years earlier.[7]

For the weakest parts of the population, interest rate risk adds to income risk (section 1), a situation compounded by the fact that debt-servicing burdens are unevenly distributed. Over and above these considerations comes the fact that household servicing costs depend also on the nature and clauses of mortgages and other loans, which financially weak households:

- Don't know how to negotiate,
- Or have no clout for doing so.

Another critical element of the debt culture is the unsustainable explosion of personal liabilities. In the United States, for example, household debt rose steadily from just under 80 percent of disposal income in 1986 to almost 100 percent in 2000; and by 2007 it soared to 140 percent. That same year in Britain it stood even higher, at 170 percent:

- Once asset prices started to come down and credit conditions tightened, excessive borrowing made households extremely vulnerable, and
- The *wealth effect* had enhanced the American and British economies' resilience, but it turned negative, damaging the psychology of households when asset prices began falling seriously.

Notice that this is not a characteristic only of Anglo-Saxon nations. In terms of ratios of household debt to disposable income, those prevailing in Britain and the United States have been put to shame by that in the Netherlands, which rose from 110 percent in 1995 to somewhat over 260 percent in 2007. That same year it stood at over 140 percent in Spain, 100 percent in Germany and France, 90 percent in Austria, but less than 60 percent in Italy.

(The ratio of household debt to disposable income should not be confused with the ratio of household debt to gross domestic product (GDP). In both the US and Britain in the late 1980s household debt to GDP stood at about 60 percent. Two decades later, in 2007, it had grown to 100 percent in both countries. By comparison, in Japan in the late 1980s it was 50 percent and in 2008 65 percent, after having peaked at 70 percent in 2000 – but Japanese public sector debt is 172 percent.)

Affordability is a prime criterion in any investment, and a frequent mistake made by households has been failure to account for the cost of carrying debt. While the debt-to-disposal-income ratio increased, many consumers found themselves obliged to pay the bank's interest and capital amortization out of a reduced current income – and in several cases debt payments reached 15 percent, 20 percent, and up to 30 percent of a household's income after tax:[8]

- Not only does it become tough to pay back the principal when debt reaches for the stars, but paying the interest becomes problematic also.
- The easy (but unwise) solution is to compound interest and capital, till eventually the total becomes unaffordable.

In America, for example, between 2000 and 2007 consumers actually added 40 percentage points to their previous debt ratio – or almost 6 percent per year. Even worse has been the case in the Netherlands where they added 13 percent per year, a staggering level. The households' record high debt ratios explain why personal defaults are rising so sharply in a recession. No wonder therefore that by late 2008 many banks were expecting:

- Lower write-downs,
- But higher write-offs from credit losses.[9]

As homeowners fall into negative equity, house loans are the first to suffer, turning from secured to unsecured borrowing. Moreover, unlike subprime mortgages, which were securitized and sold on, banks tended to keep home-equity loans on their books. But to get at the collateral, they have to buy out the lenders of the primary mortgage first, which is an expensive and risky process:

- For banks, this comes at a time when exposure to commercial property has also reached disturbing proportions.
- For families, the picture is grim because of concerns about unemployment and deteriorating consumer confidence.[10]

The extent to which households with overstretched balance sheets will have to retrench is hard to predict, but it is dramatized by the unscrupulous way personal loans were given with regard to creditworthiness, and the way credit cards were pushed down people's throats. The worst example is the one of so-called ninja loans, described in Chapter 2.

As with all loans, with mortgages banks assume more than credit risk. *If* they are given at fixed interest rates, *then* there is interest rate risk. And there may be mismatch risk associated with it if they buy short-term money while mortgages are typically long-term.

Moreover, during the go-go years of mortgage financing, banks overestimated the effects of the securitization of mortgages.[11] In their opinion, securitized instruments tapped a global pool of savings, permanently lowering rates and increasing the demand for housing. More pragmatic financial experts had however warned that while securitization would not disappear altogether, investors would demand tougher standards, making securitized instruments hard to sell and mortgages harder to get.

3. The pain of American households

Home ownership has not been the only reason for household indebtedness. From mid-2001 to nearly the end of 2006, during the housing boom, American banks raised credit card limits at a blistering pace on the excuse that it was justified by the surge in home equity. Consumers lost no time in returning the compliment.

As home prices ballooned, banks also bombarded their customers with a record number of offers to open new card accounts. Then they guided credit card borrowers to tap into rising home equity, putting their homes at risk. "Reckless extension of credit is contributing to the financial vulnerability that many families are facing," said Travis Blunkett of the Consumer Federation of America.[12] In the aftermath, the mix of:

- A high rate of debt, and
- Meager home equity

squeezed the American families' balance sheets. Whether in buying a home or in buying appliances, electronics, and vacations using the growing value of their mortgaged homes, private citizens were tricked into taking out loans they could not afford, and at the same time failed to understand the risks they were assuming.

To be fair to the American consumer, as far as his or her inclination to buy real estate is concerned, people have just two choices – rent or buy. In the years immediately after World War II when leverage was considered to be a weakness and an unwanted type of exposure, the relevant criterion for buying a house was the monthly payment, and the biggest swing factor in that payment was the interest rate.

By the 1980s all that post-war prudence was thrown out of the window, as both for households and for banks leverage had become an embedded culture. In 1990, a thorough analysis by the Office of the Comptroller of the Currency (OCC),[13] a US regulator, had shown that in addition to Third World debt, where banks such as Chase, Citibank, Chemical, and Manufacturers Hanover had made provisions for less than half their total exposure, the banking industry's stability was weakened because of loans defined as *highly leveraged transactions* (HLT).

The Comptroller's office focused on highly leveraged transactions warehoused in credit institutions' portfolios because there was plenty of evidence to be worried about:

- Bank of Boston had 252 percent of its equity in HLTs,

- Wells Fargo had 147 percent, and
- North Carolina's NCNB had 135 percent.

OCC was right to be concerned, as evidenced by the fact that many of the banks in the top HLT list don't exist anymore. Chase and Manufacturers were bought by Chemical (which renamed itself Chase Manhattan), Citi was taken over by Travelers, and Wells Fargo was acquired by another bank which took the bought company's name. But NCNB survived, renamed itself NationsBank, purchased BankAmerica and adopted the Bank of America label.

American households did not fare as badly with the 1989/1990 debacle of Savings and Loans and other banks because they were not so highly leveraged as they are today. An often heard reason for their recent ultra-high indebtedness is that in the twenty-first century incomes have been most unevenly distributed. Between 2002 and 2006 in the United States:

- The richest 1 percent benefited from an 11 percent annual real income growth in real terms, almost 2 percent per year.[14]
- On average, however, the other 99 percent got less than 1 percent over the whole period, or just 0.16 percent per year.

Seen from a different perspective, in the first 6 years of the Bush Administration three-quarters of the economic gains went to 1 percent of US citizens, who now receive a larger share of overall income than at any time since the 1920s. Arguably, every other American tried to increase his or her standard of living by going deeper into debt – with disastrous results.

Ill-advisedly, and to their own detriment, many families bought houses with less than no money, because banks allowed them to borrow more cash than they needed to pay for a new house. As banks pushed consumers to borrow and spend while supervisory authorities looked the other way, the average credit card spending limit in the US rose a cumulative 17 percent to $8,200 after adjusting for inflation.

At the same time, for a large part of the population median pay has been declining while living costs were rising. No wonder the consumers overspend themselves, and when adversity hit in July/August 2007 and house prices started a long slide down, many mortgage borrowers painfully discovered that they had little or no equity left on their homes.

Adding to their woes, an estimated 1.45 million households, many of them in California, held a particularly nasty type of adjustable-rate mortgage known as an *option ARM*, which allowed borrowers to pay less interest than the formal rate for a limited period, while unpaid interest was added to the original loan. Technically, this is called negative amortization.

When house prices were rising, that option made sense to the borrowers. If borrowers do get into trouble when they start paying off the loan in full, higher property values offer some compensation. By contrast, when house prices are falling and refinancing is difficult, as is currently the case, option ARMs turn the family budget on its head.

Some banks have paid dearly for this bad deal they pushed on consumers. Prior to going into bankruptcy, Washington Mutual saw its write-offs for option ARMs zooming from 0.49 percent in the last quarter of 2007 to 3.91 percent in the second quarter of 2008. And that was not even the worst news, because the real crunch comes when mortgages recast, forcing borrowers to start making full payments.

In fact, because loans recast after a set period, typically some 5 years after origination, or when the principal hits a predetermined ceiling, the biggest recasts wave is due to happen in 2010 and 2011 – another blow to family budgets. By some estimates:

- Borrowers' monthly payments will then surge by 60 to 80 percent, and
- With the housing industry's blues far from being changed by that time, property values may still be at, or close to, their trough.

Washington Mutual is around no more; JPMorgan Chase which acquired it will be the party facing the red ink torrent of recasts. The same is true of Wells Fargo, which bought a nearly bankrupt Wachovia Bank. (An option ARM product baptized *Pick-a-Pay* accounted for 15 percent of consumer lending at Wachovia.) Over and above that the Morgan bank and many other mortgage lenders are facing a nationwide housing slump.[15]

This can be stated in conclusion. In the post-World-War-II years, like England and continental European countries, America had regional housing booms and busts but little experience of a national slump. Stockmarket crashes are not really a precedent. At about $20 trillion, housing wealth represents around a third of all American household assets, and the damage done to housing wealth has a bigger effect on spending patterns than losses suffered in financial wealth like the stockmarket crash of 2000.

4. The housing crisis got globalized

Real estate in Britain, Ireland, Spain, and Denmark behaved fairly much as in the United States. Other states of the European Union, too, have been affected by the deteriorating expectations regarding general economic activity, housing market prospects, and tightening of credit standards – but to a lesser degree.

In Europe as in America, the securitization of mortgages has been particularly hard hit. A review of the wholesale mortgage market for the British Treasury, by James Crosby, released at end of July 2008, makes interesting reading. It says that since credit crunched in August 2007 only one British bank has managed to sell off a package of loans (and that was a paltry £500 million worth); moreover:

- Banks are unable to continue lending at anything like their previous pace, and
- Capital markets are now sucking money out of the diminished pool available for mortgage lending.[16]

As so often happens, households in some EU countries suffered more than those in others from the housing bust. According to the experts, the banking and credit crisis had an even greater impact on Britain than on the United States or any other EU country, partly because house price inflation has been faster. British household mortgage debt stands at 125 percent of disposable income, compared with:

- 104 percent in the US,
- 65 percent in France, and
- Considerably less in other European countries.[17]

Britain is also facing severe headwinds in terms of financial and economic forces. Its banking and insurance industries account for 6.5 percent of gross value added compared with 4 percent to 5 percent in other European countries. And with the financial industry in a tailspin London's economy suffers; to appreciate what this means one must know that London's economy represents about 20 percent of British national GDP.

The house price bubble has hit other British cities too, and evidently households who got mortgages and bought homes without paying a deposit. Instead of making a quick pound, they now face the fact that flats they bought in 2005 for £300,000 ($600,000 at the time) are back on the market for less than £200,000, and some are offered for as little as £120,000, particularly in auctions.

Britain aside, demand for loans to households for house purchase has turned very negative in Spain, as a result of a considerable deterioration in housing market prospects as perceived by borrowers. Spanish banks, however, did not immediately change credit standards for consumer credit and other lending to households, probably because of competition from other banks and some unrealistic expectations about improvement in general economic conditions.[18]

Also, like Italian banks, the Spanish banks have been less exposed to losses from derivative financial instruments than their American and British counterparts.

In spite of this, the European Central Bank has kept some of the Spanish credit institutions, like Banco Santander, on monetary life support – which made British bankers clamor for similar favors from the Bank of England.[19]

In supporting Santander, the ECB has also been helping British banking, as the Spanish bank already owns Britain's Abbey National, has bought Alliance & Leicester, and has cherrypicked the assets of B&B.

Other Spanish companies have not been that lucky. Martinsa Fedesa, the top housing developer, declared bankruptcy. Across the country some 700,000 homes cannot be sold, and in the Castilla La Mancha region nearly 70 percent of the houses built over the last three years remain on the block.

In Denmark, Roskilde Bank, a medium-sized regional bank, announced that it faces bankruptcy over its bad mortgage loans, and was kept open by an emergency credit line from the Danish National Bank. (An estimated two-thirds of Denmark's banks are on a watch list of the Danish Financial Oversight Institution, because of their real estate and other credit exposures.)

Spain and Denmark are interesting cases because along with Ireland they have been at the forefront of the housing boom and bust. In fact, if one looks at statistics only in terms of residential investment as a percentage of GDP, all three countries have been way ahead of Britain and the United States, as Figure 7.1 shows. It is a universal law in finance that:

- Markets that soared over the past decade are falling back to earth, and
- Investors or households who got overexposed to the market's turns and whims pay a stiff price.

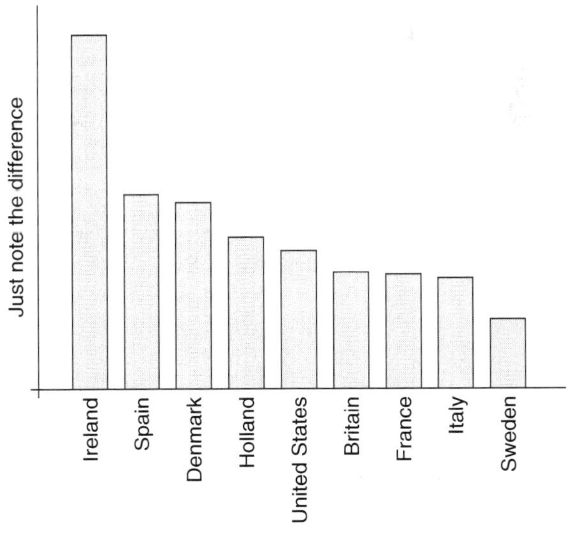

Figure 7.1 In terms of value peaks in house prices during the 2003–7 boom, Ireland led the pack (the US was in fifth position).

In Eastern Europe, too, once-sizzling housing markets are cooling rapidly. Much further east, in India and southern China, prices are no longer climbing. With stockmarkets down sharply all over Asia, families do not have much cash to plow into property. In New Delhi and other towns of northern India, prices have reportedly fallen 20 percent year-on-year, October 2007 to 2008.

All these examples provide evidence of how quickly things can go bad. On one hand the Asian consumers may have better financial staying power than their western counterparts, because they are not credit-driven. Compared with the United States and the EU, in developing countries financial innovation and the use of leverage are much less of a problem. This reflects Asia's position as a high-savings region with:

- Current-account surpluses,
- Rising foreign exchange reserves,
- Low loan-to-deposit ratios, and
- Relatively low corporate leverage.

On the other hand, however, Japan and South Korea have (unwisely) copied western habits. Japan features a ratio of mortgage debt to GDP of 40 percent, below Britain and the US but well above other countries in the globalized economy. After Japan comes South Korea with a ratio of 27 percent. By contrast, in Egypt mortgage debt is so low that it falls off the radar screen; in Brazil it is 2 percent; in Mexico, 4 percent; and in Chile, 16 percent.

The major challenges therefore lie in western countries and in those that imitated them – while, as the preceding references suggest, the problems in the housing markets are far from over. A gloomy statistic which emerged in October 2008 was a 21.5 percent annual fall in pending American home sales, a figure that is a leading indicator for actual sales. The prevailing opinion has been that house prices will surely fall further and defaults increase, as homeowners struggle to cope with higher mortgage rates.

In this environment forecasting has become an art dangerous to the forecaster's name. Back in 2005, Ben Bernanke, the Fed chairman who then was economic adviser to George W. Bush, was asked about the possibility of a decline in house prices on CNBC, the financial television channel. His answer was, "We've never had a decline in housing prices on a nationwide basis. What I think is more likely is that house prices will slow, maybe stabilize."[20]

Instead, home prices have descended to the abyss.[21]

5. Learning a lesson from bad experience

Oliver Wendell Holmes, a US Supreme Court justice, once said: "The life of the law has not been logic; it has been experience." Useful experience can be gained by analyzing not only what has happened when risks escaped prudent management, but also what was the origin of those risks that hit the housing market and real estate owners during the last couple of years:

- Some people say that, like capital, risk is a concept which can be seen through its aftereffects but cannot be touched.
- Others however maintain that careful study can reveal its nature, frequency, amplitude, and influence, starting with decisions which created the risk(s) and conditioned the magnitude of loss(es).

One population that suffered have been the developers. Whether they appreciated it or not, from late 2005 onwards builders were faced with three issues: the extent to which housing production outpaced underlying growth demand; the implications in terms of the classic oversupply backdrop that has characterized the tail-end of every investment mania known to mankind; and the fact that affordability for the first-time homebuyer has been deteriorating to levels not seen since the tail-end of the housing boom of the late 1980s. The latter induced banks selling mortgages to be so much more:

- Creative in involving new strategies, and
- Destructive in terms of their clients interests – and of their own.

The securitization of mortgages has been no new instrument or innovative decision. This practice started prior to World War I, flourished in the 1920s, went into hibernation after the First Great Depression, and came back in full swing in the 1980s with junk bonds. What has been new is:

- Its large-scale industrialization without regulatory limits, and
- Vertical integration within the banking industry, with particular emphasis on mining raw material – the subprimes, ninjas, Alt-As, Pick-a-Pays, and the rest.

Because it takes two to tango, another significant decision has been that of households that run to sign up for these exotic names without really appreciating the notion of risk. They therefore found themselves without a compass as their real estate holdings confronted rough weather. In the aftermath, they not only faced rapidly rising mortgage costs but also found themselves with no reserves to fence off foreclosures.

A third interesting decision which led to the housing debacle is that made by banks in regard to unwinding excessive lending associated with the housing bubble. Two factors lie in the background: banks run out of money, and home prices are unlikely to appreciate from current valuations over the next 5 years or more. The only positive factor is that as long as employment remains healthy, the spread of subprime problems could be slower than many people fear.

Employment has always been a crucial factor, and the way a Merrill Lynch study put it in mid April 2008:

> We are likely only one-fourth of the way into the recession. Moreover, we have seen just 20 percent of the anticipated employment retrenchment, and the consumer pull back is just starting. That means we still have a long and hard downward trek ahead of us, fraught with unexpected obstacles.[22]

During March and April 2008 in America, lenders sent several hundred thousand letters advising borrowers that their home equity lines of credit were frozen. Mortgage firms like Washington Mutual, IndyMac Bank (both now defunct), and the Greenpoint Mortgage Unit of Capital One said that declining property values obliged them to cut off credit. ("Obliged them," but did not save them from bankruptcy.)

The puzzle is that nobody, including people in the government, has clear ideas on what to do with the problems of repossessions. America, Britain, Ireland, and Spain are the four jurisdictions most severely hit by the housing bubble, and all four governments are searching for a remedy, which proves to be elusive. Following the mid February 2009 hearings by Congress, several American banks decided to put a moratorium on repossessions till March 2009. On 18 February 2009 the Obama Administration came up with a $75 billion package to help homeowners in distress.

(While the type of real estate loans in the portfolio of an American credit institution varies from bank to bank, a sample taken of loan mix indicated the following share: 38 percent commercial, 32 percent first-lien residential, 11 percent home equity, 3 percent second-lien residential, 3 percent other revolving credits, and, in a class of their own, 8 percent credit card and 5 percent other consumer loans.)

Nouriel Roubini, of New York University, is worried that the tsunami of foreclosures could spawn $1 trillion to $2 trillion of additional financial losses, creating a systemic banking crisis. As home prices have tumbled in many parts of the US,[23] examined from each bank's own perspective its management was right to rescind credit lines under the terms of contracts struck with borrowers. But at the same time, in a market-wide sense, frozen home equity lines:

- Intensified the stress of failures,
- Increased the consumer spending downturn, and
- Put added pressure on an already weak economy.

Between themselves these three bullets practically meant that banks, who already suffer from self-inflicted wounds, will be suffering even more if the housing problems in America, Britain, Spain, and other countries deteriorate.

Because however the worst cases come from inordinate leveraging and huge derivatives exposure, governments do the wrong asset allocation when they put all of taxpayers' money in the banks' treasuries.

Nobody really knows how many people would walk away from their homes when they are under water. Therefore what I personally consider as the only sensible out-of-the-box idea presented so far, is to keep the owners in as tenants paying rent, and turn back to them the property titles when the situation improves.

Key to this would appear to be a law that encourages homeowners with impaired mortgages to forfeit the deeds to the lenders but allows them to stay in their homes for the next five years, against rent instead of mortgage payments:

- For the lenders the deal would be mandatory.
- For renters, the solution can be appealing, depending on the level of rent and what can be applied in the buyback.

To make sure that real estate speculators don't use the safety net, this solution could be limited to the primary residence of families. If a secondary residence is also included, then a criterion of how long a family spends in that house could be helpful in screening those qualifying, like Monte Carlo has a law that to qualify as resident one has to spend in his/her apartment in Monaco half the year plus one day.

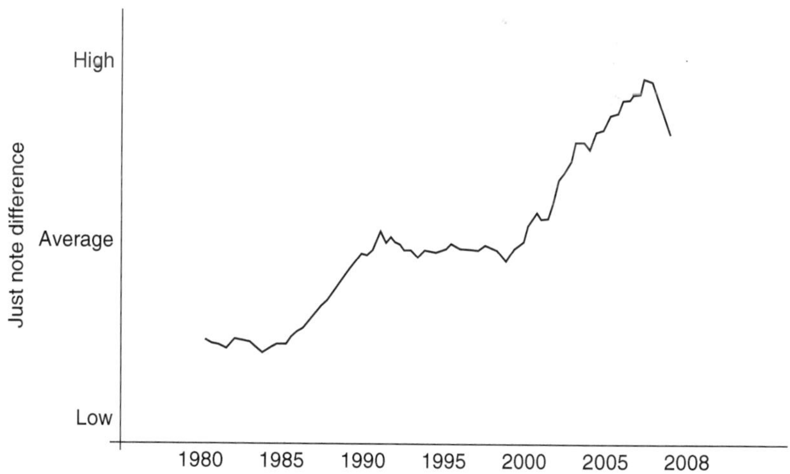

Figure 7.2 As a share of their assets, the trend line of real estate loans by credit institutions in the US increased exponentially between 1985–90 and 2001–7, leading to busts.

Financial companies which did not overexpand their balance sheets by increasing leverage, and concentrated their growing asset base in residential real estate, should not qualify for the safety net. Banks should be taught a lesson they have been incapable of learning from their experience in the mid to late 1980s when the rapid expansion of real estate loans as a share of their assets, shown in Figure 7.2, led to the crash of 1990.

6. Is negative equity here to stay?[24]

Since the late 1990s banks have been offering new mortgage products targeted at a larger number of households than ever before. One of the main objectives of this marketing strategy has been to remove two previous obstacles to borrowing:

- Offer a greater number of mortgages, at higher ceiling with little or no down payment, through higher loan-to-value ratios, and
- Allow middle- and lower-income borrowers to alter repayments relative to their financial resources, while borrowing larger amounts than might have been possible in the past.

The second objective has been achieved mainly by extending the average loan maturity, up to 30 or 35 years in some countries, with severe implications for the sustainability of household debt. Regarding the first goal of lenders, banks have been increasingly offering a variety of types of innovative mortgage products ranging from variable-rate mortgages, with the option of keeping the monthly installment constant, to deferred starts, payment breaks, or reduced starting payments – including *payment holidays*, and *interest-only* (or amortization-free) mortgages. They also permit deferral of the payment of the principal for a given period or even until the end of the loan.

The residential real estate bubble which burst, examined in the preceding five sections of this chapter, is linked closely to these mortgage "innovations" as well as to the credit default swaps (CDSs) discussed in section 7. The same is true of the concept of negative equity examined in the following paragraphs:

- *If* negative equity becomes common practice,
- *Then* a meaningful discussion has to start with its causes and lead to its aftereffects.

Equally important is to define the population to which new mortgage products have been appealing. For instance, a study in the Netherlands indicated that 41 percent of outstanding mortgages were interest-only, and these tended to be more common among lower-income households. They were also frequently used in combination with another type of loan, or as a second mortgage, for example, to finance renovations.

That's the general line. The details vary across Europe. While Dutch banks tend to grant interest-only mortgages with rather conservative loan-to-value ratios, in Spain most mortgage lenders offer a wide range of products with more flexibility in repayment schemes. As in America, the latter include mortgages under which borrowers pay only interest for a period of one to three years.

By contrast, in France loans with a deferred capital repayment have only been granted in special cases, like government-subsidized loans and student loans, as well as to investors for buy-to-let purposes to take advantage of particular fiscal schemes.[25]

Notice however that quantitative information on the aforementioned mortgage products in France and the rest of euroland is scarce, making it difficult to assess the overall financial stability implications.

A market opinion (not necessarily well documented) is that the road to negative equity is paved with adjustable-rate mortgages (ARMs), permitting the borrower to select a repayment scheme whereby payments in the initial period might in extreme cases cover only a part of the interest payment. The fact is that higher-risk ARMs have been offered to riskier borrowers, who:

- Don't understand them in the first place, and
- Subsequently face great difficulties adjusting to the rise in their monthly payments at the end of the initial period.

One of the unwanted consequences leading to negative equity, even under good economic conditions, is the so-called *negative amortization* of the loan, whereby the outstanding balance increases over time instead of decreasing, as a result of accumulated deferred interest payments. Whether we talk of American or European residential real estate, the impact of this and similar features increases rapidly when general economic conditions deteriorate.

Furthermore, contrary to a widely held belief that the most recent housing bubble is responsible for the value of the mortgage exceeding the market value of the home, this has been a steady case in the US, albeit at very small percentages. Based on statistics by First American Real Estate Solutions:

- In 1990, 6 percent of US home mortgages had negative equity.
- This increased to 6.7 percent in 1995 and 7.3 percent in 2000.
- Between 2001 and 2004 it fluctuated between 8.3 percent and 8.5 percent but went up to 10.6 percent in 2004.
- Then in 2005 it jumped to a wholesome 29 percent,[26] on first signs of possible problems with overleveraging in residential real estate.

As the forerunner of oncoming real estate problems, 2005 was critical in many aspects. Among the most important was the fact that instead of cooling down the market by becoming more careful in granting housing loans, banks pressed on with new financial instruments to lure clients even when the specter of negative equity grew more menacing.

About 65 percent of all people who bought homes in the Washington, DC area in 2005 used interest-only or option mortgages, many of which have adjustable interest rates. That's way up from 2.5 percent in 2000, according to statistics compiled by Loan Performance, a real-estate information firm. Borrowers:

- Were attracted by the fact such loans generally have lower monthly payment requirements than traditional fixed-rate loans,
- But they paid no attention to the aftereffect because (as already explained) such mortgages carry the risk that payments could jump steeply and unexpectedly.

Homeowners had been told by mortgage lenders that they were getting a break, but in reality deferring part of the interest payment was a bad deal since the deferred interest was added on to the balance of the loan and leverage grew. With this, there were two reasons why the mortgage debt swelled above the home's value and caused a negative equity:

- Compound interest, and
- Lower market value of the home.

The explanation of what the home owner's exposure is is not found in black and white in prospectuses. Instead, what one often reads is "New Price," "Just Reduced," "Priced to Sell." Once unheard of, such tags have been cropping up ever more often in the property sections of America's newspapers and in the real estate agents' promotional literature.

Adding to the reasons for negative equity are questionable practices by real estate agents. To attract houses-on-sale, some tell the owner: "To sell your house add $50,000 to what your neighbor's house sold for, and then add 10 percent to the asking price. If your house is worth $500,000, you ask for $600,000." Then the realtor tells the person who is thinking of buying the house, "Offer $650,000, because somebody else would buy the house. Anyway the rising market will forgive you."

- The loan is made for $650,000 with buyer's equity often waved, and
- That loan is underwater from Day One. Its equity is negative.

If this happens with mid-price-range homes, and it does, it is practiced much more frequently with cheaper homes where also other gimmicks like teaser rates of 1 percent play a role. Their buyers are less sophisticated and they don't appreciate that after the pre-arranged period of time the ARM resets to a higher interest rate. That could increase the interest amount due monthly by such a great amount that the borrower cannot pay the mortgage.

By then, the homeowner with negative equity has exhausted his options. He or she cannot *pay* the mortgage, because the mortgage has become too onerous; cannot *sell* the home, because even if the homeowner could find a buyer at market price, he would still owe part of the original mortgage attached to the house; cannot *refinance* the house, because in good times the bank would see that the home has a market value less than the existing mortgage – and in bad times the bank would simply not lend new money.

The homeowner is trapped while market conditions turn more and more against him or her. By the time he understands that purchasing the residential real estate was a bad mistake, all that is left to him is to lick his wounds – probably homeless.

7. Real estate property credit default swaps

The race to create derivatives in the real estate property market started in mid-2004, at least in Britain. While there were several attempts during the 1990s to develop such products, only in September 2004 was tax treatment under British law changed to make them attractive. Till then, capital gains tax was payable on profits from property derivatives, while losses did not qualify for relief.

Another push in the direction of real estate property derivatives in Britain has come from the Financial Services Authority (FSA), which allowed insurance companies to use them for portfolio management. With a smile from supervisors, and tax advantages assured by law, to my knowledge Britain became the first country in the world with a fully formed property derivatives market.[27] Back in 2004 and 2005, bankers and traders were in high spirits about this development, suggesting to whoever would listen that investors looking to make money on a downturn in housing had no better alternative than derivatives that rise and fall in value based on the likelihood that homeowners will pay back their mortgages.

The pros say that *credit default swaps* (CDSs) offer a good solution. They present them like insurance policies which allow investors to protect themselves against defaults on packaged pools of home loans. However, the reader knows by now enough to appreciate that this is an overstatement (see Chapter 5 on CDSs).

Originally the residential CDSs focused on the riskiest part of the market for home equity securities, backed by adjustable rate loans to people with shakier credit. We have already seen that this class has grown as mortgage lenders have actively pursued high-risk borrowers with easy financing. Among the biggest players have been:

- Hedge funds specializing in debt trading, and
- Speculators who try to profit from global macroeconomic trends.

Even prior to July/August 2007, however, some investors were wary of credit default swaps, if for no reason other than because the gap between the prices at which dealers buy and sell "insurance" was relatively wide, potentially cutting into expected gains. For instance, a dealer might offer to buy protection on $20 million in bonds for $500,000 a year, and sell the same protection for $600,000 a year.

In addition, at the beginning of the residential CDS era the market (and court decisions) had yet to be tested by a wave of defaults. Even in the relatively more mature market for credit default swaps on corporate bonds, payouts were frequently disputed – while, according to the critics, the advent of credit default swaps on mortgage-backed securities opened a Pandora's box of potential conflicts of interest.[28] Notice, however, that real estate swaps were not the first financial instrument based on the property market. Barclays had offered bonds and Abbey National saving products where the payout depended on movements in property prices, but:

- Prior to the CDSs, financial products did not allow investors to bet *against* the property market, and
- Swaps made it possible to take positions such as reducing exposure to retail warehouses and increasing exposure to offices.

Within the aforementioned setting, 13 January 2005 saw the completion of the first property swaps deal consisting of a £40 million contract that involved the exchange of exposure to the property market without transfer of physical assets. Theoretically, swaps of that type enabled traders and investors to instantly alter their position with regard to real estate property. Practically, they served to pile risk upon risk.

Promoters of the new instrument capitalized on the fact that real estate is a very illiquid market in which deals can take months, with charges reaching 6 to 8 percent, in terms of physical property transactions. By contrast, the real estate derivatives swap is done without the costs and delays of a physical deal. In this specific case of a 3-year swap:

- An unnamed life insurer wanted to decrease its exposure to property by £40 million, and
- Acting as counterparty, a property company wanted to increase *its* exposure.

That deal's structure was relatively simple. If returns from the UK property market outperformed the Libor interest rate, the insurer would simply pay the difference. If the returns trailed Libor, the property company would pay the difference. In both cases, the investor's estimate of how the market would move provided the difference between winning and losing.

The 13 January 2005 contract for difference was arranged by Deutsche Bank and Eurohypo, the German bank specializing in real estate. (In October 2008 Eurohypo had to be rescued through a massive injection of cash; this however was not enough and on 18 February 2009 the German government prepared a new law to nationalize Eurohypo). After the deal, experts estimated that in Britain alone this market's potential size could range from several billion pounds to £3 trillion.

Other banks were quick to try to engineer similar moves, in Britain, Sweden, and the US; and many investors were interested in becoming players. Back in early 2005, several said that real estate swaps came at the right time, as an estimated £4 billion was expected to be unlocked from people's property over the next 5 years, because elderly homeowners looked for ways to boost their retirement income.[29]

According to the pros, at consumer level the leveraging of real estate deals was finding eager participants in the so-called "equity release market"; and it had the potential for huge growth given that people were forced to take more responsibility for funding pensions, long-term care, and education costs. A motor behind that growth was believed to be the fact of a significant gap between current and planned:

- Pension provisions, and
- People's needs for cash.

Indeed, in their more classical incarnation equity release mortgages are aimed at homeowners who may have paid off their mortgage or have only a small amount outstanding. However, the pros' argument totally forgot that such deals attracted a bad name in the late 1980s because many were linked to variable interest rates, which hit a peak of 15 percent in 1989 and hit home owners on the head like a brick.

Another projection made in 2005 was that at the high end of the market, property derivative transactions would most likely take the form of risk swaps between two different sectors. One counterparty, for example, may wish to increase its exposure to business parks and decrease its exposure to shopping centers. Another may take the opposite view.

Along that line of thinking, one of the opinions was that some traders, investors, or companies would take synthetic exposure to the market rather than buying properties. And as more banks and other entities exchanged derivatives, the market could create international swaps, for instance between

London offices and New York or Tokyo warehouses, as well as assume a more complex nature by including:

- Real estate,
- Interest rates,
- Currencies, and
- Other commodities like energy.

We now know that this day of universal gratification through real estate CDSs never came. First, new financial instruments found some difficulty in adapting to the idiosyncrasies of the property market and creating for themselves a position from which they could grow. Second, the real estate property derivatives market never really had enough liquidity.

Happily for homeowners, it did not prove feasible to value estates on a regular quarterly or annual basis, while risk measurement and risk management left much to be wanted. Exposure to real estate CDSs was given a free reign but in this particular case households proved to be wiser than bankers and much more serious than their peers of the subprimes generation, who signed up to any garbage residential deal presented to them with the result that in the end they remained homeless.

8

Mea Culpa and the Abuse of the Virtual Economy's Freedoms

1. *Mea culpa*: Greenspan admits a flaw in his judgment

Who has been responsible for the devastation of American homeowners, the destruction of the American Dream,[1] and the perilous situation in which the global economy found itself as 2008 came to a close? In short, for the *triple whammy*? Dr Alan Greenspan said *mea culpa*, and he should be believed.

In a rare admission of error in judgment, made in the course of his testimony to the US Congress, the former chairman of the Fed said that he found a flaw in the ideas of the free-market economy that guided him, adding that "we are now in the midst of a once-in-a-century credit tsunami." That flaw, and presumably also some senility, guided him in wrecking first the US and then the global financial system. The congressmen were nice enough not to ask the former all-mighty chairman to pay for the huge loss he caused to the economy.

The testimony in which the, until recently, infallible "maestro" of the American – and by extension global – economy admitted that he was wrong took place on 23 October 2008. What was bad judgment on his part was to trust free markets to regulate the financial system without stronger government oversight. As a matter of fact, the *mea culpa* was not just one flaw but several.

Known to be a fervent proponent of deregulation during his 18-year tenure at the Fed's helm, Greenspan faced mounting criticism for having resisted, with George W. Bush's backing, efforts to rein in credit derivatives. Under intense questioning by Henry Waxman, chairman of the Government Oversight Committee of the House of Representatives, Greenspan said that the flaw in free market theory he supposedly found:

- Might be significant or permanent, and
- He has been very distressed by this fact, but he does not know how important that flaw might be.

In the course of his testimony Greenspan defended the use of derivatives in general, though admitting that he had been "partially wrong" in not having tried to regulate the market for credit default swaps (CDSs). Pressed by Waxman, he conceded a more serious error in his own belief that unregulated free markets create the conditions of a superior economy, stating that:

> I made a mistake in presuming that the self-interests of organizations, specifically banks and others, were such as that they were best capable of protecting their own shareholders and their equity in the firms.[2]

"In other words, you found that your view of the world, your ideology, was not right, it was not working," said the chairman of the Government Oversight Committee of the House of Representatives:

> Absolutely, precisely, [answered Greenspan, adding:] You know, that's precisely the reason I was shocked, because I have been going for 40 years or more with very considerable evidence that it was working exceptionally well.

He stated:

> In 2005, I raised concerns that the protracted period of underpricing of risk, if history was any guide, would have dire consequences.[3] This crisis, however, has turned out to be much broader than anything I could have imagined.[4]

Coming from the horse's mouth, that was very interesting evidence. During his long tenure at the helm of the central bank the CEO has been nearsighted. Such an admission of being aware of dire consequences raises serious questions. As every banker: central, commercial, or investment, should know:

- With any financial system there must be capital adequacy commensurate with the risks being taken.
- Reductions in capital because monetary authorities and regulators have kind hearts pose serious problems to financial stability (see also Chapter 9).

"Going overboard in generating change is not necessarily a good thing," says George Soros:

> Financial innovation may not be an unmixed blessing because it really prevents proper regulation. If you look at the nineteenth century, you had creative destruction going on, one financial crisis after another. But each time you had a crisis, you had an examination of what went wrong,

and you put in some instrument or some institution to prevent it from happening.[5]

This policy was instituted in the late nineteenth century by giants like J. Pierpoint Morgan. By contrast, the policy Greenspan and other dwarfs set in motion in our time ravages, and continues ravaging, on all fronts, including the debt mountain.

(In mid October 2008 the United States Treasury reported that the country's budget deficit stood at a record $455 billion for the year ending 30 September. Figure 8.1 shows the exponential trend. The deficit is expected to swell in 2009 once the short-term costs of the government's bailout of the banking system are factored in. Ironically, America's debt clock in New York's Times Square has been given an extra digit, since the sum has topped $10,000,000,000,000.)

As for investments, because bankers and traders are always one step ahead of regulators, each financial innovation that came along became the object of speculation fuelled by cheap money and deregulation. Investors who bought products they did not understand, attracted by theoretically "higher returns," assumed major risks for superficial rewards. This has been capitalism's *naive capital*.

Even the model structure of Greenspan's legacy started to crack with the case of Reserve Primary Fund documents. *Reserve Primary* has been the oldest American money market fund; on 16 September 2008 it also became the first

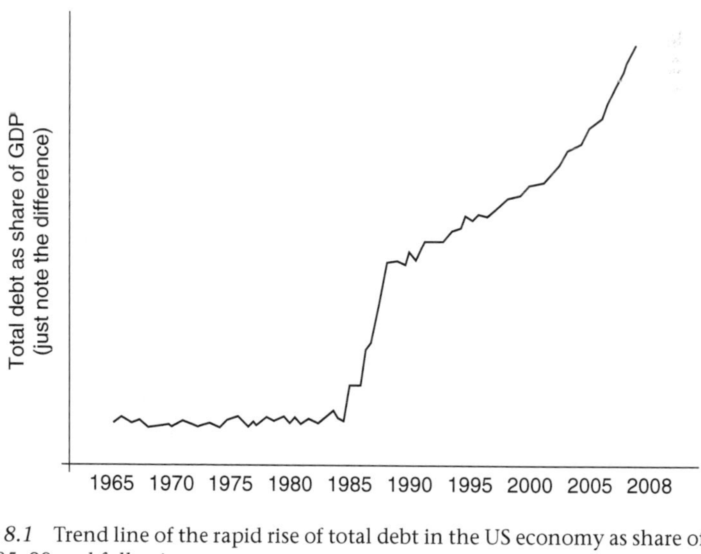

Figure 8.1 Trend line of the rapid rise of total debt in the US economy as share of GDP, in 1985–90 and following years.

in 14 years to cause its investors to lose money, because of Lehman's default. After writing off $785 million in Lehman Brothers debt, "it broke the buck," its net asset value falling below 1 dollar a share.

Reserve Primary was not alone in its Lehman sorrows. The Republic of Italy had an investment of €3 billion ($4.5 billion at the time) in Lehman which went up in smoke; Germany's state-owned KfW, €2.5 billion; and Freddie Mac, $1.12 billion. BNW Mellon Institutional Fund followed Reverse Primary's path, after being hit by Lehman's losses, in breaking the buck.

All this has been part of Greenspan's legacy; and the reader should appreciate that we aren't talking about just one flaw. "*Mea culpa*" is a honeycomb of compounding errors because of the lack of prudential supervision and the use of novel products which, after so many years of being profitable to the insiders, ran into the ground.

Another Greenspan legacy has been the added level of complexity associated with credit default swaps. Financial products were created that paid out if CDOs went into default. Bankers and trades bet on anything. The worst of all legacies has been to consider the virtual economy as having an existence separate from the real economy, and to promote this separation through lobbying.

2. Real economy, virtual economy, and lobbying[6]

Dating back some 7,000 years, the first *real economy* was organized agriculture and, along with it, trade in agricultural goods and artifacts. The domain of the earliest supervisory authority, established just prior to 400 BC in ancient Athens, was trade in agricultural products. Its boss was Anytos, the accuser of Socrates and a general in the Peloponnesian War.

With the Industrial Revolution, manufacturing replaced agriculture as the foremost sector of the real economy. This altered several supervisory duties because, in contrast to early agricultural deliverables, success in manufacturing and marketing required rapid progression towards development and the implementation of criteria of standardization, quality, conformity to schedule, volume production, transportation, sales engineering, maintenance, and after-sales service.

Among the most notable breakthroughs in manufacturing have been standards of performance, ranging from management planning to research, innovation, market analysis, cost control, investment budgets, time studies, productivity standards, safety criteria, inspection standards, reliability engineering, and more. Contributed by engineering, a fundamental advance of the physical economy has been in connection with the effort to regulated:

- The way physical products are designed, documented, and produced, and
- The real economy's operating procedures, including combinations and permutations of physical standards.

Once again, a great deal changed in terms of the supervisory chores required with the advent of the virtual economy. The latter has copied some of the real economy's ways and means, but it has also created its own supervisory requirements – without advancing (at least so far) a comprehensive system for normalization and control. W.E. Gladstone, a British late-nineteenth-century prime minister, advised wisely enough about what was coming: "Money has ever posed problems. Not even love has made so many fools of men."[7]

Theoretically, the virtual economy of the money business, which incorporates the whole financial and banking system, is supervised and regulated by the government. Practically, this is only half true. Take as an example Fannie Mae and Freddie Mac, the two giant US government-sponsored mortgage companies, taken over at the twelfth hour by the Treasury to save them from bankruptcy. They were supervised by a special agency: the Office of Federal Housing Enterprise Oversight (OFHEO), which employed 236 people. OFHEO did not fail because it was understaffed, but because:

- It lacked authority, and
- Its entire staff earned less in aggregate than Fannie's chief executive, who masterminded its disorderly expansion and bust.

OFHEO was known to be a weak supervisor, but this (till recently) did not apply to the mighty Securities and Exchange Commission (SEC), which during the last few years failed utterly in the supervision of investment banks. The reasons for such failure are many, well beyond the incentives misalignment which led to:

- Plenty of toxic waste,
- Complex structured products,
- Irresponsible trades,
- Hard sale to investors,
- Reduced transparency for everybody, and
- Minimal capital adequacy through off-balance-sheet vehicles.

With the emergency rescue of Bear Stearns in March 2008 and bankruptcy of Lehman Brothers in September, the SEC came under heavy fire. In its defense, the Securities and Exchange Commission answered that it had a voluntary program for monitoring the balance sheets of the companies it oversees. "Voluntary" in what? In honest financial statements and disclosures?

Under that "voluntary" program, which proved totally inadequate, the SEC monitored risk management, cash reserves, size and types of positions being held, and how those assets are valued by investment banks. However, under the watch of George W. Bush and his appointed SEC chairman, such monitoring became totally ineffectual – in spite of the fact that, as the SEC stated, since the fall of Bear Stearns it:

- Strengthened the liquidity requirements for investment banks relative to their funding needs, and
- Started obtaining funding and liquidity information daily, which admittedly happened quite late on.

Critics have responded that they wonder whether this program worked adequately if two of the big firms under the SEC's supervisory authority collapsed, a third urgently merged into a commercial bank to avoid the same fate, and the other two needed an infusion of taxpayer money to stand on their feet. No wonder, then, that there has been finger-pointing at the SEC, with many people questioning whether the agency was fully aware of:

- Lehman's real exposure, and of
- The tricks which could have enabled it to avoid capital charges.

The fact that many of these tricks are opaque and incomprehensible to outsiders is the virtual economy's problem. Of course, the real economy too has its challenges. One of them is overcapacity; another is price fixing. The latter is punishable by law, and plenty of executives have been to jail for that offense.[8]

As for overcapacity, the penalty is administered by the market – with an immediate effect on prices and producers. By contrast:

- The virtual economy addresses overcapacity by warehousing financial instruments for 30 years, as happens with interest rate swaps,[9] and
- Makes a mockery of the letter of the law, first because laws and regulations are way behind novel products, and also because thousands of lobbyists stop the government from taking action.

Never underestimate the power of lobbying. As Jeffrey Birnbaum writes in his book, the word "lobbyist" had become an unwritten part of almost any CEO's job description:

> Asked why he lobbied in Washington, Robert Malott, chief executive of the FMC Corporation of Chicago, cited the comment of Reginald Jones, a former chief executive of the General Electric Company: I can do more for General Electric by spending time in Washington and assisting in the development of responsible tax policy[10] than I can by staying home and pricing refrigerators.[11]

Lobbying has become so effective because the virtual economy is dominated by a handful of big players. Like Russian oligarchs, a small group of big banks write the rules of the game the way it suits them and use lobbyists for pressure on governments and for public relations. Members of this group always find among themselves a counterparty to do senseless transactions arranged in such a way that:

- Both parties in the transaction win, and
- They make accounting profits big enough to pay large bonuses at year's end.

It is the regulator's job to see that this is does not happen. Supervision is not a matter of looking at cooked numbers and giving indulgences, but of investigating and understanding what lies behind them. How unsuccessful Christopher Cox has been as SEC's chairman is documented by the fact that when in 2005 he took over from William Donaldson there were five big Wall Street banks. By October there 2008 remained only two:

- Converted into bank holding companies, and
- Fed with taxpayer money to keep them from dying.

One of the main criticisms of Cox lies the widely held belief that, as far as supervision is concerned, he took a hands-off approach. He also acted too slowly to address claims that investment banks and hedge funds were busy in naked short-selling of stocks,[12] in effect driving share prices to the ground. Many experts now suggest that:

- *If* the SEC had put in place at an early date a rule against naked short-selling, and reintroduced the "uptick" rule aimed at stopping unrelenting short selling,
- *Then* Bear Stearns, Lehman, and Merrill might have withstood the market pressure and survived in spite of their overleveraging and wide exposure to toxic waste.

Behind Cox, however, stood George W. Bush and the lobbyists. Quite likely the head of the SEC had not forgotten that his predecessor was ejected for having planned to initiate rules to register hedge funds and combat potential abuses. The result of this absence of supervisory control has been a most severe financial crisis which took its toll on traditional banks. In the US alone more than one hundred banks are insolvent or at the edge of the precipice, unable to restructure their balance sheets.

3. The virtual economy overtook the real economy in the 1970s

The financial industry grew and prospered as the intermediary of the real economy: agriculture, manufacturing, and (later on) services. Since the mid nineteenth century financial crises which happened prior to and in 1929 had in their background speculation in the real economy, often associated with megaprojects. An example is the building in the United States of railroad networks with an enormous and overlapping capacity.

The late 1920s also saw the first efforts by the banking industry to unstick itself from the real economy – a reason why in 1933 the Roosevelt Administration passed the Glass –Steagall Act which separated investment banking from retail and commercial banking. There have been other legislative measures as well, including the institution of the Securities and Exchange Commission (SEC) as an equities trading watchdog.

Absorbed by the reconstruction effort, for slightly over a quarter century after the end of World War II the banking industry kept to its role as an intermediary. For more than two decades, banks that became global did so because they followed their client manufacturing firms in their international expansion. But in the early 1970s several things put the more aggressive credit institutions on a new track.

The consequences of this change have not been immediately visible because the process of adjustment of the international financial system has been in flux. Key factors were bank-to-bank trading, as well as the scale of cyclical pickup and slowdown in the west's economies particularly that of the United States. As long as there was no crisis, frictions between the financial system and the real economy passed by unobserved. Better yet:

- A boom in finance lifted other sectors of the economy, and
- Some financial turmoil did not bring industrial activity to a stop, though it had a negative impact on the macroeconomic outlook.

Initially, the real economy was able to withstand the rougher wind blowing from financial markets, but as the latter impacted more within the gross domestic product, it became evident that central banks and regulators must apply a wide-ranging knowledge and knowhow to prognosticate, overcome, and assess periods of stress for the financial system.

Some clear minds warned of latent risks. One of them was Hyman Minsky, one of the few economists of his generation to think seriously about financial crises. In 1982 he had observed that the most significant economic event since World War II was something that had not happened: there had been no deep and long-lasting depression.

The likelihood of a financial earthquake increased as it became apparent that crucial aspects of the virtual economy escaped the monetary policymakers' and regulators' oversight. One of them was the sharply decreased transparency; a second was the unfulfilled need for a much more sophisticated system of risk management; a third was superleveraging (Chapter 5); a fourth was the looting of both the virtual and real economies by some of the players (sections 3 and 4).

One of the first steps that sent the banking industry on a course of independence from government supervision was the Smithsonian Agreement by the Nixon Administration, which ended fixed exchange rates and the dollar's convertibility into gold. In one stroke, this opened up a huge market for trading and speculation, which today stands at $3.5 trillion per day. The first oil shock of the 1970s, and even more so the second, brought banks into a business they had scarcely exploited before in a massive way: the recycling of a large amount of petrodollars. By a strange coincidence, at about that time derivative instruments were becoming of age, after a formula had been found to price options (the Black–Scholes algorithm). Eventually, the manipulation through derivatives at global scale has been augmented through leveraging 30, 40, or 50 times the capital of institutions – banks and hedge funds – with much of that capital being borrowed.

The next big step in the banking industry's globalization drama came with a bull market in shares and bonds propelled by falling interest rates, new information technology, and corporate restructuring. In the twenty- first century, cheap money saw to it that banks, hedge funds, and other financial entities could take on more and more debt, which made trades and investments very profitable but also increased exposure by leaps and bounds:

- Combining debt and derivatives, big banks created a new perpetual motion machine that could originate and distribute prodigious quantities of risk to a growing range of counterparties.
- For any practical purpose, the seeds of the self-inflicted financial industry disaster were sown in the 1980s, when all sorts of entities – from banks to hedge funds and manufacturing companies – began an unsustainable growth pattern.

Analysts tracing the rise of the American financial industry's share of total corporate profits, from 10 percent in the early 1980s to 40 percent at its peak in 2007, are now assessing the bust that followed that boom. They point out that over the same timeframe the US financial industry's share of stockmarket value grew from 6 percent to 19 percent. Yet, financial services count for:

- Less than 15 percent of *corporate America's* gross value added, and
- A mere 5 percent of *private sector jobs*, which talks volumes of how much the virtual economy and the real economy became unstuck.

Bankers, traders, asset managers, and investors rushed into high-risk transactions, simply forgetting the first basic financial principle that the higher the expected benefit the greater the risk one is assuming. The same parties who got burned with the year 2000 stockmarket crash invested in real estate and mortgage-based securitization – in violation of the second basic financial principle: there has never been a tree as tall as the sky.

As should have been expected, irrational exuberance in the virtual economy has been followed by financial market turmoil, which began July/August 2007 and spread from the US to the global economy like brushfire. Initially, this was viewed as a correction because of the previously overly optimistic assessment of risk. But in the second half of 2008 the consequences for the real economy became evident and they extended well beyond and intensified the contraction in housing construction.

Continental European countries, Japan, and the emerging economies have all been affected, and the dynamics of the downturn in the global economy have been upstaged by the failure of big financial institutions in a mix of:

- Widespread mismanagement, and
- Unprecedented conflicts of interest.

Trillions of dollars, pounds, and euros got lost with the collapse of the shadow banking system whose tools can be found in a soup of names like SVPs, SIVs, conduits, ARMs, CDOs, CDSs, and more. The lion's share of responsibility lies on the bankers' shoulders, but part of the blame goes to the supervisory authorities who failed to rigorously monitor the drifting of the financial system.

Greater regulation, adapted to the virtual economy, is inescapable if the authorities truly want to be in charge, but so far this issue has not attracted the right amount of attention (Chapter 9). As Martin Wolf suggested in an article in the *Financial Times*, an integral part of any new regulation should be a shift in the psychology of supervision away from the presumption that institutions know what they are doing. In particular, far more attention must be paid to behavior that:

- May appear rational to and for each particular entity,
- But tends to become destructive if all institutions are engaged in it at the same time, all over the global financial market.

This issue of new regulatory perspectives is of utmost urgency because if not settled *now*, then it will not be settled till the next and more severe crisis. As soon as the credit crunch improves, big commercial banks, investment banks, hedge funds, and other heavyweights will regroup and build up walls to regulation. The Sarbanes–Oxley Act of 2002 was passed in the wake of Enron, Adelphia, WorldCom, and other scams. It would have never made it through Congress two years after 2002.

4. Bankers have abused their prerogatives

In the first 7 years of this century bankers abused their money creation privilege in a big way. They granted loans without consideration of the borrower's creditworthiness or the loan's objective, invented new forms of credit which left in the dust time-honored lending practices, practiced massive securitization with scant attention to quality, over-relied on short-term commercial paper for long-term commitments, created a horde of structured investment vehicles, and unstuck the money supply from the gross domestic product of America and of other countries.

Big and easy money led to a vicious cycle of more greed and carelessness, generated a false sense of massive liquidity, and enriched the bankers' pockets (as well as those of their business associates) to the detriment of their shareholders, employees, and society as a whole. All this was done without any risk of punishment because government authorities and supervisors became accomplices – though there is (as a rare exception) a single case of a bank manager being convicted (who in June 2008 hung himself in prison).

No wonder therefore that in the aftermath the US and global economy is in terrible shape. Practically, nothing is moving, as if there were a common accord that everything should stand still. On 12 November 2008, Jamie Dimon, JPMorgan Chase CEO, said that the coming recession (read: the Second Great Depression) will be worse than the ongoing credit crisis – which brings to mind a WWII joke: "Enjoy the war. Peace will be dreadful."

Trying to do things halfway, in the hope of redressing the balances, has led to confusion. Nobody knows what to do anymore. Dr Martin Feldstein, of Harvard University, was right when he said[13] that precedents for the current crisis are practically non-existent. Few lessons filter from the Great Depression, because the US economy has changed a lot since 1929:

- It is no longer an industrial economy,
- It is a service economy and nobody really knows which levers to pull.

In fact, like Britain's, it is a virtual economy, and virtual assets facilitate their own abuse. Unlike in the case of real assets, the virtual economy's representations can be easily multiplied, divided, combined, reinvented, and employed to simulate the most peculiar deals. This is done:

- By uncoupling the economic features of debt from a formerly rigid physical state, and
- By cutting, dicing, and recasting debt in novel forms, as has been the case with the subprimes.

"Formal property rules require assets to be described and characterized in a way that not only outlines their singularity but points out their similarity to other assets, thus making potential combinations more obvious," says Hernando de Soto.[14] This is true for real assets, not for those of the virtual economy, which offer themselves to a previously unthinkable level of leverage, exploitation and abuse.

Along with that comes moral hazard. The fact that western governments and central banks have been massively bailing out financial institutions (Chapters 9 and 10) which failed because of mismanagement and greed suggests that the so-called global banks have turned themselves into syndicated public beggars, who expect to cover up the red ink in their balance sheets through government handouts. Some experts and a large part of the public are appalled at this decadence.

The low level of prevailing morality is evidenced by the fact that the high life at the top of financial companies which went bust because of excesses, and were given a lifeline of public money, continues as if nothing had happened. AIG has been bailed out of bankruptcy with $153 billion in taxpayers' money so far, while its executives have not abandoned their big-spending practices.

An outcry in the US put a temporary stop to AIG's Las Vegas and California posh resort retreats, but it did not stop a lavish shooting party at a British country manor. The way an article by Maureen Dowd had it, London's *News of the World* sent undercover reporters to track down eight of AIG's financiers on their $86,000 partridge hunt as they feasted on pigeon breast and halibut.

They stayed at Plumber Manor, a seventeenth-century country house in Dorset, and in the 4 days they were there spent $17,500 on food and rooms alone. The private jet to get them there cost another $17,500, and the limos added $8,000 more. An AIG big cheese held court at the bar and told an undercover reporter: "The recession will go on until about 2011, but the shooting was great today and we are relaxing fine."

In Britain, in spite of the company's near-bankruptcy the AIG party went on. This contrasted starkly with what happens in the US where Andrew Cuomo, New York's attorney-general, got AIG to reverse itself and cancel 160 conferences and other events that would have cost more than $8 million. The company has also been obliged to give information on compensation, bonuses, and other payments.

"We stopped a $10 million severance payment to Stephen Bensinger, the chief financial officer," Cuomo said in a statement. "There's a phenomenon when senior management sees the corporation deteriorating and they concoct a version of looting the company to take care of themselves." Cuomo also stopped a $19 million payment to AIG-fired CEO Sullivan, who is using a state "claw back" law which allows him to recover contracts and rescind payments if there was unjust compensation.[15]

In France, at the end of October 2008, the Caisses d'Epargne (the central treasury of the savings banks) admitted having lost €685 million[16] in high-risk transactions. Afraid that this might be only the tip of the iceberg, the French government rushed to recapitalize it with a cash infusion of €1.1 billion. Reportedly, Nicolas Sarkozy, the French president, was informed of the losses while flying to Canada for an official meeting with that country's prime minister (prior to the Camp David conference with President Bush) and he asked for the heads of the bank's chairman and its CEO.

According to published reports Charles Milhaud, the CEO, first resisted the liquidation but then decided that it was better to take the money and run.[17] Several board members rejected that request, making reference to the CEO's serious errors. The chairman offered a compromise: half the money. This, too, was rejected (minus one vote): "Not a penny" was the board's answer. Shortly thereafter the CEO made public a declaration that he:

- Assumed full responsibility for the losses, and
- Asked for no indemnity.

This has not yet been heard of in America, where golden parachutes are still the order of the day, in spite of draconian clauses in the Sarbanes–Oxley Act of 2002. Not without reason, therefore, many people are now seeking to bring to court the Wall Street executives and other bank managers who are responsible for the torrents of red ink that have hit the American economy, and for the ensuing mess.

One can hope that the political climate will be changing as the government feels great pressure to put a few money men in the dock. The FBI is probing more than two dozen firms but no concrete court case has yet been advanced. Market regulators, state attorney-generals and the Department of Justice are also working to unearth wrongdoing, sifting through emails and seeking whistleblowers at firms such as Fannie Mae, Freddie Mac, American International Group, and Lehman Brothers (the only Wall Street firm so far allowed to go bust).

At least 17 former Lehman executives, including Dick Fuld, its former CEO, have received grand-jury subpoenas.[18] Investigations focus on disclosure and valuation, including public statements they made even as they knew their firm was in trouble. (But to constitute fraud there must be intent to deceive, and proving that beyond reasonable doubt is not easy while even pitifully sloppy risk management is not illegal.)

5. Extravagant pay but no disgorgement

Imported from America where it flourished in the go-go 1990s and continued going strong in the following decade, extravagant executive pay has more recently taken hold in Europe. Critics say that this is the twenty-first century's version of theft in the executive suite; and a mockery of "shareholder value."

Down to basics from fat salaries to perks, options and bonuses, executive pay can be seen as a measure of society's excesses. This does not mean the concept of paying for performance is wrong – but it should be kept within what society judges as fair, and be based on a real test of whether a business is run in ways profitable for its shareholders and society at large.

Are the boards approving extravagant salaries, options, and bonuses really motivating the company's top brass to perform better, or are they doing so because they cannot stand up to the chief executive and his cronies over pay? Politicians in Germany, France, the Netherlands, and more recently also America, think that boards are being weak when they decide to gratify with tens of millions of dollars or euros quite average executives whose performance should have been censured rather than rewarded.

In mid June 2008 John McCain, the Republican presidential nominee, complained that at big firms failed senior managers are packed off with \$40 million or \$50 million for the road. Horst Köhler, the president of Germany, and Nicolas Sarkozy, the president of France, have publicly denounced extravagant executive pay. Jean-Claude Juncker, president of the European Commission's Eurogroup of Finance Ministers, called excessive pay a social scourge. Yet it continues to grow unimpeded.

When *L'Expansion*, the French business weekly, stated that pay for the country's bosses went up 58 percent in 2007, Christine Lagard, the finance minister, commented that it was scandalous and threatened regulation. But in Germany Angela Merkel, the chancellor, resisted the Social Democratic Party's push for legislation to clamp down on executive pay; in Britain even though the Labour Party is in power practically nothing has yet been publicly stated against extravagant compensation for meager results; and in America business continues as usual.

Nowhere is the pay-and-bonuses business more profuse than in battered banking and finance. Research done at the University of Chicago has shown that in 2004 nine times as many Wall Street executives earned over \$100 million as did chief executives of public companies. The top 25 hedge fund managers earned more than the chief executives of all the companies in the Standard & Poor's 500 combined:[19]

- This study's findings are startling.
- The conclusion to be drawn is that the beneficiaries earned such salaries and commissions by taking enormous risks with other people's money.

Not all big-ticket beneficiaries have performed trivial feats. John Paulson, founder of Paulson & Company, a hedge fund, made \$3.7 billion in 2007,[20] probably the richest reward in Wall Street history, by betting against subprime mortgages, complex financial products and banks that held them. That could be looked at as the reward for observing the fragility of the financial industry and acting before the debacle occurred.

John Paulson is an exception. What is indeed regrettable is that even the average types of bankers and hedge fund managers have redefined the notion of wealth they thrust upon themselves. Apart from the fact that they don't deserve it, this underscores the gaping inequality between:

- Millions of people facing stagnating wages and home foreclosures, and
- A self-appointed financial elite that thrives in good times and bad.

Fed hand-to-mouth by manipulating the mechanics of the free market, the richest executives and traders keep getting even richer. The way Jenny Anderson had it, in 2007 – in plain market turmoil – to make it into the *Institutional Investor Alpha* magazine's top 25 list a hedge fund manager needed to earn at least $360 million, more than 18 times the amount in 2002. By contrast, that same year the median American family earned $60,500. Combined, the top 50 fund managers in 2007 earned $29 billion.[21]

If the *Alpha* list guys and dolls are the outliers, those at the body of big wealth's self-distribution gratify their extravagant desires for themselves and their families (often brought into the deal) through lavish share options which also carry plenty of moral risk. Originally the aim of share options was to fill in for the diverging interests of managers and owners. This, however, is now a thing of the past.

In America, Britain, and continental Europe options have been much used and misused, with the result that it is not at all clear that they work any longer as intended. Both in regard to options and in the case of bonuses, companies have devised ingenious rather than upright compensation schemes allowing CEOs, their immediate assistants, and other big company egos to reap handsome rewards even if they foul things up.

The House Banking Committee chairman was on the right track when on 22 October 2008 he urged that banks forego the year's bonuses as risk-taking had backfired. Other critics of the bonus system which has run wild have pointed out that in many financial institutions the higher value of warehoused positions might be no more than 10 cents to the dollar – an unprecedented loss. But has anybody been listening?

The money paid out in unwarranted lavish handouts strains the treasury of financial companies, which is already in the red and survives by offering new equity and debt or through the injection of government money. In 2008 it was the taxpayer who footed the bill of an unprecedented $700 billion salvage plan to avoid a systemic crisis while big banks who benefited from this plan were unwilling to forego 2008 bonuses to their traders.[22] Quite to the contrary, there should have been disgorgement. The best cases on record of penalties and disgorgements hitting Wall Street date back to April 2003, though it took nearly a year until the sentence fell – announced in a packed press conference at the Securities and Exchange Commission, in Washington, DC. It was an event waiting to happen. Somebody had to be held accountable for:

- Hundreds of stocks which had collapsed, while heavily promoted by brokers, and
- Trillions of dollars investors lost in overpriced equities, which led to the stockmarket bubble of 2000.

In a way, the penalties were expected because almost everyone already knew who had done what and, more or less, what the punishment would be. Opinions were even expressed, mainly in academia, that the big Wall Street banks welcomed these penalties as a means of getting over the wave of criticisms about disregard of shareholder value or even malfeasance. Without acknowledging any guilt, the ten Wall Street firms agreed to pay a total of $1.4 billion in fines, to pay back of ill-gotten profits, and also to make further payments to support:

- Independent research, and
- Investor education.

Curiously enough, there have been no similar penalties and disgorgements connected with the king-sized financial manipulations that led to the banking crisis of 2007, credit crunch of 2008, and deep recession of 2009. The argument that the financial industry is still reeling from the crash and could not afford to pay penalties is a non-starter. Its top executives have pocketed among themselves tens if not hundreds of billions and disgorgement should have been the order of the day.

6. 23 February 2009: disgorging the illegal bonuses

Most damaging to the standing of the banking industry has been the case of bonuses paid to executives and traders of investment banks in spite of the torrents of red ink which ran during 2008 – and at whose origin have been little-understood instruments, excesses, inordinate risks, and plain bad management. By being unwarranted and extravagant, these bonuses further documented the fact that in the twenty-first century:

- Bankers have been living in a make-believe world, sometimes called cloud-cuckoo-land, and
- "Their world" is totally disconnected from the real world of Main Street, consumers, and society's needs at large.

On 23 January 2009 Ken Lewis, the CEO of Bank of America, ousted John Thain, former CEO of Merrill Lynch and his heir apparent, after the merger of the two banks. Thain had made $4 billion of bonus payments for 2008 to Merrill's investment bankers – in a year the brokerage company had bled white from a torrent of losses and, to avoid bankruptcy, found refuge in a merger with Bank of America.

A month later, in the week of 23 February, 2009 Andrew M. Cuomo, attorney general of New York State, pressed Thain to reveal the names of the beneficiaries of these irrational and illegal bonuses. They were illegal because they were done in secrecy, they were not authorized by the board of directors, and, most particularly, they were paid with taxpayers' money. That money came out of the $700 billion authorized by Congress to save the mismanaged and self-wounded big banks from outright bankruptcy.

The way the financial news had it on 25 February 2009, John Thain underwent hours of questioning at the New York attorney general's office. What the authorities wanted particularly to know were the names of the 5 top Merrill executives who took the lion's share of the $4 billion. Not only did Cuomo grill Thain, but also a day later Ken Lewis, the CEO, had to appear before the attorney general to answer questions. (One of them has been about Lewis having allegedly authorized single-handed the illegal Thain handouts.).

All this came at a very bad time for Bank of America as the company was also confronted by the need to replenish its equity capital, which had dropped to between 2.6 percent and 2.8 percent of assets, versus a minimum of 3 percent demanded by regulators and the US Treasury. (At 1.5 percent Citigroup was much worst off, while at about 3.6 percent JPMorgan Chase was above this minimum limit.)[23]

What all this proves is that the top management of big banks not only damaged severely the institutions and the institutions' assets that were under their charge, but also violated ethical rules as well as long-established capital requirements. Yet none of these people has so far been brought to justice. The moral risk runs high when one sees that what senior executives care for is huge salaries and unjustified bonuses for themselves and their pals, in violation of the management principles that:

- Bonuses should be paid only on evidence of factual and documented performance.
- They should account fully for long-term assumed risk and for the market value of transactions.
- They should be spread over the life of the trade, and not given on the spur of the moment.
- They should be paid in shares, not in cash; but neither should they be distributed as options that have been widely abused.

- They should include clawback clauses, obliging recipients to pay back bonuses that turn out to be earned for the wrong reasons and/or by assuming excessive risks.

In short they should be associated with exceptional performance, not the rising tide of the markets, they should be transparent, and their administration should be made part of the Sarbanes–Oxley Act. In addition, as in any other industry when a company goes bankrupt, executives, traders and everyone else should lose their bonus – while public authorities summon the courage to enact the disgorgements.[24]

7. The 2008 manipulation of Libor by wounded banks

Since the mid 1980s each morning a handful of banks, 16 to be precise, quietly decide how much it costs to borrow money all over the world.[25] In late May 2008, however, a troubling question came to the public eye, prompting the British Bankers' Association (BBA) to examine the way it sets the rate at which banks borrow money from each other.

- Known as the London Interbank Offered Rate, or *Libor*, this interbank cost of bought money affects the rates banks charge on transactions ranging from home mortgages to corporate debt and other borrowings.
- But in May 2008 evidence started filtering through that some of the elite rate-fixing members were lying about one of the world's most important interest rates, by providing false or misleading estimates to hide their own precarious financial positions.
- According to an analysis performed by the *Wall Street Journal*, Citigroup, JPMorgan Chase, HBOS, WestLB, and UBS were among the banks that reported significantly lower borrowing costs for the London Interbank Offered Rate than they should have. All five banks, members of the aforementioned panel that reports rates used to calculate Libor in dollars, were supposed to be objective and truthful in their answers; but they were not.

That's another of the virtual economy's freedoms that have been violated, and it came as a shock because the British Bankers' Association's system for setting Libor had worked well for more than two decades. The fact that banks manipulated their input meant that rates subsequently charged on thousands of financial contracts were artificially low. According to Sean Maloney, a bond analyst at Nomura in London:

- "There are definitely incentives for banks to push the rate lower."
- "They would get the rate down while still charging their customers more."[26]

In turn, this meant not only that credit rating by independent rating agencies became unreliable but also that the London Interbank Offered Rate went through its worst credibility crisis since its creation in 1986. Yet, more than two decades ago it was the big global banks who asked the British Bankers' Association to come up with a benchmark rate to price syndicated loans and derivatives. Libor was unscathed by the 1987 stockmarket crash, the 1994 bonds crisis, and the 2000 dotcoms hecatomb. But with the 2008/2009 credit crunch the standards bent.

Critics say that this Libor affair amounted to a bought money fraud, which is part of a more general banking fraud. They also point out that while nobody was brought to justice with the Libor scam, in late August 2008 federal prosecutors in New York charged two former brokers at Crédit Suisse with securities fraud. The pair had allegedly asked investors for money to put into low-risk securities backed by student loans (which in itself is a rather risky investment). Instead, the two brokers used the funds to buy higher-yielding (read: junk) mortgage-backed collateralized-debt obligations (CDOs) which have been at the eye of the storm of the credit and banking crisis.

The Libor banks and the pair of brokers were by no means the only black sheep. As the banking and credit crisis unfolded, official comments by plenty of senior bankers proved to be untruthful. Instead of speaking their minds, they lied as they sought to sooth the markets and the public in the hope that:

- Light-headed investors could be lured into buying again, and
- Banks could unload more of their worthless securities on their customers.

Back in April 2007 Richard Fuld, CEO of the now bankrupt Lehman Brothers, was quoted as having said: "The worst is behind us." Jamie Dimon, JPMorgan Chase's CEO, claimed that the crisis "may be 75 to 80 percent over." John Mack, Morgan Stanley's CEO, commented that the turmoil would last "a couple of quarters longer." Lloyd Blankfein, Goldman Sachs's CEO, stated "We're closer to the end than to the beginning."[27]

Veiled by such statements lies the fact that the big banks' leadership began to appreciate that the financial crisis is only one aspect of a much larger economic earthquake: the destabilization of an economy based on debt and on leverage. The CEOs who tried to misguide public opinion knew very well that the badly wounded global financial structure was being kept alive through a combination of trillions of taxpayer money and a supervisory system bent on:

- Allowing banks to hide their losses, and
- Always looking the other way as the US capital market could cope no more with the rapidly increasingly demand for cash.

A month prior to this false good news, on 19 March 2008 the Financial Services Authority had announced an investigation into potential market manipulation by spreading false rumors. The FSA was also investigating unusual share trades in financial equities, after the HBOS share price fell 17 percent amid speculation that it had sought emergency funding.

The stock's heavy losses led the Bank of England into the unusual action of calling news organizations to deny that it had held emergency meetings to discuss the viability of specific UK banks, including HBOS, describing these rumors as an absolute fantasy. (HBOS's woes proved themselves not to be a fantasy at all. Six months later Britain's former premier mortgage lender was forced into merging with Lloyd's TSB to avoid bankruptcy, and also benefit from a handful of taxpayers' money.)

A similar message about the destructive power of false news (really false or alleged to be so) was given by the Securities and Exchange Commission, which warned that it was looking into trading which had taken place ahead of the 14 March collapse of Bear Stearns. The SEC was probing whether false or misleading information was disseminated to investors to manipulate markets. Its probe also covered potential insider trading and market manipulation by Bear Stearns ahead of its sale to JPMorgan Chase.

8. The huge loophole of over-the-counter derivatives

The 1990s have seen an explosive growth of over-the-counter (OTC) derivatives trades, a trend which increased by leaps and bounds in this century. These are primarily custom-made products that are tough to price and nearly impossible to mark-to-market – a fact which has created frequent headaches for central bankers and bank supervisors. Side-by-side with the pricing challenge, to which there has so far been found no effective solution, are three other concerns:

- The continuing expansion of this market, which puts the supporting infrastructure under stress;
- Consistently substandard risk control, connected to the impossibility of knowing the instruments' fair value; and
- The fact that failure of a counterparty to honor its commitments would cause chaos, an example being the just-avoided failure of Bear Stearns (March 2008).

Every one of these bullets connects to other failures. One of the reasons for infrastructural strain, for example, is sloppy trade processing systems and procedures. While the OTC market grew to extraordinary proportions, very few banks cared to make their networks and computer systems more resilient, and to drastically reduce settlement risks. (The latter may change with a 31 July 2008 agreement engineered by the Fed, which will take some time to implement fully.)

As of mid 2008 only 50 percent of all OTC interest rate trades, which constitute the big bulk of bank-to-bank derivatives deals, were executed automatically. Much greater attention, however, was paid to credit default swaps. According to informed sources nearly 90 percent of CDSs were handled by computer, roughly double the amount of 3 years earlier. But they were not regulated.

The big question for governments, central bankers, and regulators is whether or not they want to close the huge OTC loophole by mandating that all financial transactions are handled through the exchanges. ISDA's standardization initiative points in this direction, but for the time being the so-called alternative transactions and settlements (ATSs) – also known as dark liquidity – steal market share from the exchanges. It is projected that if the current bank-to-bank trend continues, by 2011:

- 38 percent of transactions will be ATS-executed, double today's statistics, and
- The balance of 62 percent, which will still be in exchanges, will tend to shrink in favor of unregulated dark liquidity.

This poses two questions: should this trend be reversed? And: how far can OTC trades be regulated? Without much doubt, for reasons of transparency and risk control, the answer to the first question is "Yes!" Exchanges are supervised while ATSs are not.

The response to the second query is more complex. Given that OTC transactions are secretive and bank-to-bank, and there is no publicly available information on such trades, the ability to supervise OTC trades is practically zero. Nothing is going to change unless OTC ends and all transactions are exchange-based. On the other hand, as several experts now suggest:

- OTC is not regulated, but what could be regulated is the product, and
- Provided that the product is standardized, this is doable, even if banks cry that this stifles innovation (which, as an argument, is a red herring).

Instead of being against it, top management should welcome and promote normalization and exchange-based trades, because this makes its job so much more effective, which is to assure that each new transaction, product, and service is developed with safety as well as profitability in mind. Weaknesses need to be identified early, so that *if* they cannot be corrected *then* the new instrument can be dropped before the bank gets too committed to it. Exchange trading helps in killing two birds with one well-placed stone:

- Greater transparency, and
- More effective risk control.

Prior to the deterioration of the banking and credit crisis in 2008/2009, which brought to light very serious abuses of the virtual economy's freedoms and some horrendous practices, nobody would have thought of accusing the bankers of bundling up loads of toxic-waste securities and peddling them as AAA investments. But now this has happened, it is wise to be doubly careful:

- The culture of deals for deals' sake will change slowly, and
- Over-the-counter transactions provide the ideal mechanism for hiding the skeletons.

The law to punish wrongdoers has been available for half a dozen years, but it has not been applied. Passed in 2002, the Sarbanes–Oxley Act (SOX) was a response to a number of accounting scandals, including some major ones like Enron. Among other things, SOX:

- Tightened disclosure requirements in corporate financial reporting made it mandatory (with penalties) for the CEO and the CFO to sign the financial statements, and
- Extended the obligations of external auditors.

But there has been no rush to implement it. Notice as well that SOX applies not only to listed US companies and their foreign subsidiaries, but also to foreign companies listed on a US stock exchange or the NASDAQ. There is no equivalent to it in euroland or in other EU countries, and this is regrettable – but given that by a large margin trades in toxic waste took place in New York, the Sarbanes–Oxley Act was plenty, *if only* the government had wished to apply it:

- Sound risk management depends as much on the legal infrastructure as on the way businesses and governments comply with the rules.
- Had Sarbanes–Oxley been put into effect, as it should have been, then CEOs and traders ought to have paid back their bonuses and compensated their customers' shareholders.

Not only did this not happen, but also during the last few years the SEC has been under fire from lawmakers and business groups who blamed the Sarbanes–Oxley Act for driving the costs of compliance higher, and for pushing firms to relocate to less-regulated markets overseas. In the end the Securities and Exchange Commission issued new guidelines, along with the revised auditing standard from the Public Companies Accounting Oversight Board (PCAOB).[28]

Bending the *audit standards* is counterproductive and dangerous. Internal and external audits should be done to well-established standards. The argument that the audit is no more than a contractual agreement between a company and its auditor, with standards subject to negotiation, is sophistry. For the public good – and for the benefit of financial markets – audit standards must be uniform for all companies and in all countries. They should also be made far stricter than they have been so far.

9. Marking-to-market: bankers don't want to hear the bad news

Big banks that found it difficult to face heavy write-downs resulting from the rotten transactions they had done over the past 6 years have raised a great deal of criticism against *marking-to-market* – essentially, fair-value accounting. Marking-to-market obliges them to value their warehoused assets and liabilities at the price they would fetch if sold now, rather than at historic cost.

The fate of Lehman Brothers, American International Group (AIG), Washington Mutual, and plenty of others provided irrefutable documentation that many of the instruments in a bank's portfolio are worth 10 to 20 cents to the dollar, and some only 5 or 6 cents. Therefore, if one wants to know about the "assets," fair-value financial reporting is a "must." It is very dangerous to let the banks define at will the value of *their* "assets."

- *If* they are not marked to-market,
- *Then* the way to bet is that posted values are fake.

Marking-to-market is not easy, particularly for OTC trades, while for other "assets" it often provides painful messages about how little inventoried positions are really worth. This has led to a chorus of big banks against marking-to-market. In reply, both the Financial Accounting Standards Board (FASB) and the International Accounting Standards Board (IASB) answer that the nature of instruments in which banks trade makes it impossible to apply classical accrual accounting.

In their banking books, credit institutions are using *accrual accounting*, whereby they wait until loans actually go bad before reducing the value given in their accounts. This is the historic-cost approach and it means one big go of write-offs in contrast to several write-downs. No matter which accounting method one has used, red ink remains red ink.[29] Essentially, what the anti-marking-to-market politicians and bankers are saying is that IASB and FASB could have added in their response that accrual accounting is by no means a sweeter financial reporting scheme for a wounded bank, or any other company with a damaged balance sheet. The rapid increase in loans which went sour is a harbinger of bad news which has to be revealed to the authorities and the public one way or another – even if it is detrimental to the entity in which bad news originates, or to the whole banking industry.

It is important for all banks to appreciate that accruals accounting, too, can be a messenger of painful news, because the credit crunch has moved on from a phase of mainly market losses to a more traditional phase of credit losses. The forced sale of Wachovia, America's fourth-largest commercial lender, in October 2008 reflected concerns about its loans, which banks almost always carry using accruals rules, not fair value:

- The fact is that banks don't want to release information on their losses at all, and
- They prefer to keep their financials close to their chest, without appreciating the fact that this makes the market more nervous than it has been.

A senior banker told me that in a downturn fair-value accounting forces his institution to recognize all losses at the same time, impairing its capital and triggering a fire sale of assets which in turn drives down prices and valuations. This argument is half-baked. Whether marking-to-market or accrual, the accounting system only mirrors a bad situation; it does not create it. The banks can only blame themselves for the red ink.

The fact that banks would have to mark their securities to the prices Lehman receives as it is liquidated, and this is most likely going to be awfully low, reflects only the reckless trades and crazy "investments" the banks have made. The banks have clear reasons to worry. In April 2008 the Institute of International Finance (IIF), the banking industry's Washington-based lobbying group, sent a confidential memorandum to FASB and IASB as standard-setters. This practically said:

- Markets had failed, and
- Therefore companies should be allowed to suspend fair value for "sound" assets.

As this stance not only was self-serving but also lacked credibility, Goldman Sachs resigned from the IIF in protest at "Alice in Wonderland accounting."[30] Goldman was right. A few months later Merrill Lynch sold to LoneStar, the vulture fund, $30 billion in subprimes-based securities at 21 cents to the dollar. But as we have already seen, at the same time it advanced to LoneStar, as a loan, three-quarters of the amount it was about to receive. Therefore, in reality:

- Merrill Lynch sold its portfolio of damaged securities at slightly over 5 cents to the dollar, and
- It has a potential claim on a loan to the vulture fund, with all this represents in credit risk.

Politicians don't seem to appreciate the implications of *5 cents to the dollar*, otherwise they would not have brought the accounting regime directly into their line of fire. It is indeed regrettable that in America the bailout package revised by Congress would give the Securities and Exchange Commission the power to suspend fair-value rules. This makes a mockery of the "free economy":

Suspending fair value leaves bank balance sheets at the whim of speculators. Standards setters should resist the cancellation of the rules – and in this they must be supported by institutional investors and accounting firms. (It is enough, and it is really regrettable, that IFRS are inconsistently applied across Europe, though standard setters hope to reach a definitive set of rules only by 2011.)

Whether it is the bankruptcy of Wachovia and of Washington Mutual or the bankruptcy of Lehman Brothers and a lifeline thrown to AIG, Fannie Mae, and Freddie Mac by the US authorities, investors want to be able to distinguish "good" from "bad" institutions. That's a basic principle of free markets and it is the investor's right to become more selective within the banking universe. The contagion from hidden toxic waste could harm the better-quality securities.

Investors don't want, either, to hear about the so-called *proforma* financial statements, which are a cheat; or to be misled by embedded value (EV), which represents shareholders' funds plus the (highly uncertain) value of "future profits." When individual companies are allowed to pick their own assumptions on things like investment returns, the results are highly biased and this is anathema to investors. What the latter care about is:

- A sound accounting system able to promote market information and market discipline, and
- Dependable financial reporting which reveals whether a company's condition is strong or weak, and what its market stress level is now or might be in the near future.

The bad news can serve a purpose, if one acts upon it promptly. As Chapter 1 brought to the reader's attention, in the early 1990s Riksbank, the Swedish central bank,[31] immediately confronted the developing banking crisis in the country through transparency and *high interest rates*. This proved to be an excellent policy and Swedish banking returned to profitability.

By contrast, also in the early 1990s the Bank of Japan chose precisely the opposite approach. It permitted the country's banks to hide their huge losses. "To help them," BoJ kept investors in the dark and interest rates to a minimum. As a result, the Japanese economy entered a vicious cycle. Repeated jump starts cost more than 100 percent of the country's GDP in public debt terms, and 18 years down the line the Japanese economy is still in a coma.

9
The G-20 Conference, Central Banks, and Garbage Collection[1]

1. Partners in averting a catastrophe

Speaking to union members in Italy on 11 November 2008, President Lula of Brazil warned his audience that they should not expect major results from the meetings of Group of Twenty (G-20)[2] nations in Washington at the week's end. Lula admitted that the G-20 would not be able to make a perfect diagnosis of the causes of the global financial crisis, though he added that:

- This first meeting was at least a promising start, and
- The G-20 nations now appeared to be taking over from the G-8, as the main forum for tackling the crisis, a fact that was (in his opinion) to be welcomed.

Lula knew what he was talking about because a few days prior to that statement he had welcomed in Rio a preparatory meeting of G-20 finance ministers. (The Group of Twenty was created after the Asian and other emerging markets financial crisis of 1997/1998, mainly with the objective of looking after exchange rates and (less so) cross-border capital flows. Even restructured, it is by no measure the perfect forum for today's problems, some of its members like Argentina being chronically mismanaged. On the other hand it is true that the G-7 is too narrow and should be enlarged with Russia (which is in the G-8), China, India, and Brazil (the BRIC), plus South Africa and Saudi Arabia.)[3]

Other heads of government were much more enthusiastic and hopeful than Lula, speaking of the gathering as Bretton Woods II (BWII). The comparison is meaningless, however, because the problem is so different from what it was in 1944. Then, there were three victors, two of which, America and Britain, took upon themselves to decide on how the finances of the world should be organized and run when peace came – to avoid another Great Depression.

(The other nations that participated in Bretton Woods were for any practical purpose taken along as stage hands.) Moreover:

- Bretton Woods painted a picture (right or wrong) on white canvas, and this was done by known artists, namely John Maynard Keynes and Harry Dexter White.
- The artists had full backing from two political giants: Franklin D. Roosevelt and Winston Churchill, a species now extinct.[4]
- The conference itself was preceded by more than two years of grueling technical work, which laid the ground for (what was then) a new global financial structure,[5] and
- There was an underwriter with huge prestige and ample financial resources to lift the world economy and guarantee its solvency and liquidity. With all due respect, such an underwriter is not around today.

What is around is Snow White and the seven dwarfs. Or, more precisely twenty-one dwarfs who were present at the Washington conference – and who don't make a giant even if one steps on the shoulders of others like a famous act in the Chinese circus. Therefore, it is presumptuous to talk of BWII. The best that could be expected is a workable compromise and even that cannot be certain, as section 2 documents.

Critics say that the supposed BWII agenda is incomplete and superficial. Others consider it to be vague, repetitious, and sprawling, made to please political leaders sitting around the negotiators' table. Others still believe that nothing would come out of discussions which started with platitudes and are constrained by complexity as well as by self-interests connected to competitiveness and sovereignty. These were reasonably absent in the original Bretton Woods negotiations.

Nobody would really disagree on the general lines,[6] such as the need to limit the ongoing financial and economic crisis. *The devil is in the detail.* "We are witnessing a fundamental reassessment of the value of every asset everywhere in the world," said Kevin Warsh, a governor of the Federal Reserve.[7] Warsh is right. Can a committee of 20 or 30 do that? A committee has neither a soul to blame nor a body to kick.

Added to this shortcoming is the fact that each big bank today is (or at least was) richer and more powerful than the large majority of UN member states, and that all nation-states jealously guard the right to oversee their own banks. Different reasons lie in the background: prestige, suitability of bank regulations to local conditions, and taxpayers' money thrown at the problem by the fire brigade. When a financial crisis comes, who will foot the bailout bill?

The more serious critics of BWII are pointing out that what really bothers them about these G-20 talks is that the agenda itself is vast and half-baked (section 2). And above everything else, any effective solution will be primarily political and only then economic and financial. The original Bretton Woods did not come standalone. The political arm was the United Nations. But the United Nations today is another old coots' club. It cannot fulfill the same mission.

Besides, it should not be lost from sight that while big banks were motivated by lust and greed in their destruction of the global financial structure, in the background there have been the $60 trillion or more of world-wide debt – plenty of it at family level (Chapter 1). This debt hangover will continue increasing exponentially, as people want to live better (which is reasonable). The only way to bend the debt curve is to establish global birth control – as Mao did in China. Who is going to do that? The G-20?

Closely associated with this priority is the need for a major political choice. Is our generation, and those coming immediately after, opting for the State Supermarket (Chapter 1) as the social and economic model? *If yes,* who will pay for it, and what sort of banking system do we need to have in this case? *If no,* then how will social restructuring be done, and how should be defined the role of:

- A bank?
- An insurance company?
- A hedge fund?
- A private-equity fund?

Critics of the Washington event also lament the fact that the Bank for International Settlements (BIS) – evidently including the Basel Committee, insurance supervisors, and the Financial Stability Forum – was not given a prominent role on 15 November 2008. As far as banking regulation is concerned, the World Bank and the International Monetary Fund are irrelevant:

- They are bureaucracies of another age, and for a different purpose, and
- Bureaucracies cannot be effectively recast. Too many invested interests and too much stonewalling don't permit it.

True enough, the Basel Committee's Basel II has been no success, for reasons briefly discussed in Chapter 5 and further explained below in section 3. It is a flawed agreement because too many hands (precisely, the commercial banks' own hands) manipulated it – ironically to their own disfavor. Hence, while it is not yet in full force, it already needs major repair. This is particularly true of its two main failings:

- Reliance on independent rating agencies, and
- Allowing banks to develop and use their own models of the risks they are carrying, and the capital adequacy that these require.

To correct (up to a point) the failure identified by the first bullet, I propose the Delphi Method.[8] Its wide use will permit the replacement of one party's biased credit rating by community intelligence. In regard to the second bullet, a universal risk model should employ the best artifact available from the physical sciences, namely quantum electrodynamics (QED), on which I am currently working.

Its adoption and implementation should be a chiefs-of-state decision, precisely the kind of agreement the 15 November 2008 conference aimed to reach. But attention: the modeling solution based on QED must be holistic, applied *as is* (without deviations and incompatible versions[9]) by every bank – permitting all regulators to look at systemic risk in an integrative manner, not just one bank at a time, which has been the way done so far.

A universal model, its results unambiguous and understood by everyone, would allow the building of confidence; and business is built on confidence. In terms of methodology, QED should go to the core of the problem, rather than limiting its application to hitting the headlines. Attacking the core of the problems has been precisely the strategy followed in physics.

2. The 15 November 2008 conference in Washington, DC

There have been several positive effects from the 15 November 2008 G-20 meeting of heads of government in Washington DC: the recognition of the world's increasingly interconnected financial services, the fact that if left to its own devices the current crisis is likely to create major systemic risk, and the existence of responsibilities which go along with prudential supervision of the banking industry as well as with the management of the banks themselves.[10] In counterparty, there have been six negatives:

1. *The final communiqué is both unfocused and modest.* The mission given to finance ministers is so confusing that they should be excused if they deliver nothing by the 31 March 2009 deadline (more on this later). Rarely have so many words been put together to mean so much in headlines and so little in practical terms.
2. *The financial industry has been looked at from a very narrow and ill-defined perspective.* Which banks are precisely targeted? The big, the medium, the small? All of them at the same time? Retail, wholesale, investment? And why only banks? Insurance companies must be included, as well as hedge funds, mutual funds, endowments, and other entities dealing with large amounts of money. In short, non-bank banks.
3. *Not only have hard details not been touched upon, but also alternative choices that exist have not been identified.* It is up to the chiefs of state, and not to the ministers of finance and their underlings, to make these choices. *If* however the CEOs don't define precisely what they want regarding the study of alternatives, *then* the answers they will be getting are bound to be ineffectual if not outright meaningless.

4. *The practice of deviating from the main theme – which is the credit crunch, banking, and the economic crisis – by calling on the World Trade Organization for a successful conclusion to the Doha Development Agenda – is unprofessional.* Running after too many hares is the best possible prescription for catching none.[11] As the English recipe for cooking rabbits advises: "First catch your rabbit." Doha was not Washington's rabbit; banking and the economy were. "Instructing the trade ministers" to revive "Dead Cat Doha" is equal to providing everybody with the excuse to play dead cat.
5. *Most vital to the avoidance of future crises is strict control of national debt and household debt. This is utterly missing from the Washington conference's goals.* As Chapter 7 has documented, in several countries – particularly the US, Britain, Holland, and France – household debt is reaching for the stars. This cannot continue without severe consequences. National debt, too, is running out of control. A more stringent type of euroland's Growth and Stability Pact would help to put a limit to debt's unstoppable rise.
6. *As every manager worth his salt knows, the goals should be very few and very clear – so clear that every member in the team understands exactly what is expected of him or her, as well as what are the rewards and penalties.* Reading the 11 pages of the communiqué one gets the impression that it has been written by busybodies who probably want the whole effort to fail. Lobbyists, maybe. The text is unfocused, repetitious, with plenty of platitudes and a fair amount of contradictions. Pity any finance minister who might try to understand which way to go.

   There is as well the suspicion that the communiqué is overstuffed because some of the 21 nation leaders wrote in bits for electoral consumption at home. "At a G-20 meeting in Washington on November 15th, Mr Brown is expected to seek agreement from other leaders on the need for an international round of tax cuts," said an article in *The Economist*.[12]
7. *A large part of what is written in the joint communiqué is nothing more than "apple pie and motherhood"; it is not a plan of action with precise deliverables.* There exist as well some platitudes that are difficult to untangle. In a conference on the rapidly deteriorating global economy, statements such as "We remain committed to addressing... climate change" break all records of irrelevance. Is climate change taking precedence over the banking and economic crisis, or is it something to be kept in the background?

Such deviations are dangerous because they indicate that what the Washington conference has built may well be a castle in the air. Rather than on climate change and Doha, the heads of government who met mid November 2008 should have focused their attention on ways and means to:

- Bring under the wings of bank regulation *all* financial entities, their instruments and vehicles,

- Study in order to decide whether the current deflationary backdrop can morph into outright consumer price index (CPI) deflation in 2009, and whether this might become self-perpetuating.

The fact that deflationary forces may be in motion is no call for inflationary spending, which at the end of the day has always proved to be ineffectual and damaging to the economy. In addition, the fragile national economies simply cannot afford simultaneous garbage collection by central banks (sections 5 to 8) and big fiscal stimulus at the same time. However, some easing could be acceptable *if* it is:

- Focused,
- Rapid, and
- Temporary.

Heads of government, their finance ministers, and central bankers should try to keep an open mind on this topic, and the only effective way of doing so is by spelling out possible strategies, as well as the costs and deliverables of each of them.

Regarding the regulation of industry sectors, those that were the biggest beneficiaries of decreased regulation during the past two decades are likely candidates for greater regulation in the period ahead. Among them are financials, transport, communications, energy, and healthcare. Insurance companies are also likely to be targets in the wake of some of the recent problems in that industry, exemplified by AIG. The mission to the finance ministers should be to:

- Come up with a concrete proposal for regulation of all sectors of the financial industry, and
- Identify correlations, links and aftereffects of regulations between the aforementioned industries.

That's the short term. Regarding medium-term objectives, a fundamental question begging for a factual answer is: should our society put a limit on company size, so that companies can be better managed? Many people now suggest that companies must not be bigger than the state, and no CEO should be paid more than the country's president – even if he had a better year:

- The question of salaries was vaguely mentioned in the communiqué,
- But the more relevant issue of company size was nowhere to be seen.

As cross-border financial flows have expanded, big financial institutions have by far outgrown both their original purpose and their domestic markets. Their boom and doom has become more unsettling than the multinationals of the real economy because (as Chapters 6 and 8 explained) the virtual economy is wide open to layer upon layer of leverage. The G-20 conference failed to address the issue of whether these are the sort of companies we wish to have when we know that:

- Finance is inherently unstable, and
- Today the financial industry is the most globalized part of the world economy.

Other basic choices, too, have been left in a state of vagueness in the communiqué. The statement is made: "Regulation is first and foremost the responsibility of national regulators..." Hence the Washington conference accepts that the current fragmented regulatory system will persist. There will not be the "global sheriff" George Soros has asked for – yet he is right:

- In the global economy somebody has to regulate the regulators, and
- Short of that the supposed internationalization of "this" and "that" will be a half-baked solution.

Also making funny reading is the reference to the "strengthening of international standards, where necessary." Who is going to decide what *is* and *is not* necessary? This might very well have been a mission given to the ministers of finance for their study and 31 March 2009 report. Instead of asking for deliverables, the communiqué skids to the next issue: "to protect against adverse cross-border, regional and global developments."[13]

From the record there also transpires a disagreement about two views theoretically opposing each other: the American for "boosting oversight" and the European for "increased regulation." With the exception, of course, that because Bush has now left office, his words may not represent tomorrow's American position. In conclusion:

- Either the Washington economic conference has been a goodwill initiative and nothing will change,
- Or it is much more ambitious for what 21 semi-equals can achieve, but in this case they should know that the undertaking is full of risks.

In an article in the *Financial Times* Martin Wolf had good advice for Barack Obama and the G-20 meeting of 2 April 2009.[14] Here is his opening paragraph about what Obama should say to the other heads of state, according to Wolf: "My fellow leaders... Let me get a big point out of the way: yes, the US is messed up. We thought we knew about sophisticated modern finance. We were wrong. On behalf of my country I apologize... We must learn the lesson and look ahead, not backwards."[15]

An assembly which leaves sovereignty behind and strikes for a new order based on multilateral economic and financial cooperation has to contend with the fact that this calls for a vast plan. Its execution requires unity of command and the utmost in managerial skills. It is not at all sure that each of the 21 heads of government has decided to leave sovereignty behind on the doorstep before entering the temple.

The needed change will not come with calls for "due diligence" and "better risk management," as the G-20 communiqué suggests. These are empty words to impress the gallery. What is needed is two or three precise goals which *must* be achieved, expressed with great clarity and accompanied by a firm timetable. *Good timing* requires a detailed schedule of deliverables, which was missing from the communiqué.

3. Basel II[16] failed to account for modern risk's polyvalence

Basel I and Basel II have been introduced in Chapter 5. This section brings to the reader's attention the likely aftereffect of ongoing efforts aimed at restructuring the financial system and most particularly its supervision – of which the Basel capital accords are an integral part. This is important inasmuch as Basel II is based on three pillars and all of them would be affected *if* a global agreement could be found:

- Pillar 1 addresses capital adequacy.
- Pillar 2 provides for regulation, at the discretion of each jurisdiction.
- Pillar 3 targets market discipline.

Pillar 1 is aimed at aligning the bank's capital adequacy with the amount of risk they are taking. This contrasts with Basel I's goal, which was more limited – calling for a flat capital ratio of 8 percent for internationally active banks – without accounting for the riskiness of each bank's assets.

What has been the result of this more sophisticated approach? For several reasons (some of which are discussed in this section), the answer is not positive. Basel II tried at first to be sensitive in risk terms, rewarding banks that take fewer risks with lower capital requirements. Pretty soon, however, that proved to be wishful thinking because:

- Each bank has been permitted to develop its own capital models.
- Credit decisions, and credit rating, have been biased on the side of imprudence.
- Banks found plenty of ways to game the system, including model manipulation.
- By increasing their amount of leverage they simply send risk to a stratospheric level, higher than ever before.

Many of the big banks' strategies have backfired. Key among them have been too-lenient loans, disregard for liquidity (section 4), and the fact that longer-term commitments have been financed through short-term commercial paper. None of these was adequately controlled by Basel II rules.

Analysts reckon that in October 2008, 14 months after the credit crisis started, there is a $6 trillion overhang of committed lending facilities to be drawn down, most of it at more generous terms than borrowers could get at present. According to reports circulating in the banking industry, for evident reasons corporate customers are not interested in refinancing. Banks, however, run scared because default risk is now high.

Under the Bush Administration, the Treasury made commitments way beyond appropriations by Congress. During the 10 February 2009 Bernanke hearings by the House Banking Committee, representative Carolyn Maloney, a Committee member, said that by some calculations the US government has guaranteed $7 trillion. Other estimates put the gearing higher, to over $8 trillion. This is by no means the end. Rather, it looks like being the beginning.

Basel II had not foreseen these management failures on the banks' side; therefore it does not provide for appropriate guarantees in regard to capital adequacy. Neither was much thought given to the fact that banks will hide a great deal of their exposure through off-balance-sheet vehicles and instruments, reducing by so much their capital resources and their solvency established by Basel's regulatory capital requirements (Basel I, Basel II).[17]

Using lobbyists, political pressure and smart stratagems, big banks managed to hide a horde of risks they were assuming from supervisors' eyes, till hell broke lose. In addition, a very weak element of Basel II has been that it handed much of the responsibility for assessing counterparty risks to credit rating agencies and to the banks themselves. The subprimes meltdown demonstrated that both these parties' credentials as risk controllers are questionable.

As proof of some of Basel II's flaws, critics also point to the role played by universal banks in brokerage. A rule change in 2004 allowed Wall Street firms to use new risk calculations, but this rule change was so imprecise that financial reports continued to show these banks as being well capitalized, on a risk-adjusted basis, even as their exposure skyrocketed. European universal banks followed closely on that practice, and in the end such a twisted rule had fatal consequences.

Another criticism is that, Basel II or no Basel II, the meddling with massive amounts of money by central banks and governments with the way markets work has long-term consequences – such as making capital adequacy standards irrelevant. An interesting and unsettling result of all this intervention has been to make it hard to find out just how risky assets are now that:

- The state is underwriting the system, and
- The practice of marking-to-market assets and liabilities has partly been turned off.

The ill-advised government action in the second bullet comes at a very bad time because the markets ask for a higher not lower level of transparency. True enough, steps are being taken to strengthen risk charges for assets held in banks' trading books, and to improve banks' liquidity management. There are also discussions on how to dampen procyclical effects, and Swiss regulators are now requiring that their biggest banks introduce a leverage ratio. But, altogether, Basel II is out of step with current realities.

Moreover, while Pillar 2 of the new capital adequacy framework has been taken as evidence that the rules are flexible, allowing national supervisors to turn the screw on capital as necessary, this has proved to be a weakness. In some jurisdictions regulators have used that clause to favor their own banks at the expense of their foreign-based competitors. Rather than appeasing the financial markets, such nepotism has triggered a wave of uncertainty:

- The investor community has been saying: "Show me the money, or I won't believe you," and
- The only way to buy credibility is to raise capital and improve each bank's liquidity position, even if in the medium term this is dilutive for its shareholders.

For its part, Pillar 3 was supposed to provide for market discipline, but subprimes, CDOs, and CDSs have shown that that's a hope rather than a fact. In addition, the virtual cancellation of marking-to-market is the worst thing that could happen to market discipline. It is simply dishonest to say the market will exercise discipline when it is denied reliable fair-value information.

Another factor negatively affecting transparency and market confidence has been the postponement of integration of off-balance-sheet exposure – where a myriad of skeletons hides – into the banks' balance sheets. The reason for hiding bad news is that it is hard to see how the overhang of debt is going to be cleared. The amount of paper for sale is far outstripping the market's buying power. Every time one of the lists of assets for sale circulates, the market drops. Investors believe that:

- The price of warehoused loans and derivative instruments has lost touch with the levels of default; and
- This psychology sees to it that debt is trading at levels that assume corporate defaults will hit numbers last seen during the First Great Depression of 1929/1933.

Part of the reason for the strong linkage between risk aversion and debt is that credit markets are unwinding from excessive leverage. One of the shortcomings of Basel II is that it made no provision for the effect of high leverage on banks' capital adequacy, and it says practically nothing about how deleveraging affects the survival of a credit institution.

A basic characteristic of the continuing stress conditions in banking and the economy, which has been missed by government authorities, central bankers, and analysts, is that the rapid disappearance of leverage from the market is having as many perverse effects as its piling up. Something else that Basel II did not account for is that by its very nature the balance sheet is not a precise mathematical document. Much of what is written is invalid, the result of manipulation:

- Making it easy to hide leverage,
- But hiding deleverage has not yet been perfected in creative accounting terms.

Arbitragers, who in the go-go years would have been actively hunting mispriced assets, cannot get access to money. For bankers, too, liquidity that was ample across the globalized market has become nonexistent and regulators have to factor in the likelihood of markets being illiquid. In addition, as excess leverage is being unwound there are many forced sellers of bonds, precious metals, and other commodities, and this is creating huge dislocations in prices. None of these events is accounted for in calculating capital adequacy under Basel II.

4. Principles of liquidity risk management by the Basel Committee

Incorporating liquidity facilities into banks' internal liquidity risk management is an important requirement, indeed an indispensable one. In addition, the growing prevalence of new instruments like the originate-to-distribute business model, has led to the increased interdependence of the availability of financial resources with emphasis on:

- Funding liquidity, and
- Market liquidity.

Funding liquidity risk is the risk that an institution will not be able to meet efficiently both expected and unexpected current and future cash flow and collateral needs, without affecting its daily operations or its longer-term financial condition. By contrast, *market liquidity risk* is the risk that the entity cannot offset or eliminate a position at fair price, because of inadequacies in the debt market or an outright market disruption.

As the events of July/August 2007 and of subsequent months have shown, a large number of financial institutions had considered funding neither liquidity risk nor market liquidity risk, and therefore they were in difficulty in satisfying their obligations as they became due. Moreover, many of the most exposed banks did not have in place an adequate framework for sound liquidity risk management.

For their part, since their inception Basel I and Basel II lacked mandatory liquidity directives. In June 2008 the Basel Committee on Banking Supervision issued a draft for consultation *"Principles for Sound Liquidity Risk Management and Supervision,"* which outlines 17 principles, 13 of which are addressed to commercial banks and 4 describe the role of supervisors.

The Basel document names, as the fundamental or *first principles* for the management and supervision of liquidity risk, the bank's liquidity responsibilities. These include the establishment of a robust liquidity risk control framework, high-quality liquid assets, and strength to withstand a range of stress events. Liquidity is defined as the ability of a bank:

- To find increases in assets, and
- Meet obligations as they come due, without incurring unacceptable losses.

The Basel Committee makes the point that virtually every financial transaction or commitment has liquidity implications for the institution. Also brought into perspective is the fact that a liquidity shortfall in one entity can have aftereffects on other banks, leading to systemic repercussions.

These principles have been known but they were not applied. The Basel document underlines the need for identification and measurement of a full range of liquidity risks (including those contingent) and for stress test scenarios (more on them later) which could provide foresight on impending liquidity problems.

Basel's *second principle* on liquidity risk management is that a bank should clearly articulate a liquidity risk tolerance that is appropriate for:

- Its business strategy, and
- The role it plays in the global financial system.

Liquidity principles 3 to 7 state the reason why a financial institution's funding strategy must be characterized by effective diversification in the source and tenure of funding. It is senior management's responsibility to develop strategies, policies, and practices that allow effective management of liquidity risk. Also, to steadily review information on the bank's liquidity and to take effective measures to redress poor liquidity approaches.

Furthermore, a financial institution should incorporate in its product pricing, as well as in its new product approval, liquidity costs, benefits, and risks, comprehensively projecting cash flows arising from assets both on-balance-sheet and off-balance-sheet. It should also match exposures and funding needs within and across:

- Currencies,
- Business lines, and
- Legal entities under its control.

Liquidity management principles 8 to 12 state that the bank should actively manage its collateral positions and track liquidity exposure intraday, with the objective of meeting payment and settlement obligations on a timely basis. This should be done both under normal conditions and under stress. Therefore, a financial institution should regularly conduct stress tests for its own specific and market-oriented scenarios:

- Identifying sources of potential liquidity strain, and
- Adjusting its liquidity risk control practices.

Adjustments should integrate into a formal contingency funding plan that sets out policies for addressing liquidity shortfalls in emergency situations – including high-quality liquid assets to be held as insurance against a range of liquidity stress conditions. Principle 13 interfaces with market discipline in liquidity management, stating that a bank must publicly disclose information on its liquidity position and liquidity risk management framework.

The role of supervisors is described in principles 14 to 17, which specify the performance of ways and means for comprehensive assessment of a bank's liquidity risk management framework and liquidity position. Emphasis is placed on supplementing regular assessments by monitoring a combination of:

- Internal controls,
- Prudential reports, and
- Market information.

Additionally, Basel says, supervisors should intervene to require effective and timely remedial action when deficiencies in liquidity risk management are identified in a given financial institution. They should also communicate with other supervisors and central banks, within and across jurisdictions, to enable effective cooperation regarding the oversight of liquidity.

Without explicitly saying so, the concept underpinning the 2008 liquidity rules is that the banking, credit, and liquidity crisis which started in July/August 2007 has demonstrated that financial institutions had no clear understanding of contingent liquidity risk exposure arising from their contractual and non-contractual relationships at large and their commitments with special-purpose vehicles (SPVs) in particular.

In either case the bank should incorporate cash flows related to the issuance, repricing, exercise, or maturity of derivatives contracts in its liquidity risk analysis. This must include the potential of a demand for additional collateral in cases of a decline in the price of the underlying asset, a downgrading in credit rating, or other reasons affecting liquidity criteria and the institution itself. Examples of where a bank should consider liquidity risk on a consolidated basis are those of:

- Providing liquidity to a special-purpose vehicle (SPV) characterized by a maturity mismatch between short-term and long-term obligations, and
- Providing liquidity facilities to third-party SPVs like conduits, structured investment vehicles (SIVs), and asset-backed commercial paper (ABCP) transactions.

Regarding liquidity stress tests, the Basel Committee recommends that they must enable management to analyze the impact of extreme events on the bank's consolidated group-wide liquidity position, as well as on the liquidity position of controlled entities and business lines. Such tests should:

- Reflect accurate timeframes for settlement cycles of assets that might be liquidated, and
- Incorporate the time needed to transfer liquidity across jurisdictions.

Operational and settlement disruptions must also be considered. The same is true of a number of assumptions necessary for the effective execution of a stress test, like the likely and unlikely response of other market players to events of market stress, and the likelihood that such response might amplify value movements and exacerbate market strain – for example, creating runoffs of funding, eroding the value of liquid assets, leading to the unavailability of secured and unsecured wholesale funding sources, and creating additional margin calls and collateral requirements.

In addition, an integral part of stress-testing funding liquidity risk is that of liquidity drains associated with complex financial products and transactions, the likely impact of credit rating triggers, the operational difficulties the bank finds in monetizing assets, and the changes to the policies followed by central banks in terms of making available liquidity under stress conditions – the theme of the next four sections.

5. Repositories of last resort: the European Central Bank

The new regulations that section 4 brought to the reader's attention are still at the draft stage. Since July/August 2007, liquidity has been scarce, and liquidity risk has topped the list of central bankers' concerns for new regulation.

The best-managed commercial and investment banks have always considered liquidity one of their overriding concerns, the guiding principle being to lock in time deposits and borrow for the longer term. But poorly managed banks did the opposite:

- At the end of fiscal 2007, Bear Stearns, the fifth-largest US securities firm, had relied on repos for 26.7 percent of its borrowing.
- Lehman, the third largest, had the highest reliance on repo funding in the US investment industry, at 27.2 percent of liabilities.

When other market participants became skittish about Bear and Lehman finances, they became less willing to engage in repo transactions, depriving the New-York-based companies of a key source of funding. In 2008 both of them crashed; one in March and the other in September. So much for Greenspan's guiding principle that "free markets" are able to regulate themselves (Chapter 8). European banks have shown the same propensity to forget about sound government principles. Confronted with a nearly impossible situation in terms of market liquidity, on 9 August 2007, after an alarming leap in interbank interest rates, the European Central Bank signaled its readiness to provide the banking system with liquidity. During the following months, the Fed and other central banks followed the ECB in collecting as collateral all sorts of dubious financial paper, though a year on the credit crunch continues.

The pros say that the central banks' willingness to provide liquidity by bending the rules guiding the quality of collateral they accept has prevented financial markets from melting down completely. In the opinion of critics, this policy has overflowed with moral hazard. No doubt, in the years to come, this policy will be one of the hottest topics discussed and debated by economists:

- Was garbage collection necessary because the financial system was not as robust as most regulators thought, and major risks were hidden off-balance-sheet?[18]
- Or was the "no bank left behind" policy one which bends central banks' credibility, resting as it does on their ability to do two unpopular things: raise interest rates to control inflation, despite the economic pain; and let financial institutions fail.

It is not the objective of this text to take sides but rather to review the facts and let the reader decide (though a couple of comments have been unavoidable). The fact is that first the European Central Bank, and a couple of months later the Federal Reserve, added a new twist in their provision of liquidity to the market: that of acting as collateral depositors of last resort, for non-investment-grade paper presented to them by commercial banks as guarantee of the loans which they take.

Theoretically, the logic behind assuring a broader liquidity provision is simple. It is the means of breaking a vicious circle of market fear and forced selling, as the traditional system of credit provision becomes dysfunctional. In the aftermath of a major crisis generated by the banking industry itself, investors had plenty of reason for refusing to hold all but the safest government bonds.

The downside which made itself evident, a few months after this practice started, is that commercial banks exploited the central banks' goodwill by placing freshly created asset-backed securities (ABS) in the monetary institutions vaults. Eventually, this became a new sort of leveraging. An Australian bank, for example, used as collateral at the ECB securitized Australian receivables.[19]

Some banks even employed the same rocket scientists who projected the CDOs to design instruments specifically for warehousing at central banks; and there have been other abuses. In mid November 2008 Volkswagen confirmed that, via its banking subsidiary Volkswagen Bank, it would seek to tap the ECB facility for liquidity by tendering €2.8 billion in securities backed by car loans in Germany as collateral. The ECB has included asset-backed securities in the list of eligible assets that can be monetized. This transaction will make VW the first German manufacturer to get liquidity from the central bank; it is likely to be followed by BMW Bank and Mercedes-Benz Bank:

- VW claimed that it is considering using the plan to optimize its refinancing costs, given the attractive conditions offered under the scheme.
- Analysts said that while any funding the plan will reduce the technical pressure on VW to issue and help support new car sales, the adverse fundamental situation will continue to look bad.[20]

Let's make one thing clear at this point. Since its institution, the main aim of the European Central Bank has been to maintain stability. Even at the time of the European Monetary Union (EMU), which was first proposed in 1962 and instituted by the Maastricht Treaty, European finance ministers had agreed that:

- Monetary orthodoxy would prevail, and
- Monetary policy will be based on strict anti-inflation criteria.

At the heart of the problem is the fact that ECB and other western central banks have been accepting as collateral, in their refinancing operations, a wide range of assets including ABS, for which there is temporarily little or no trading. The only provision, in the ECB's case, is that the tranche is the most senior and graded A- or above by one rating agency, which means nothing at a time when even junk has got AAA credit rating. According to published reports, this has led a large number of banks to design ABS tranches purely for central bank consumption.

JPMorgan Chase has estimated that, as of mid June 2008, of €208 billion ($320 billion at the time) of "eligible securities" created for the above-mentioned purpose, less than €6 billion has been placed with investors. In December 2007, for example, Rabobank, Holland's huge agricultural bank, issued €30 billion ($44 billion) of mortgage-backed securities, 90 percent of which were designed exclusively for refinancing with the ECB.[21]

The central bank's readiness to help in terms of liquidity by accepting second-rate collateral has been treated with disrespect and impunity by commercial and investment banks. Therefore, it has come as no surprise that at end of August 2008 the ECB announced that it would tighten its rules for collateral to assure that what it offers to banks is strictly liquidity support. But the Volkswagen case put a question mark over the effectiveness of this change.

A particular worry is that in countries where housing bursts have made investors wary of mortgage-backed assets, like Spain and Ireland (both euroland members), banks continue creating securities for the express purpose of gaining central bank funding – and they use their government to exercise pressure for their acceptance. This:

- Exposes the ECB (and other central banks) to too much credit risk, and
- Stalls market recovery for mortgage-backed assets in a global sense.

For instance, the supply of central bank cash to Spanish and Irish banks more than doubled from August 2007 to August 2008, both in size and as a share of the euroland total, while creditworthiness has taken a dive. In May 2008 Fitch, the credit rating agency, said that standards for newly structured Spanish mortgage-backed securities had slipped since the credit crunch started in July/August 2007.

This issue of garbage collection for liquidity's sake is complex, because the ECB is essentially the central bank of euroland's central banks. Critics say that it should shield its constituent central banks from the risk of loss if one of the commercial and investment banks depositing toxic waste as collateral defaults, and also assure that commercial banks:

- Do not shift their credit risk onto the ECB vaults on favorable terms, and
- Benefit from an unwarranted subsidy, while they are at fault.

In the opinion of some economists, a good approach for avoiding moral risk is that the Fed, the Bank of England, and the ECB should ban the use of securities that seem to have been created to take advantage of central bank funding, starting with the rule that only a small fraction of any ABS of corporate-bond issue could be permissible. At the same time, central banks should require that collateral is backed by income streams in local currency, which would curb one of the ways banks use to game the system, using central bank money to finance doubtful loans they still make around the world.

6. Repositories of last resort: The Bank of England

Section 5 provided evidence that the European Central Bank and the Federal Reserve have too few tools and procedures to cope with the problem of commercial bank and market illiquidity, and at the same time there are too many questions posed about the wisdom of accepting all sorts of toxic waste as collateral in order to let banks off the hook. The Bank of England did something similar.

In April 2008, the British central bank set up a Special Liquidity Scheme (SLS), subject to some restrictions. Subsequently, it widened the range of collateral it accepts provided that the illiquid financial products were held in the commercial banks' balance sheets before the end of 2007. Essentially the Bank of England has followed in the footsteps of the Fed and the ECB in accepting bad money in exchange for good money. The first installment amounted to £50 billion ($90 billion at that time), the only requirement being that any beneficiary should:

- Recapitalize themselves, and
- Restructure their balance sheet.

Experts suggested that this £50 billion was no more than the beginning, and the experts were right. Midway through 2008 came the news was that British banks were preparing up to £90 billion of mortgage-backed bonds to send to the Bank of England, and that piece of news created a doomsday mood in the market.

Less than 2 months down the line, securitization analysts estimated that through the Special Liquidity Scheme banks could draw down more than £700 billion of liquid government bonds, in exchange for existing *and* newly created mortgage bonds. Some experts considered that number to be astronomical, while others stated that it showed the depth of the banking crisis in Britain.

Criticism mounted as news leaked out that all three central banks – the Fed, the ECB, and the Bank of England – were highly concerned about the quality of collateral they were holding in the aftermath of commercial and investment banks' excesses, while buyers of this type of toxic waste had all but vanished from the market. Like their counterparts in America, the British banks created a lot of fake double-A and triple-A products.

Faced with an impossible situation, the Bank of England provided a temporary relief for overleveraged and overexposed commercial and investment banks. Several economists warned however that this could not go on forever;

if it continued it risked engulfing the western central banks themselves in a downturn which would throw a huge amount of oil on the flames of inflation.

On 11 September 2008, Mervyn King stated that the Bank of England would offer short-term liquidity insurance to British banks but could not give commercial banks long-term help in funding.[22]

For this he referred them to Gordon Brown, the British prime minister. A week later, like the Fed and the ECB, the Bank of England sought to stem the fallout from Lehman Brothers's slide into bankruptcy:

- Many British banks were short of cash because they had lent Lehman money which was then tied up in bankruptcy proceedings.
- Not all of that money was necessarily lost, but the central bank has had to tide British banks over until it becomes clearer how much they will ultimately recover.

At the same time, while the Bank of England stated that it was closely monitoring market conditions and would take actions to ensure that the overnight rate is close to its bank rate, worries were raised about the effects of the steady injection of good money, which also risked toppling the British government's already frayed fiscal framework.

The experts' worries were increased by rumors that up to early November 2008 British banks may have tapped a low three-digit number of billions in Bank of England funds. The way such rumors had it, the central bank had found itself obliged to put on the table extra reserves to help stabilize conditions in the sterling money market.

When, following a torrid day on 7 October 2008, Alistair Darling and the Treasury set out their plan to recapitalize British banks that had propelled themselves to the edge of the abyss, they envisaged having to inject up to £50 billion of public money to bolster banks' capital. But already by mid October 2008 a big amount was needed to beef up the capital of just three banks: Royal Bank of Scotland (£20 billion), HBOS (£11.5 billion) and Lloyds TSB (£5.5 billion), assuming shareholders made no contribution. And whereas the initial plan had envisaged the state acquiring safer interest-bearing preference shares, £28 billion out of the £37 billion were in riskier ordinary shares.

Moreover, who else would be invited to join? And under which conditions? The first news was that Britain's biggest banks have all signed up to the new capital injection, while the government planned to help free up the market for short-term liquidity by lending to banks for up to three months. Then it was revealed that:

- RBS, HBOS, and Lloyds TSB would participate to the plan and share among themselves the £37 billion.
- To the contrary, Barclays chose not to participate, looking instead to raise £5.4 billion (later upped to £6.5 billion) from private investors through a shares offer.

Indeed Barclays issued a statement that its "proforma" Tier-1 capital was more than 11 percent. This left the market puzzled because proforma is a murky way to compute financials, being totally at the discretion of the company making the announcement. It was used in the dotcom boom and bust to report on EBITDA (earnings before interest, taxes, depreciation, and amortization), making upstarts of heavily indebted internet companies.

The British government said that the share it took in the country's big banks would not be permanent;[23] it would be diversified over time. But the effect on the economy could not be hidden. The first installment alone raised debt by 2.5 percent of GDP, as the Treasury had to borrow to finance its recapitalization of the three banks.

The increase in the British government's liabilities[24] was accompanied by the risk to taxpayers that loan losses would destroy some of the capital supplied to the three banks and the support provided for Northern Rock and other institutions. In 40 banking rescues studied by the International Monetary Fund (IMF) the taxpayer typically recouped some but not all of their cost.[25]

As with the Fed and the ECB, there has also been plenty of moral hazard in mitigating the banks' funding liquidity problems though rescue operations conducted by the Bank of England. The moral hazard is greater if liquidity injections are carried out at rates that are lower than prevailing market rates (elevated because of liquidity hoarding). An additional problem was that interbank trading activity might shrink further, with the risk that the financial system would become increasingly reliant on the funds provided by central banks.

7. Repositories of last resort: the Federal Reserve

Commercial banks that needed money in a hurry and could not buy it on the market classically used the Federal Reserve's discount window, which has lent daily. Banks however have long considered access to this facility to be a stigma, an indication that they are in financial trouble. This changed with the severe 2008/2009 credit crunch and banking crisis. Borrowing from the Fed's discount window suddenly became an everyday practice with both commercial and (more recently) investment banks queuing up for money.

The Federal Reserve has thrown open its emergency lending facilities to investment banks, and it is also accepting in its open market operations a much broader range of collateral than it used to (including complex credit derivatives). Besides that, all sorts of firms have been converting themselves into bank holding companies in order to take part in the central bank's liquidity drive.

In the week of 10 November 2008 the Federal Reserve gave American Express the go-ahead to turn itself into a bank holding outfit. The decision gives America's only remaining big independent credit card firm greater access to government funding. But is this sensible? A week earlier, General Electric became the first company to borrow from the Federal Reserve's new Commercial Paper Funding Facility. GE is also the world's largest issuer of commercial paper, and it is engaged in an effort to reduce *its* exposure to it. All this is characteristic of the fact that topmost in the minds of CFOs these days are the queries:

- Have we got enough cash to make it through the night?
- Will our counterparties grant us credit?
- What are the chances of us going bust?

These are the legitimate worries of chief financial officers, but it is not the central bank's mission to provide the answers, let alone to offer them the solution on a plate. But that is exactly what the State Supermarket does, with its policy of no one being allowed to fail (Chapter 1). Because nobody is allowed to fail, small policy errors are now becoming major ones.

The smaller policy errors started when central banks acted as repositories of last resort of the toxic waste developed, sold, bought, and warehoused by financial institutions.[26] This was done without the benefit of a global plan and without establishing in advance well-thought-out criteria and limits. Prior to being launched, the liquidity policies needed:

- Harmonizing,
- Refining, and
- Limiting to assure that moral hazard is being weeded out.

The time to do so was well before December 2007, when the Fed announced its Term Auction Facility (TAF) to supply one-month loans to deposit-taking banks. As cash loans backed up by bond collateral, the TAF deals are rather conventional, even if they are for a longer time and the eligible security is more liberal than is the case with the discount window.

Suddenly, without the benefit of a clear redefinition, in March 2008 the money available to the Term Auction Facility was expanded to $100 billion from the previously announced $60 billion. The Fed just said it would increase the amounts offered if conditions warranted, and TAF auctions would continue "for at least the next 6 months," unless evolving market conditions indicated clearly that such auctions were no longer necessary.

Also, in March 2008, the Fed announced that it would lend an additional $200 billion of Treasury securities to its primary dealers through a new Term Securities Lending Facility (TSLF). These loans were projected for a 28-day period, with looser collateral requirements. For TSLF loans the central bank decided to accept federal agency debt, federal agency residential-mortgage-backed securities (RMBS), and non-agency AAA/Aaa-rated private-label residential MBS.

TSLF, the Fed added in its announcement, has been intended to promote liquidity in the financing markets for Treasury and other collateral, and thus to foster the functioning of financial markets more generally. At the same time, the Fed expanded its currency swap agreement with the European Central Bank to $30 billion, and a similar agreement with the Swiss National Bank to $6 billion – the increases being $10 billion and $2 billion, respectively.

The cash-strapped banking industry looked at these as steps as positive and innovative, but not nearly large enough to make a big difference. Though in tens and hundreds of billions, the stated amounts must be compared with a total MBS market of $6 trillion, comprised of $4.1 trillion in agency MBS and $1.9 trillion in non-agency MBS. Some analysts said that the fact the Fed would be accepting only AAA was less constraining because plenty of this mortgage debt is now mis-rated as AAA anyway.[27]

It should be note referenced, however, that the TSLF is different from previous facilities for central bank liquidity injection because it is a bond-for-bond arrangement – albeit nearly worthless MBS for Treasuries – aimed explicitly at providing liquidity to markets beyond those where cash is traded. This process has the effect of:

- Deepening the pool of Treasuries, which are in strong demand during liquidity crises, and
- Easing markets that have few buyers, by providing a temporary home for illiquid bonds.

According to critics, however, the scale of the TSLF operation raised concerns that in its attempt to reduce liquidity risk the Fed was taking on too much credit risk. Swapping pristine government bonds for rather questionable assets lowered the quality of the Fed's balance sheet. In fact, on a totally different occasion on 31 October 2008 Ben Bernanke himself had said that the relative lack of capital by government-sponsored entities (GSEs, such as Fannie Mae and Freddie Mac) proved their downfall.

8. The $2 trillion gaping hole

The measures discussed in section 5 had no immediate effect, as spreads widened alarmingly in 2008; in terms of higher volatility the VIX hit an unprecedented value of 70, and different reasons underpinning market nervousness fed upon one another. The Fed tried to break that cycle by offering US Treasury bonds while holding unwanted securities deposited as collateral by wounded banks seeking liquidity:

- The pros said that by taking them as collateral for "temporary loans" at a discount, the Fed would lose money only if there is a bankruptcy among institutions borrowing Treasury bonds.

- Critics respond that the risk of losses can be significant and this carries major moral hazard, because it induces commercial and investment banks to behave in a more risky way.

The same critics added that it is a bad policy to administer the liquidity programs in reference without counterparty by the banks, in the sense of immediate tougher regulation, better-focused accounting rules, and more rigorous supervision. Banks were still left with a lot of wriggle room when it came to reporting the values of and profits from complex loans and securities, while their losses were not always based on hard numbers but rather on debatable judgment calls. Moreover, the market needed to develop mechanisms that would allow participants to:

- Distinguish between different types of counterparty creditworthiness, and
- Apply fair margins in transactions, making central-bank lending more expensive than in the interbank market.

"If banks are too big to fail," said Dr Henry Kaufman in a Bloomberg interview on 17 March 2008, "then they must also be managed well so that they don't get themselves in trouble." However, as the subprimes and credit crunch experience has demonstrated, banks are prone to get themselves into impossible situations.

Several economists have also been uneasy about the likelihood that the Fed might decide to lend taxpayers' money directly to non-banks via the Term Auction Facility, something the central bank last did in the 1930s. We cannot rule out the Fed being forced to revive this option, but the benefits of such action would need to be weighed against the headline shock of bringing back a Depression-era measure, said one of the experts – and he had a point, though at the time this statement was made nobody imagined how big the gaping hole might be.

Then, in the first week of November 2008 some disturbing news broke. The Federal Reserve refused to identify the recipients of an urgent salvage amounting to a cool of \$2 trillion. An alternative version was that the assets of the Fed had more than doubled to \$2 trillion, which meant a blown-up, highly leveraged balance sheet with unprecedented dollar overhang on the economy.

What really seems to have happened makes interesting reading. The Federal Reserve did indeed refuse to identify the recipients of almost \$2 trillion of emergency loans financed with money taken from American taxpayers. This was in spite of the fact that two months earlier Bernanke and Paulson had said they would comply with congressional demands for transparency in a \$700 billion bailout of the banking system (Chapter 10).

Bloomberg news requested details of the Fed lending under the US Freedom of Information Act, and on 4 November 2008 it filed a Federal lawsuit seeking to force disclosure.

> "The collateral is not being adequately disclosed, and that's a big problem," said Dan Fuss, vice chairman of Boston-based Loomis Sayles. "In a liquid market, this wouldn't matter, but we're not. The market is very nervous and very thin."
>
> "It's your money; it's not the Fed's money," added Ted Forstmann, of Forstmann Little. "Of course there should be transparency."[28]

In terms of statistical evidence, in the first week of November 2008, for the first time, total Fed lending topped $2 trillion – rising by $1.17 trillion, or 140 percent in the 7 weeks since Fed governors (in mid September) relaxed the collateral standards. The difference included an assumed:

- $788 billion increase in Fed loans to banks (!), and
- $474 billion in other lending, largely because of the central bank's purchase of Fannie Mae and Freddie Mac bonds.

Market rumor had it however that part of the money which created the $2 trillion hole had found its way into hedge funds, to provide them with badly needed capital. (I saw no documentation to support such rumors.) Hedge funds or not, the exponential growth in the Fed's lending is significant because the central bank did not have the authority to spend extravagant amounts of money. Moreover, it stepped into a rescue role:

- That was the purpose of the $700 billion Troubled Asset Relief Program, and
- It did so without the safeguards put into the TARP legislation by Congress.

According to market information, the beneficiaries included Citigroup, JPMorgan Chase, and Lehman Brothers – the last named is now bankrupt and that Federal money has been lost. Banks seem to oppose any release of information with their name on the line, because it might signal weakness, spur short-selling, or lead to a run by depositors. Their argument, which by all evidence the Fed has bought, is that one has to balance the need for transparency with protecting the public interest. But on the other hand, taxpayers have a right to know where their money is going.

It is quite likely that banks have been getting an unwarranted large-scale financial aid with both hands: one in full secrecy by the Fed and the other transparent to the public eye – precisely the $120 billion in capital from the TARP. From the latter source, those who benefited in a big way were Citigroup, Bank of America, JPMorgan Chase, Wells Fargo, Goldman Sachs, Morgan Stanley, Bank of New York Mellon, and a score of other financial institutions:

- None of them has been asked to present a believable plan for redressing its financial staying power, as should have been the case.

- Some of them fared very badly in the market *after* the Treasury's injection of $25 billion (Citigroup's stock fell to $4.71 on 20 November 2008).
- The Treasury seems to have failed in determining who to save and who to let go bankrupt, just like it has failed to put a limit on where to stop with bailout capital.

To these shortcomings the Federal Reserve has added the controversial issue of lack of transparency. "Taxpayers have the right to know what sweetheart deals Bernanke's been giving out," stated an internet posting.[29]

The Bloomberg lawsuit argues that the collateral lists are central to understanding and assessing the government's response to the most catastrophic financial crisis in America since the Great Depression, but politicians seem inclined to secrecy.

In an interview on 6 November 2008, Barney Frank, House Financial Services Committee chairman, said the risk the central bank is taking on is appropriate in the current economic climate. Frank added that the Fed should not reveal the assets it holds or how it values them because disclosure would give people clues to what the pricing is and what they might be able "to sell us." All this took place a week prior to the 15 November 2008 G-20 meeting in Washington, which called for transparency, transparency, and even more transparency. The court decision may cut the Gordian knot.

10
Trillions of Dollars, Euros, and Pounds Thrown at the Problem

1. Public money that has been thrown away

In September and October 2008 a lot of damage was done to market confidence. Bankers, traders, politicians, and government officials were telling everyone who would listen that the financial system was falling apart and the economy at large, at the edge of the precipice, could be saved only through massive injections of capital out of the public purse. But it was not difficult to perceive the lack of any precise plan on how to achieve a turnaround.

One of the similitudes between 1929 and 2008 has been that governments and politicians have steered clear of punishing those who wrecked the financial system, concentrating on asking the taxpayer to foot the bill and letting employees suffer loss of jobs, of savings, and of pensions. In an interview he gave on 13 October 2008 to CNBC, Julian Robertson, of Tiger Management fame, said: "We are going to have 10 to 15 years of poor economy," adding that "80 percent to 85 percent of Americans are broke" – largely because they had overleveraged themselves during the good years (Chapter 7):

- The so-called "American consumers' resilience," of which Alan Greenspan was so proud, had appeared as a monolith.
- But by later in 2008 it had become a house of cards.

Faced with the likelihood of losing their jobs, as unemployment started to increase rapidly, consumers wanted to save but they could not because they had to pay back their loans. In mid September 2008 Hewlett-Packard said it would cut almost 25,000 jobs as it pushed forward its integration with Electronic Data Systems, with around half that number in the United States. Two months later on 17 November Citigroup announced it would fire 50,000 people, after having already eliminated 28,000 in the previous months of 2008.

In Europe, things have been no better. In the wake of the banking and credit crisis, London banks planned to slash 62,000 jobs as the recession continued and deepened. In euroland, too, the trend towards lower unemployment was reversing, as one country after another fell into recession:

- Panicky governments have sent tens, hundreds, thousands of billions in good money running after bad money, and
- Not everybody is convinced this is the way to go. Many are now asking: "Have the governments gone too far?"

Banks have bankrupted themselves, and we need a banking system. But is throwing a great lot of money at the problem the solution? Or has this been done on the spur of the moment, without much thought given to the consequences? The first question is:

- Is recapitalizing and nationalizing the big banks the best course available?

Nobody would argue that as of February 2009 the world's financial markets are not in total disarray. There is a flight to cash and security, out of all risk assets, even bonds. Any way one looks at it, stocks have fallen to deeply discounted levels, and everything seems to depend on whether the authorities can take steps to stop the fear from spreading to every corner of the economy. But not everyone is convinced that recapitalizing the fat cats is the best way to bring back business confidence. The second question is:

- How are governments going to get out of these bank nationalizations, which have been heralded as "temporary"?

Government ownership creates inefficiencies without eradicating lust for power and greed among those in charge. Worst, nationalized banks are used by politicians as milk cows and to reward close friends with top jobs. If evidence is needed, look at the scandals which shook and sank Crédit Lyonnais in France in the François Mitterrand years. The third question is:

- How can reputation be enhanced, so that when someone of authority talks he is listened to?

A government and central bank's greater support comes not from the status book but from the reputation enjoyed in public opinion and among other central banks, enhanced by the competence of the men in charge. Judged by the way privatizations of nationalized banks have been handled in the past – for instance by the Balladur government in France – one is permitted to doubt the outcome. The joke has been: "When they swim in red ink we nationalize them, and when they are profitable we privatize them." The fourth question is:

- Why have governments rushed to throw big money at mammoth banks without asking them first to sign firm commitments about compliance, processes, and products?

On 15 October 2008, less than two days after a huge recapitalization of big American banks to the tune of $250 billion, the news was that they still weren't giving out loans and that Hank Paulson, the Treasury secretary, lacked the leverage to force them to put Federal money in the frontline for loans. Recapitalizing the banks with taxpayers' money and having them resume their role as intermediaries are two sides of the same coin.

Paulson did not foresee that both sides of the coin could be tarnished at once. This is surprising for a man who was CEO of Goldman Sachs for 8 years. The first thing to happen before a penny was dropped into the big banks' treasuries should have been that they sign a contract stipulating that all Federal money would be used for loans to companies and people. This would include Goldman Sachs and Morgan Stanley because to get taxpayers' money they had converted themselves into bank holding companies.

Moreover, such a contract should have been characterized by a longer-term perspective. Standard & Poor's, the rating agency, has said that although more people and companies would have to seek refinancing in 2008, the real peak would not occur until 2011 to 2014. By all likelihood, well before that time the Tamerlanic destruction of the Western financial landscape by *collateralized debt obligations* (CDOs) would be exceeded by an even greater eruption, that of *credit default swaps* (CDSs, Chapter 5):

- Lessons have therefore to be learned from the CDOs, and
- They should be proactively applied to the CDSs, as well as *interest rate swaps* (IRSs) whose overhang is a high multiple of CDSs.

Another prudent measure should have been placing limits on the amount and type of derivative financial instruments that the banks can gamble with – as well as the counterparties they can take in their games.

These are elementary precautions to avoid repetition of the same catastrophe, but nothing has been done about establishing a regime of strong bank supervision, *prior* to giving out public money.

2. Where has all the money gone?

If big banks in America, Britain, and continental Europe urgently needed recapitalization to avoid bankruptcy, then where have all the equity and reserves they had gone, as well as their depositors' money? Also, who has been responsible for the negligence in spoiling that capital and therefore for the pain and loss the taxpayer has subsequently had to suffer?

I have asked both questions to lots of cognizant people. The answer to the second question has been nearly unanimous: this is a case of unprecedented bad management, amplified by lack of supervision. Only a couple of answers have referred to fraud, and even if this was in no way generalized the result nonetheless has been disaster.

The majority of answers to the first question have been: "I don't know," followed, in terms of frequency, by: "To the subprimes, fat salaries, and huge unwarranted bonuses". That's likely but not certain. The fact that many bankers became super-rich is not enough to explain the disappearance of hundreds of billions – in fact, of trillions. Only two people gave me an answer which, while it does not exclude excesses, is out of the box. The missing money has gone to the *deficit living* of our society. The State Supermarket (Chapter 1) is living way beyond its means:

- The first two decades after World War II's end were dedicated to the reconstruction after a great war's ravages, providing work for nearly everyone and resulting in a 2 percent to 4 percent average annual increase in the standard of living.
- From the mid-1960s onward, however, that extra reconstruction work practically disappeared, but no government dared to say publicly that the increase in the standard of living – which had become a pillar of liberal democracy – was ending.

Young people, including recent college graduates, could not find a job? No problem. From the mid 1960s onwards the government would deficit-finance them to have a good time doing nothing. "This" or "that" industry wanted subsidies? The government would provide them also through deficit financing. And the same has been true of early retirement, good pensions, medical care for all – the State Supermarket could promise and provide everything .

Firm monetary and fiscal discipline causes pain, but this is preferable to an inflation and currency depreciation where nearly useless debt paper money is turned into even more leveraged useless financial paper. This accumulation of leverage and debt (Chapter 5) has been no concern of any western government. Let future generations pay for it as long as at present voters are nice enough to reconduct the incumbent party into the seat of power.[1]

The public was satisfied because it had never had it so good. Even the students who in May 1968 revolted in Paris against the consumer/producer society turned themselves into producers and subsidized consumers as they aged. They also found a way to improve their standard of living by getting deeper into debt, which banks were all too happy to finance.

This of course had to end one day and that day of reckoning came closer as social inequalities became increasingly visible, all sorts of irregularities increased, imbalances between supply and demand caused an inflationary overhang, and the middle class was crushed under direct and indirect taxes. In an effort to make the ends meet for as long as possible and keep social unrest under lock and key:

- Governments abandoned pledges they had made about financial stability,
- Companies adopted the Modigliani–Miller theory that debt is vastly preferable to equity, and
- Consumers continued loading themselves up with all sorts of loans.

"Stability is not everything, but without stability everything is nothing," said Karl Schiller, a German economist and Social Democratic minister (1966–72). Other socialists however bet on currency instability through budgetary deficits, and by throwing money at the problem they made these deficits worse than they might have been.

Whether by training or by experience, few people are in a position to appreciate that slowly but surely this leads straight into a bottomless pit. Governments, companies and households joined the chorus. Just as an example, the $2 billion injected into Washington Mutual in April 2008 by TPG, a private-equity fund, represents the largest one-shot loss ever by a firm of its kind. It will be surpassed by more than two orders of magnitude by the $700 billion of Treasury handouts (section 4).

Once it starts, the draining of money has the nasty habit of accelerating, and when this happens the economy trends to shrink. Once it entered into the Great Depression, between 1929 and 1933, America's economy shrank by more than a quarter. Many economists however don't appreciate that even worse was the post-WWI year of 1921, when the US economy contracted by a quarter in that single year alone.

We are not at that point, but an impaired banking system makes the slump longer and deeper and nobody is taking action against those responsible for gross negligence and for bringing the early twenty-first century economy to its knees. The crash of Savings & Loans in the late 1980s was a low-key affair compared with the current crisis. Yet it led to a number of convictions and prison terms.

Convictions are not going to right the economic balances, but along with the end of bonuses and redimensioning of huge salaries, they will give to common people the message that the justice system works. These have been the bankers who not only made highly risky trades but also in the years preceding the crash have been drumming up the slogans:

- "Where vision gets built"
- "The strength to be there"

- "You can count on us"
- "The short term has no future"
- "As the American dream grows, so do we"

and ended by killing the American dream along with the British, French, German, Spanish, Italian, and so on. It was the now dismembered and defunct Fortis Bank which asked: "Here today, where tomorrow?" The answer is in hell – precisely where all the money has gone.

The other side of the salvage plans, which we study in the following sections, is that God-size bank bailouts not only constitute moral hazard and unduly penalize the taxpayer but they also prevent the markets from acting in a responsible way. Nor do they allow the courts to look into the balance sheets of companies, to establish possible fraud and personal responsibilities. Sloppy in their conception, they are just giving the lopsided impression that everything can be corrected with a blank check:

- Without a thorough plan for restructuring and for supervision,
- Without detailed criteria for credit allocation and expected performance, and
- With the government-financed action buying only the bad part of portfolios, not the good parts which can have an upside.

Critics say moreover that the possibilities for further and greater amounts of fraud remain wide open with Ben Bernanke's statement that the $700 billion voted by US Congress would be used to buy junk assets "above fire sale prices," without explaining why in a market economy the taxpayer should pay "more" than the market price, how much more is "more" and at whose discretion this will be established. (Probably on these considerations the Treasury decided to switch to a program of loans whose details are equally imprecise.)

3. Can the economy afford huge bailouts?

For its part the Group of Seven (G-7) leading industrialized nations was set up in the 1970s[2] so that leaders of its member countries can contemplate economic development and resolve their differences. But it is more a discussion group than a war room that can make urgently needed monetary decisions in real time. Therefore, it came as no surprise when it was not convened during the acute crisis of the "historic weeks" of September/October 2008 on Wall Street.

By contrast, the 15 November 2008 international economic conference did take place at a peak of the crisis, but so far it can be seen solely as a public relations event, as none of the G-20 state leaders came along with concrete ideas, or even expressed a firm standing on bringing large-scale speculators to justice. Both are important if a deeper crisis is to be averted before it becomes a guillotine hitting the common citizen.

Nobody among the heads of government seems to have remembered the words of John Maynard Keynes, who wrote in his *General Theory*: "Speculators may do no harm as bubbles on a steady stream of enterprise. But the position is serious when enterprise becomes the bubble on a whirlpool of speculation."

Somebody will have to pay for this big-time speculation, and this somebody is the nation-states. But can they afford it? The majority of the industrial nations as well as most of the developing countries are in the red. Counting 2008 budget deficits as a percentage of GDP (the way they are at present projected), that of Italy is −2.5 percent, France −3 percent, Japan −3 percent, the United States −3.5 percent (probably much more with the $700 billion, without even counting the Fed's $2 trillion)[3], and Britain −5 percent.

Only Germany hopes to close the year with a timid +1 percent, but Germany also has a national debt equal to 64 percent of GDP. Among major nations only China features an enviable national debt, of 22 percent of GDP. As for 2009, deficits promise to be even more dismal.

Accumulated national debts and budgetary deficits count a great deal. Take as an example the US Treasury's $700 billion bailout of cash-strapped financial institutions[4] (sections 4 and 5). A majority of economists and financial analysts believe that it is likely to have severe fiscal consequences in the long run, particularly because the Fed had already swapped almost half of its safe US Treasury securities for private sector assets via:

- The TAF program,
- The discount window, and
- Direct loans to wounded banks.

While the billions of dollars in handouts are largely meant to offset the private sector credit contraction, they also put long-term inflationary forces in motion. US economists are estimating a $500 billion deficit for the fiscal year 2009, reaching 6.2 percent of GDP. On top of a large fiscal deficit, the US also runs a large trade deficit, and foreign capital inflows into the US are likely to play an important role in the aftereffects of the crises.

Another sore point, and a direct result of the lack of open public discussion on how the large amount of funds authorized by Congress should be used, is its allocation. In an interview he gave on Bloomberg on 16 October 2008 Dr Alan Blinder, a former vice chairman of the Federal Reserve, expressed the opinion that too much of the $700 billion is given to banks:

- Leaving too little to refinance mortgages,
- While at least half the $700 billion should have gone to solve the mortgage crisis through mortgage guarantees.

Nothing of what is written in the preceding paragraphs about current trends is good news for the US currency, and therefore for the American economy. Here are the thoughts of three German bankers had to say about the currency: "A stable currency is the condition for our daily bread," said Hans Luther, Reichsbank president in 1931. Hjalmar Schacht, another Reichsbank president, put it a little differently: "States and governments perish for two reasons: war and bad finances."[5] "There can be no hard currency without hard measures," added Karl Blessing, the Bundesbank president, in 1966.

Critics of the worsening state of the western economies say that there are other ills as well. By recapitalizing big banks, governments will be lavishing money on the very people who got American and western Europe into this mess – and while the bloated financial sector will continue shrinking, accountability will remain at its lowest. The fact that big, well-known banks got practically nationalized means that:

- These entities were in such a bad state that nobody wanted to buy them.
- Under these conditions, why should the taxpayer come up with the money in a deal he can hardly afford?

In addition, once the government got into the business of supporting banks or any other companies to avoid bankruptcies, it would not know where to stop. And in regard to toxic waste auctions, it would find it hard to stop sellers from rigging them, if only because no two lots of nearly worthless securities are exactly the same.

- Taxpayers would pay over the odds, and
- Banks would be rewarded for their gambling stupidity.

There is as well the overriding question of the final bill to the economy. The better way to answer the query regarding the total economic cost is to look for historical evidence about fixing a broken-down financial system. In the early 1980s loose rules and decision delays brought the bailout of Argentina's banking to:

- 55 percent of GDP.

The pros say that one reason why in emerging markets bailouts cost big money is inadequate safeguards against abuse. Critics of bailout practices answer that in developed countries, too, there may be indecision and inefficiency. The bailouts and restructuring of Japan's banking system (1991–2007) cost a staggering:

- 130 percent of GDP.

Decisive action by the government and the central bank can cut that by almost 98 percent. In the early 1990s the bill for fixing Sweden's and Norway's banking systems was (in each case) 3 percent of GDP. It should be note referenced, however, that both countries kept costs low by acting swiftly with *drastic* and *painful* measures – which has not been the case in the US, Britain, Belgium, and elsewhere where money was thrown at the problem.

For its part, a study by the IMF puts the average cost of resolving banking crises around the world at 16 percent of a country's GDP. Averages, most evidently, mean nothing because countries and their banking problems are so different from one another. Also, so much depends on the resolve of central banks and governments to get out of the credit crisis even if the pain is high, and eventually out of commercial bank ownership altogether.

4. Preparing for the $700 billion US bailout

On 23 September 2008, in the course of the US Senate hearing on the $700 billion authorization to spend taxpayer money to ease the pains big banks suffered from their self-inflicted wounds, one of the senators asked Paulson, Bernanke, and Cox: "Do you think Wall Street owes the American people an apology?" Ben Bernanke answered that there should be a commission to study what went wrong. It has been one of the golden rules of bureaucracy that if you don't want something to be done you delegate it to a committee or commission.

Paulson's opinion has been that the financial instruments traded by Wall Street were too complex to be properly understood; but he said so without explaining why in the 7 years he was president and CEO of Goldman Sachs (1999 to 2006) he authorized the development and trading of these instruments. Paulson added to his congressional testimony: "We will fix the problem, it will not happen again," knowing very well that these were big words.[6]

In answer to a question posed by another US senator, the Treasury secretary repeated his opinion that structured financial instruments and complex derivative products are awfully misunderstood by bankers. The next question was: "How do you calculate the price of a troubled asset?" The answer has been that confronted with asset complexity one should use a variety of tools – which of course means nothing.

On the other hand, the Federal Reserve faces some constraints. Like most central banks, it is generally prohibited from unsecured lending, but it more or less gets around this by lending to its own off-balance-sheet vehicle, which holds the unsecured commercial paper. If this limit is legal, another one is political: several politicians in the House of Representatives object to their central bank displacing private lenders – a reason why the $700 billion bailout was voted down the first time around.

Another constraint about which little has been said is of a financial nature. Throwing money at the wounded banks has risks, as we saw in section 2. The Treasury and the Fed could suffer equity and loan losses so great that the central bank would need recapitalization, as central banks in Chile, Hungary, and the Philippines have in the past. The Bank of Japan avoided this by purchasing much private-sector debt earlier in this century.

The US Congress imposed its own constraints and provisos when granting the $700 billion authorization through the Troubled Assets Relief Act (TARA) of October 2008. One of them, intended to sooth the electorate, has been the piggy-backing of another spending bill aimed to help homeowners and consumers. Other changes were specific to the Treasury's plan:

- The first authorization is $250 billion.
- The second of $100 billion will be almost automatic.
- But Congress has the right to reject the final $350 billion.

The Treasury is authorized to get equity in banks, but there must be limits to golden parachutes and executive pay in those institutions which benefit from the handouts. Other changes, however, have been counterproductive, like doing away with marking-to-market the toxic waste, which makes the quality of banks' assets more opaque and questionable rather than increasing transparency.

There have been uncertainties connected to the handouts. One of primary importance is the effectiveness and impartiality of the party or parties responsible for them. On 22 September 2008 Senator (and then presidential candidate) Hillary Clinton said in an interview on CNBC that a $700 billion plan cannot be run by the Treasury. It must be managed by an independent agency under proper supervision through an oversight committee reporting to Congress. But nothing has followed this statement, so the Treasury has been given *carte blanche* after all.

At par in terms of importance has been the issue of how that wholesome $700 billion should be used. The Treasury wanted to be free to buy equity in big banks, give them loans, and through auctions purchase their toxic waste. In the week of 10 November 2008 Henry Paulson, however, said that the government's rescue plan for the banking system:

- Would no longer involve purchasing *toxic mortgage* debt from banks, and
- Would instead focus on providing banks with capital by buying stock directly.

Acceptable candidacies have been extended from publicly quoted institutions to private banks, with a deadline set for 8 December 2008. Some 3,600 private banks could apply for a share of the $700 billion bailout; previously they had been unable to ask for funds because the program involved stock purchases. (As long as a bank's application to become a bank holding company or a savings and loan was with federal regulators by the deadline, it became eligible for the bailout program.)

Reference to such midway decisions and U-turns is revealing, inasmuch as it documents how little there was in terms of a plan for using the $700 billion to turn the economy around in the best possible way. Yet the cost is tremendous. Neither is this $700 billion the only big-spending scheme to extinguish the fires of the financial crisis. On 6 October 2008 the Fed doubled to $900 billion the planned size of the loans it auctions to banks. A day later it said it would, for the first time in decades:

- Make unsecured loans to companies, including banks, and
- Do so by buying commercial paper that they are unable to refinance.

Subsequent to this, the Federal Reserve joined other leading central banks in a concerted effort in cutting interest rates, lowering its target for the federal funds rate from 2 percent to 1.5 percent; in a fortnight the latter dropped to 1 percent. Some analysts suggested that another rate cut will follow bringing the funds rate below 1 percent. (A rate cut is a conventional response to the growing risk of a deep recession.)

And yet not everything that may need to be done has been factored in. Back on 29 September 2008 Professor Edmund Phelps of Columbia University said in an interview that the $700 billion plan did not address borderline insolvency, now faced by many banks – and it may even make it worse. Neither were the Treasury's and Fed's plans targeting unemployment.[7] Other critics have added that a big bank bailout of $700 billion will have perverse influence on:

- The US economy, and
- The way a free market works.

Since it is almost certain that the current authorization will be followed by others, a spike of over $1 trillion in public debt will shake the market's confidence in the US government, and it might crash the dollar. In addition, buying equity in wounded banks with murky balance sheets, as Paulson wanted to do (and did) in order to support banking stocks, may well be the seed of further troubles:

- It is a bailout of banks in disguise, and
- Eventually the government will be under pressure not to limit support to the banks.

Other industries like autos and airlines, as well as several states of the Union, would like to be part of the Federal government's generosity. In the

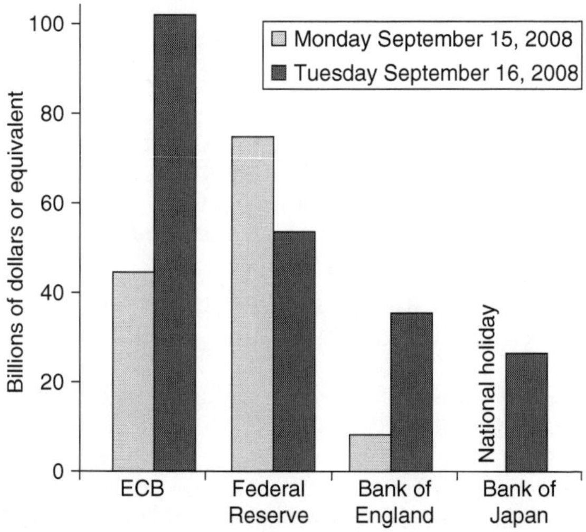

Figure 10.1 Liquidity injected into money markets by central banks over two consecutive days, in the wake of the Lehman Brothers collapse (mid September 2008).

opinion of several experts, these are gifts which have nothing really to do with financial problems; and they are gifts because nowhere has it been shown how the companies that benefit from direct cash injections will pay back the government.

As Figure 10.1 shows, in September 2008 the European Central Bank, the Federal Reserve, the Bank of England, and the Bank of Japan all made important liquidity injections into capital markets to calm down their fever from Lehman's bankruptcy. All that money, the billions and trillions, are on top of other handouts in disguise made to big commercial and industrial banks as central banks have turned themselves into philanthropic institutions ready to buy any sort of garbage from poorly managed financial companies.

5. A troubled "Troubled Assets Relief Program"

Right after America's House of Representatives approved the $700 billion bank rescue bill to create the Troubled Assets Relief Program (TARP), President Bush signed it into law. The reader should however notice that this law does not deal with the immediate economic threat, which is a collapse of confidence in the financial system. In the first 4 months of the lavish recapitalization program nothing has been done to help the American families at risk of losing their houses. In addition:

- Money-market funds and banks remain deeply suspicious about who they can entrust their money to, and

- This continues to stifle the supply of credit and cause more banks to fail in spite of such unprecedented handouts.

The homework has been skin-deep. Treasury Secretary Paulson first sold the proposal as a way to buy troubled bank securities via an auction, but it quickly became clear that the Treasury people had not thought about it in a fundamental sense. Without the benefit of a firm plan, the $700 billion morphed as a fund that could be deployed in different but uncertain ways to shore up the American financial system.

The failure to stress-test the results of financing is the worst possible policy in a panic. Neither is the talk that the Federal government might insure all bank deposits making much sense. Until recently the FDIC assured deposits only up to $100,000 per account; a limit which with the $700 billion authorization has been raised to $250,000. Ensuring all deposits would add another $1.9 trillion in taxpayer guarantees, which the American economy simply cannot afford.

Neither is the supposed similarity of the current crisis to that of the Savings & Loans, in the late 1980s, making much sense. Nor is the real difference the one often mentioned: that in the S&Ls case public authorities did not commit public money to the financial system until bank failures and insolvency became wider.[8] The first real difference lies in the fact that the Resolution Trust Corporation (RTC) is no blueprint for today's:

- Complex,
- Highly indebted, and
- Practically bankrupt financial world.

The second real difference, resulting partly from the first and partly from the aforementioned lack of homework, is the uncertainty surrounding the TARP. The Treasury first planned to buy huge amounts of distressed debt using a reverse auction process. The complexities of thousands of different mortgage-backed securities led to the conclusion that its results would be highly dubious, and that plan was dropped.

Then, direct bank recapitalization caught the Treasury's attention, and its managers said they will do that too. There is a clause in the TARP that allows it to buy almost anything in the interest of stability, including direct stakes in banks, as long as it notifies Congress. That is supposedly part of the "kit of all of the tools" at the Treasury's disposal – and it is highly dangerous, like the policy of shoring up capital-starved banks with large purchases of preferred stock which continues dropping in price:

- That practice surely enriches some people, mostly those already rich from looting the system.

- But it does little, if anything, to stop the worse from continuing to worsen.

Is the $700 billion only "chickenfeed," as Alan Greenspan told a US senator? If yes, then what are the limits, and what is the likely risk and return attached to each option? How much toxic waste is in the banks' vaults other than the famed subprimes and Alt-As based securitized junk? How much of that has been already transferred to the treasuries of central banks (Chapter 9)?

There is no evidence that these questions were ever resolved before the handouts started. Or that a careful plan has been laid on how and under which conditions the State Supermarket would get out of the commercial banking business – which is not its vocation in the first place. Good management practice required that banks:

- First are asked to come up with certified assets and liabilities under SOX legal clauses, and
- Then are asked to present for approval a plan on how the taxpayers' money will be used (a normal banking practice).

Nothing like that has happened, nor has there been an established channel for feedback. Everything is ad hoc, as documented by the fact that in a Senate hearing in the week of 10 November 2008 key lawmakers pressed bank executives on how they have been using government funding, adding that the banks ought to do more to directly help struggling homeowners. Senator Christopher Dodd, chairman of the Senate Banking Committee, said that banks were not using the government funds to ease credit for struggling home-owners.[9]

Plenty of evidence suggests that the only strategy the Bush Administration put forward was simply to throw money at the problem, with no questions asked. As was to be expected, the first beneficiaries have been the big banks – all *Fortune 500*. Injections of $25 billion were made to each of Citigroup, JP Morgan Chase, and Wells Fargo. Bank of America was granted $15 billion, while Goldman Sachs, Morgan Stanley, and Merrill Lynch were given $10 billion each.

Then on 17 November 2008 the Treasury said that it had dispersed $33.56 billion to 21 banks in a second round of payments as part of the $700 billion bailout program. The new (and unwarranted) distribution of public money brought the total of handouts to $158.56 so far. (The previously distributed $125 billion to nine banks was in the form of stock purchase.)

Banks that benefited in this second round of State Supermarket favors included PNC, which received $7.7 billion; U.S. Bancorp, $6.6 billion; Capital One Financial, $3.56 billion; Regions Financial Corp, $3.5 billion; SunTrust

Bank, $3.5 billion; Bank of New York Mellon, $3 billion; and more. A smaller amount went to Los-Angeles-based Broadway Financial, and the smallest, of $1 million, to Saigon National Bank.

For its part, Congress would have liked to use a chunk of the authorization for reasons other than filling the banks' coffers. In the 18 November 2008 congressional hearing the Treasury secretary clashed with lawmakers on the bailouts, stating that they were necessary but were no panacea. Paulson and Bernanke rejected the idea of using part of the authorized $700 billion for the salvage of the auto industry. (No doubt other industries too are queuing up.)

Demands for helping the US auto industry and those targeting the banks also share common ground. According to analysts at JPMorgan Chase, losses on securities tied to car loans could rise close to those on subprime mortgages. In addition, defaults on junk bonds and other commercial debt are soaring,[10] bringing nearer the day of reckoning with the $62 trillion of CDSs:

- Should these other domains of crisis be covered by the Troubled Asset Relief Program?
- Or is it better to limit it to the banking industry with its toxic securities, and let the other wounded entities stay at the street corner?

The fact that this question has come post-mortem provides further evidence that the Treasury's Troubled Assets Relief Program is itself in trouble. The proper homework would have seen to it that the major options were the first to be examined, before even asking for a given amount of money to face the crisis. Along with these major options a study should have been made of the policies, ways, and means to pay for the requested authorization – including the payback possibilities available to the government and their risk and return, namely:

- Raise taxes by a significant margin,
- Allow much higher inflation, of the sort characterizing banana republics,
- Engineer a Third World War in Asia, hoping that it reflates the economy, and/or
- Default on all debt by declaring the financial system bankrupt.

The reader should appreciate that these four options are facing all of the 21 chiefs of government who gathered in Washington for the international economic conference on 15 November 2008. Hence these lines are written also for them. It is always wise to clarify the alternative courses of action which are available at the twelfth hour. The more governments hide the truth from their citizens, the more painful will be the way out.

6. Timothy Geithner and the Stability and Recovery Program

In his first press conference as Treasury secretary, Timothy Geithner said on 10 February 2009 that the policy of the Obama Administration, in confronting the economic and financial crisis, would be comprehensive and forceful. The "Stability and Recovery Program" (SRP), which he presented, aims to replace the Treasury programs for restructuring the big banks inherited from the Bush Administration. The new framework will rest on three pillars:

- Clean up the banks' balance sheets,
- Bring in private capital, and
- Get bank lending going again.

In regard to the first bullet, banks will be required to make stress tests and to apply new metrics in measuring their exposure to toxic assets (more on this later). As with the TARP program, the capital will come from the taxpayers' purse with conditions which include the requirements to lend and to replace government money with private capital.

According to Geithner, SRP will aim to use private and government funds as well as the knowhow of private professionals to help in valuing the wounded assets. To this the Obama Administration plans to commit $1 trillion, which may be up to $2 trillion through leveraging appropriated funds. (It's a little curious to use leverage in order to clean up the mess left by previous leverage.)

Judging from the contents of the 10 February 2009 press conference, it would seem that the idea of a government-sponsored "bad bank" is in principle rejected, but not every aspect of it is off the table. What has been proposed is a government–private effort, whose specifics are still missing. (Some critics have said that the risk is that the government will end putting up the money and the private parties will reap the profits.) Geithner however cautioned that in conjunction to these general lines of a new framework there come up four major questions:

- Financing,
- Pricing,
- Trading, and
- Accounting.

The term *bad bank* is very popular these days, but it is not necessarily a rational concept. Bankrupt and nearly bankrupt financial institutions have found a way to unload on the taxpayer their deeply wounded assets, like CDOs and other useless paper, by passing them to a newly created bad bank supported by the state – while getting from the state good money for these rotten "assets." This trick would leave a financial institution which has been at edge of the precipice as a *good bank*.

George Soros knew what he was talking about when in an interview he gave at 2009 World Economic Forum at Davos, Switzerland, he said that he likes the concept of a good bank – not that of a bad bank. Most of the better known American-economists also spoke against the bad bank as "a solution", but both the American and British governments are uncertain about what they should do.

The leveraging of current appropriations left aside, the Obama Administration will need a great deal of money to get its plan rolling. More than half of the $700 billion appropriated by Congress, in October 2008, for TARP have been used or misused. The nearly $800 billion appropriated by Congress, in mid February 2009, for relaunching the economy are already earmarked and the lawmakers are not in the mood to allocate more funds.

An idea that has been floated since the Bush Administration is to continue leveraging the Federal Reserve's balance sheet; but this is already overblown, and moreover that's not the function of the central bank. Several economists now say there are major risks in asking the Fed to do too much by going way outside its remit, which is monetary policy.

At the same time, however, other economists question whether the plan outlined by Timothy Geithner goes far enough. In an article in the *New York Times* on 13 February 2009, Paul Krugman said that the stimulus bill looks helpful but inadequate, especially when combined with a disappointing plan for rescuing the banks. To his mind:

- The US is probably facing the worst slump since the Great Depression, and
- Over the next 3 years there will be a nearly $3 trillion gap between what the US economy could produce and what it will produce.

Two days prior to Krugman another respected economist, Martin Wolf of the *Financial Times*, published an article entitled "Why Obama's New TARP will fail to Rescue the Banks." Wolf encapsulated his opinion in a query in the opening short sentence: "Has Barack Obama's presidency already failed?"[11] (I hope not.)

Opinions diverge as well on whether the nationalization of bankrupt big banks is the right course, given that to the mind of American businessmen "nationalization" has been long regarded as a folly of European socialists and other leftists. This position may however be changing. While nationalization is still considered as a solution of last resort, it is now on the table.

Most likely, a great deal will depend on the results of the projected stress tests[12] – which are typically focusing on the long tail of the risk distribution. Though these have not yet been properly defined with regard to what the Treasury has in mind, a growing opinion is that the big banks will not be able to pass them, because they are known to test extreme values and their financial aftereffect.

"If you put most of our banks under a 'stress test', they're going to fail," Lindsay Graham, the Republican senator from North Carolina, told ABC News on 15 February 2009. "I would not take off [the table] the idea of nationalizing the banks."[13] (Neither would I.)

Indeed, a week after Geithner's press conference senior administration officials acknowledged that the SRP financial rescue plan could result in temporary nationalization. That's the cost of what Krugman called "the economic debacle of the past eight years" meaning the two tours of duty of the Bush Administration. One should also account for the damages created by the uninterrupted 16 years' reign by Alan "Double Bubble" Greenspan.[14]

Like it or not, the whole western economy has to bite the bullet. Adding together bank rescue plans, fiscal stimuluses, lost tax revenues from slumping output and falling asset prices, as well as higher unemployment benefits, many economists expect that the industrial countries' combined fiscal deficit will rise to 7 percent to 8 percent or more of GDP in 2009 – way up from 2008 figures.

A real worry regarding the rapidly growing US government debt is that the ultimate price tag of banking bailouts and stimulus will be much bigger than early 2009 figures have so far suggested. Even the trillions already committed may prove to be modest against the scale of the banking crisis, which continues unabated with huge write-downs unstoppable quarter after quarter.

Some analysts also draw a parallel between America's woes in 2007/2009 and Japan's in the early 1990s, including the meager returns compared with the huge costs. Officially at least, all proportions considered, by January 2009 the US government had committed less than half as much public money to the financial sector as Japan did in the 1990s. Is this too much or too little? Experts say that by all likelihood that's just the beginning:

- Goldman Sachs estimates that the total value of troubled assets in American banks' coffers is $5.7 trillion.[15]
- If so, it would mean many more trillion on the cost of restructuring and in long-term public debt – and official statistics may be lying because according to some estimates the US government has already committed $7 to $8 trillion.

Quite pessimistic as well is an IMF conclusion that western countries tend to recover only half their outlays for financial rescues. But there are exceptions. Sweden, whose banking rescue was well planned, tough and forceful, recovered 85 percent to 90 percent. America has no chance of getting near that because the whole operation, TARP included, started very poorly under Hank Paulson and Ben Bernanke.

These notions have, in a way, been confirmed in an interview the new Treasury secretary gave to CNBC on 10 February 2009 right after his press conference. In this Tim Geithner pointed out that a lesson learned from the crisis is that the government underestimated both the extent of the damage and the cost of the recovery. The interviewer did not miss the opportunity to remind him that most of the big banks need to be put in bankruptcy and recapitalized, to which Geithner answered:

- This is the core of our problem, and
- We don't know how much was lost and where.

The discussion then focused on the public/private ownership of the recovery entity, and most particularly on how to value the wounded assets. After stating that this is enormously complicated, the Treasury secretary added: "We will be open to suggestions, and we only take risks we can understand." Were the details of SRP work worked out? "No," he answered, "we are not going to put out details until we get it right." To the question about accountability for what has happened, Geithner's response has been that:

- The quality of decisions that led to this crisis is troubling, and
- There is an appalling lack of accountability at the top of the banking industry.

With all these facts in mind, Tim Geithner asserted that "this government needs to act and that is what we plan to do," but he also cautioned that the chosen strategy will cost money, involve risk, and take time to give results. What was not stated but should have been said is that no matter how much money is put on the table results will be trivial till there is a 180-degree change in today's prevailing bankrupt big bank culture.

7. Euroland tries to give birth to a common solution

Confronted, like everybody else, with a severe banking crisis and credit crunch, but lacking a central government, the 27 countries of the European Union have found it difficult to put their act together. This has also been visible in the smaller group of the 15-member euroland. By mid-October 2008, however, the chances of a common solution improved somewhat as the bigger economies unveiled plans to spend tens of billions of euros in state funds to prop up their banking institutions.

After some bickering, political leaders agreed on a menu of measures to cope with the growing financial crisis which knows no frontier. At a Paris summit on the weekend of 11/12 October 2008 leaders of the 15 countries that have adopted the common currency said they would partially nationalize their banks when necessary. Other measures to cope with the growing financial crisis included:

- State-guaranteed loans, and
- Loosening of marking-to-market rules, which (as note referenced in the US case) is irrational.

Hosting the meeting as EU president, Nicolas Sarkozy said France, Germany, and the rest of the EU would commit €1.5 trillion to bank rescues. "We must restore the capacity of our banks to lend money," he added in a news conference. France pledged €320 billion in state-guaranteed aid to banks, and €40 billion to recapitalize banks in trouble. Germany's rescue package included a state guarantee worth €400 billion to back bank loans to each other, plus €80 billion to top up capital. The principle has been:

- No system-relevant bank will be allowed to fail.
- No depositor will lose money.

Already on 6 October 2008 Germany had guaranteed all bank deposits – essentially every bank account in Germany – to a rumored amount of over €500 billion.[16] A collapse would have spread through the banking system, said Peer Steinbrück, the finance minister.

Not without reason, the German government had originally posed cross-border bank recapitalization because, as Europe's largest economy, Germany traditionally ends up paying the bills. But there had been an emergency. "Primarily it's about achieving market-based solutions where market participants should be first in line to drive recapitalization forward," said Axel Weber, president of the German central bank, in a Washington meeting.

As in the case of the United States and Britain, there can be no 100 solutions to the problem. One challenge has been that governments have lacked self-confidence. Another is that while each of euroland's countries has a central bank, these don't have the money, which is managed by the ECB, and a flood of money is needed which can only come out of the common monetary institution.

But actions by some euroland countries to get a handle on their financial problems have sometimes worsened woes elsewhere. The Irish government's broad guarantee of deposits prompted investors in other EU nations, particularly Britain, to shift their money to Ireland.[17] It has however been a positive sign that it did not take long to appreciate that to be worth its salt a solution must have a wider perspective. Nearsightedness does nothing to restore confidence.[18]

Critics also add that euroland's agreement on the salvage of credit institutions has included no clause to guarantee that Ireland's example of unilateral action would not be repeated. These are major commitments. The Irish guarantee covered around €400 billion ($575 billion) of liabilities, more than twice Ireland's gross domestic product, which the country simply could not afford.

The bad news for euroland has been that while the 11/12 October 2008 meeting put some meat and muscles on the skeleton of a common solution, nobody really had (or has) a slim idea about final cost:

> We confirm today our commitment to act together in a decisive and comprehensive way in order to restore confidence and proper functioning of the financial system, aiming at restoring appropriate and efficient financing conditions for the economy,

– that's all one could read in the statement which followed the mid-October Paris meeting.

The glue that held together this common agreement has been the hope (but only the hope) of avoiding a rerun of the Great Depression. Germany – which had already sunk €50 billion to shore up its Hypo Real Estate bank[19] – kept the door open to eventually inject equity capital worth "double-digit" billions into its banks and guarantees for debt issuance. France (together with Belgium) put up money to save Dexia from bankruptcy.[20] In the first days of October 2008, Dexia received a €6.4 billion ($9.2 billion) government cash injection.[21]

Another precedent in terms of cross-border government collaboration in financing the aftereffect of a failing bank has been the case of Fortis, the sprawling Belgian–Dutch conglomerate which had taken on billions to buy a big chunk of ABN Amro of the Netherlands in 2007 (together with RBS and Santander). With doubts rising, confidence in Fortis plunged, dragging down its share prices and making it even harder for it to attract funds.[22]

With its €160 billion deposit base, Fortis was seemingly on firm ground. But customers were voting with their feet, pulling roughly €5 billion out of the bank and taking them elsewhere. This was worrying Belgian and Dutch bank regulators. Eventually, the Dutch, Belgian, and Luxembourg governments were forced to inject €11.2 billion into the wounded big bank, which still was not enough to stem the tide:

- The Dutch ended up fully nationalizing Fortis's operations in the Netherlands (the former ABN Amro).
- On 5 October 2008 BNP Paribas snapped up the rest of the former flagship of Benelux banks.[23]

Postmortem, there has been evidence that the abyss in the Fortis treasury was so profound that the €11.2 billion it got from the Belgian, Luxembourg, and Dutch governments were a drop in the ocean (considering that the bank had €900 billion in "assets"). The cash injection represented just 1.24 percent of "assets" and it was clear that this was an interim solution designed to buy time till a more permanent one could be found. Fortis's fate was sealed.

As far as the Belgian taxpayer is concerned, Fortis and Dexia have not been the only banks hungry for cash. KBC, Belgium's second-largest credit institution, needed (and got) €3.5 billion. In Holland, the government injected €10 billion in the coffers of ING, the big banking and insurance group, against an 8.5 percent equity stake.[24]

ING's retail deposit base was thought to be large enough to prevent it from having to recapitalize. However, its share price sank after it said it expected to make its first-ever quarterly loss, forcing it to turn to the Dutch government. What came as a surprise is that the CEO and the CFO of the bankassurance did not say "Thank you, taxpayer."[25] Their somewhat headstrong attitude has been: "We are strong and now we are becoming stronger."[26]

Critics suggest, rather controversially, that the plan to salvage euroland's distressed banks is loosening some accounting rules: Under the current exceptional circumstances, financial and non-financial institutions should be allowed as necessary to value their assets consistently with risk of default assumptions rather than immediate market value which in illiquid markets may no longer be appropriate, runs a common agreement between euroland member states.

Excuses can always be found, but it should escape nobody's attention – least of all that of political leaders – that transparency is the only way for private capital to return to the market. It must also be kept in mind that money advanced by governments is hybrid and it contributes nothing to the real economy. Neither does it help the banks' profits, since they must pay interest. Essentially this money is another sort of leveraging, State Supermarket style.

8. Russia discovers oligarchic capitalism's aftereffects

Ten years after the August 1998 meltdown of Russian banks and finance, in mid 2008 many Russian companies held off raising debt in the hope that the cost of money would decrease. This led to a backlog debt by Russian banks and other firms which needed to be refinanced amid increasingly difficult conditions as western investors repriced the risk of doing business in Russia.

It was not difficult to write a follow-up scenario. The crisis was around the corner. On 18 September 2008 trading was suspended on Russia's stockmarkets[27] when shares went into free fall, and this fall was not halted even by the government's injection of capital into the country's three biggest banks. JPMorgan's emerging-markets bond index fell by more than 5 percent in the week to 16 September, giving up in a few days all the gains it had made in 2008.

Smaller highly leveraged banks and companies faced more severe problems refinancing debt. The Russian Standard Bank sought to raise $200 million in international loans, but its attempts were hampered because of its junk rating. Home Credit & Finance Bank, another non-investment-grade Russian bank, also faced severe difficulties in managing its debt.

Critics say the boys at Goldman Sachs had hand-fed Russia's debt addiction. With high leverage now put in question, the debt market was shut to second-tier borrowers, and the cost of borrowing money in Russia jumped even for blue-chip names. However, Sberbank and VTB Group, which are state-owned and have government reserves on which to fall back, were able to weather the storm. The Russian government:

- Poured money into their coffers, and
- Asked them in return to help the smaller Russian banks.

On 21 September 2008, Russia's Finance Ministry widened the provision of emergency budget funding to Russia's banking system. This was a sign that despite the rise to $130 billion of additional liquidity to the country's financial markets announced a week earlier, the banks were still under pressure. Subsequently the Finance Ministry said it would immediately provide another $24.21 billion in 3-month credit, at a minimum rate of 8.75 percent at an auction:

- In all, till mid November 2008 Russia spent $220 billion to shore up its financial services industry.
- For the same purpose Japan put up $275 billion, South Korea $100 billion, and 13 Asian nations planned to create a $80 billion fund to fight the global economic crisis.[28]

The announcement of the Russian government's multibillion package followed a meeting between Finance Minister Alexei Kudrin and the representatives of more than 20 Russian banks, who had been arguing for such a measure to be taken. Many bankers had been complaining that government credits provided to the country's top three institutions did not filter down to them, and the interbank lending market was not functioning to get liquidity into the overall banking system.

The oligarchs managed to keep their name in the news. On 28 September 2008 the *New York Times* had an article on one of them, Aleksandr Y. Lebedev, who reportedly lost $4.6 billion in the Russian stock market crash that same month after being highly leveraged and exposed to market gyrations. (He is not a beggar, as he was left with $3.1 billion in assets.) The wealthy men who run the country are headed into a period of flux, Lebedev said, predicting that if Moscow's sky-high property values deflate then 50 percent of the country's banks will fail.

Lebedev was not alone in losing a fortune in the stockmarket crash. At his side could be found the "Who's Who" of Russian oligarchs who had been gambling in the stockmarket's casino among themselves and had borrowed hundreds of millions in the hope of adding more billions to their already large fortunes: Roman Abramovich; Oleg Deripaska, of Basic Element, a conglomerate; Mikhail Fridman of Alfa-Bank; Vladimir Potanin, of Interos; and Mikhail Prokorov, of Norilsk Nickel.

As far as profits and losses are concerned, the die had been cast and the wrong number had come up. Therefore, both the personal business empires of the oligarchs and the huge loans they took out from (silly) western banks were in peril. By 17 October 2008 the value of shares pledged as collateral by ultra-rich Russians had fallen below the value of the loans. "The ground is shifting under them," said Rory MacFarquhar, an economist at Goldman Sachs in Moscow. "This could be a game changer for a lot of very, very large players."[29]

On 10 October 2008 Prime Minister Putin had said $16.7 billion would be set aside for buying shares and that the State Development Bank would place the orders. This was in line with a strategy that relied essentially on making the government's oil windfall profits available to banks, hoping they would in turn lend to companies or buy equity to maintain growth.

That same day the Russian Parliament had passed a law unlocking central bank lending to private banks in a $36 billion bailout that had been announced a short time earlier that week. Shares in Russian companies traded on foreign stock exchanges still plunged, however.

Government action was deemed necessary because early to mid October 2008 Russian shares had fallen by about 40 percent and trading was again suspended in Russia for 2 days. In a way similar to what happened in the American and western European markets, stocks were heading south because of fears that the worst was still to come, plus the fear that the government might take advantage of the crisis to buy up prime assets from cash-strapped oligarchs on the cheap. If anything, both of the Moscow-based:

- Rouble-denominated MICEX index, and
- Dollar-denominated RTS index

had dived. In spite of the government's measures to restore confidence, compared with late October (in a mere 5 months) both indices shed about two-thirds of their value. And, somewhat as in New York, London, Paris, Berlin, and other capitals, the end of the tunnel was not in sight.

Either the market did not believe what the government was saying, or there were a lot of forced sellers. The money promised for stocks uses a respectable

10 percent of the free-float on the Russian market and it should have sent stocks up; but there was more selling. In addition, while by mid to late October 2008 tightening credit had not yet as wide an effect in Russia as in western Europe, softening commodity prices were beginning to hit some industries. But the stockmarket's response to government measures was very similar.

It is however interesting to note that unlike the strategy in the United States, where bailout funds are being gathered by borrowing (which will increase the national deficit), in Russia they are being drawn from the national savings account from the period of high oil prices. Under the latest plan approved by lawmakers the central bank will dip into the national gold and hard currency reserves for loans to private Russian banks.

9. Iceland's banks have reminded everybody that given enough rope anyone can hang himself[30]

When in late September 2008 the news broke that Iceland's three bigger banks were ready to jump off the cliff and take the whole country down with them, some experts were quick to comment that Iceland is a special case because there is no domestic activity to absorb the leveraging. That may be true, but at the same time there are many countries where the banks' leveraging outpaces by far:

- Their domestic activities, and
- The ability of the national economy to support the banks' superleveraging and toxic waste.

During the last few years, in a way not dissimilar to that of the global banking industry, the country's three largest credit institutions expanded headlong abroad, particularly since two of them were privatized in 2003, amassing assets of about €125 billion ($180 billion) by the end of 2007. This compared badly with the island state's economy of just €14.5 billion – small fry.

Worse yet, many of these "assets" were funded by lenders in wholesale markets. Statistics suggest that in early 2006 less than 30 cents in every loan issued by Iceland's banks was backed by deposits, while in parallel to this Iceland's households accumulated debts amounting to 213 percent of disposable income. General bankruptcy was an accident waiting to happen; as it did. Compared with these statistics:

- Overleveraged American households owed 140 percent of GDP;
- The debt of British households was higher at 169 percent, but still well below Iceland's; and
- Rising rapidly, that of French households had just crossed the 100 percent mark (Chapter 7).

An early warning about forthcoming trouble was given in 2006, when Iceland's main banks struggled to finance themselves. At the time, government sources suggested that both the banks and the country were doing their best to steer back to safer shores, but as subsequent events have demonstrated, that "best" was not good enough and they could not make it to safety.

The aftereffect has been that Iceland's swollen banks ruined themselves in one deadly blow. In a matter of a few days, practically the entire banking system was seized by the government, starting with Glitnir, the third largest, following up with Landsbankii, and then the largest Icelandic credit institution: Kaupthing Bank. In the aftermath:

- Trading was suspended on the stock exchange, and
- The krona ceased functioning as a currency outside the country.

Not unexpectedly, inflation and debt payment have been soaring, and trade was crippled in an economy heavily dependent on imports. Britain and the Netherlands have been suing over frozen deposits held by their citizens (more on this later), while the government was trying to arrange more foreign loans to help stave off national bankruptcy.

Experts suggested that Iceland's collapse is the most dramatic washout from the global credit crunch, and a documentation of how far the crisis can demolish an economy. They also speculated about who might be next outside of Europe. Hungary and the Ukraine headed the list, but also some Asian countries which, experts suggested, are much more concerned than Latin America in leveraging terms, and therefore an easier pray to the financial firestorm.

In the second week of October 2008, Iceland's government rushed through emergency powers to nationalize banks and sack their chief executives. The prime minister said he was negotiating a loan from Russia because Iceland's allies had refused to come to its aid. This was not totally true, because some time earlier the Scandinavian countries had contributed to lift Iceland's finances and Sweden continued doing so.

In different parts of the world, Iceland's rapid rise and even faster fall were viewed in ways ranging from the aftereffect of greed and hubris, in which a nation of farmers and fishermen borrowed too much and have been paying the price, to what can happen to anybody when a global sick financial system is towering over a small economy. The fact has been that:

- Iceland's Treasury could not back its banks' obligations, hence the country could default on its sovereign debt, and
- If this happened, it would have a cascading effect on other small, debt-ridden countries.

One of the colorful aspects of the Icelandic crisis was a dispute over British savers and local governments whose deposits were frozen in failed Icelandic banks. The two sides – Britain and Iceland – said they had agreed in principle to an accelerated payout to depositors. Suddenly more than half a dozen countries stated that their residents had deposits stuck in the Icelandic banks, or that their institutions had made loans to them and might be exposed to losses:

- Hundreds of thousands of British consumers had accounts frozen in Icelandic banks that collapsed and were nationalized.
- Also stuck was close to £1 billion ($1.75 billion) held by British regional governments, police and fire departments, and London's transport authority.

British companies, too, got burned. But, according to figures released on 23 October 2008 by the Bank for International Settlements, German banks had $21 billion deposited with Icelandic institutions – more than those from any other country just before Iceland's near bankruptcy:

- As of the end of June 2008 German banks accounted for one-third of all loans made to Icelandic lenders by all foreign institutions, and
- They were also the most exposed to some other fragile European economies, like Spain and Ireland, where they were owed more than half a trillion dollars at the above date.

The parties which lost their wealth in Britain and in Germany did not belong to the same class. The loans to Iceland came from German lenders alone. By contrast, in Britain a variety of institutions from banks to common citizens, local government bodies and charities had parked money – some $4 billion – in Iceland's leveraged economy.

Among the German entities some institutions were more hurt than others. BayernLB, a state-backed bank that was saved from collapse by the German government in mid October 2008, blamed its Icelandic problems partly on a big write-off of loans. (Correspondingly, German banks had $240 billion in outstanding loans in Iceland, more than the British.)

This dual aspect of cross-border deposits and loans to Icelandic banks has been part of the latters' dual strategy to expand abroad to enlarge their intake. Iceland's banks offered savings accounts at well above local market interest rates in a number of countries in Europe, particularly where inflation and interest rates were lower.[31]

(Under EU rules, which Iceland has signed, its government is obliged to guarantee €20,000 ($26,500) of each account. The government said, however, that it might not be able to compensate foreigners. Some of these accounts involved online banking operations, like Landsbanki's IceSave in Britain, which Britain says are subject to Icelandic deposit insurance procedures. That would mean that Iceland would be responsible for about £16,000 per account.)[32]

Nevertheless, there were no signs that the Royal Navy might be steaming toward Iceland, something that indeed happened in the 1950s/1970s timeframe, when the two island nations clashed over fishing rights. But the words exchanged between London and Reykjavik were as belligerent as in the so-called *cod wars*.

By 17 November 2008, however, Iceland said it had reached a preliminary deal with Britain and other European countries on guidelines for dealing with foreign depositors in a collapsed bank. This agreement was likely to clear the way for a stalled International Monetary Fund support package for Reykjavik.

A full resolution to the near-bankruptcy issues – including the one concerning the "IceSave" accounting interesting Britain and Holland – is necessary to clear the way for Iceland to be awarded the $2 billion loan to which it had agreed on 24 October. Securing approval from the IMF is also crucial because it removes the last remaining obstacle holding other countries in the Nordic region and elsewhere from offering up to $4 billion in additional loans to Iceland.

Epilog

In mid-March 2009 (and widely reported) Josef Stiglitz, Professor of Economics at Columbia University and former Chief Economist of the World Bank condemned the lack of a coherent long-term strategy by the Obama Administration in dealing with the severe economic and banking crisis, perhaps turning it into another Great Depression, thus dashing the hopes of all those who had thought that America has finally found the right leadership to end the state of *capitalism without capital*. Four themes suggest that the UK and US governments are going in the wrong direction:

- "Quantitative easing" by Fed and Bank of England,
- Rewarding rather than punishing the wrongdoers,
- Canceling "marking to market", therefore transparency, and
- Institutionalizing the so-called "bad bank," paying for it with years' and years' worth of gross domestic product (GDP).

In the first week of March 2009, the Bank of England crossed the frontier separating a central bank's responsibility for prudent monetary policy from practical irresponsibility, by announcing the start of *quantitative easing* in Britain. Mervyn King joined Ben Bernanke and other central bank leaders in becoming a big spender of public money, lifting inflationary expectations in the vain hope of spurring lending.

Quantitative easing relies on massive quantitative measures (which are typically uncharted territory), whose effect is felt through the quantity rather than the cost of credit. Because of it, the Federal Reserve's balance sheet has soared from below $900 billion to over $3 trillion, and it continues ballooning. It is rather curious that the Bank of England decided to join the party.

Since late 2008 the American central bank took the decision to position itself outside its charter, devoting its time in expanding its already bloated financial assets while no one in two successive administrations (Bush and Obama) complained. The British central bank followed suit. According to *The Economist*, quantitative easing:

- Alarms many people, who fear that the border being crossed may be an inflationary Rubicon, and
- Though the Bank of England will pay for the purchases by crediting the accounts of commercial banks, it is creating money just as surely as if it were printing notes.[1]

In America, "Rambo Fed put the printing presses full speed" read the ticker at *Bloomberg News* on March 20, 2009. That came a day after having thrown $1.15 trillion to the hydra of the big banks' toxic waste: allocating a cool $750 billion to buying mortgage-backed securities of subprime fame, making agency purchases (read: defunct Fannie Mae and Freddie Mac "assets") for another $100 billion, and devoting the rest to the purchase of US Treasury bonds.

"Such actions may have prolonged the crisis by not addressing the fundamental problems at the banks," wrote John Taylor, Professor of Economics at Stanford University, with reference to quantitative easing. "These extraordinary measures have the potential to change permanently the role of the Fed in harmful ways."[2]

In the meantime, those who left the banking system in tatters and brought the economy to its knees are rewarded with massive bonuses and golden parachutes. In the week of March 16, 2009 over $220 million was showered as "2008 bonuses" to executives and traders of AIG's financial products division – the very people who between September 18 (after the company was nationalized) and December 31, 2008 lost $49.5 billion to Goldman Sachs, Société Générale, Barclays, Deutsche Bank and other gamblers in the Grand Casino:

- This has been US taxpayers' money, and
- The banks which "guessed right" in the credit default swaps wheel of fortune, showered their members with bonuses.

Shortly before those aberrations it was revealed that Fred Goodwin, the man who more or less wrecked the venerable Royal Bank of Scotland (RBS) and got fired (or was 'retired'), was awarded nearly $1 million per annum for life to feel comfortable in his retirement over the next decades (he is about 50).[3] All this is not just outrageous; it is revolting:

- Rewarding for hubris and mismanagement is the worst possible policy.
- *"Nothing emboldens sin as much as mercy,"* Shakespeare wrote in *Timon of Athens*. It was true then, and it is true now.

Instead of being brought to court and from there (when found guilty of economic sabotage) to prison, big bank bosses are pampered and featherbedded. No wonder, then, that they are emboldened. On March 21, 2009 America's big bank CEOs had the nerve to attack the government and Congress for wanting to limit and tax their "bonuses" – which, it seems, are for them a God-given right.

The public is not that stupid; it knows what is going on and it is angry. In the week of March 16, 2009 a crowd of shoe-throwing demonstrators gathered outside a conference center in Canada, as George W. Bush spoke to businessmen.[4] This was his first speech since stepping down as US president, but not out of public sight.

One can but hope that Barack Obama is not going to go down the same route. But the rampage continues. In mid-March 2009 JPMorgan Chase congratulated itself for having made a profit of $5 billion with derivatives. Forgotten in that message was the likelihood that behind that one-digit profit may be hiding a high two-digit loss in billions to be paid by the US taxpayers after JPMorgan fails and is "saved" through huge government subsidies – the usual end:

- It would have been rational for US and British governments to close such leakages before refilling capitalism's empty pool with new capital.
- With loopholes left wide open to wheeling and dealing, the Federal Reserve and Bank of England will never end having good money run after bad money.

The reinstitution of prudential regulation is long overdue, but it has been held hostage by lobbyists and conflicts of interest. The booming market for credit default swaps (CDSs) provides evidence that the Casino Society continues unabated, and beggars have become choosers. Good sense advises that:

- The CDS market is immediately and thoroughly regulated.
- *If* for any reason this cannot be done, *then* the CDS market should be closed down. Either way the lottery must stop.

Neither will things be any better with nationalization without tough regulation. After being salvaged through lavish outlays of public money, the UK mortgage company Northern Rock continued with its bad past practises of highly risky loans which brought it to bankruptcy. On March 21, 2009, its auditor said that the wounded bank had again engaged in risky mortgages and other dubious "assets" to the tune of nearly £2 billion.

Another novel and ill-advised policy on both sides of the Atlantic is the fierce opposition by bosses of self-wounded big banks to *marking to market* – an accounting standard which has helped to reveal the horrendous contents of big banks' portfolios. This was meant to show transparency, and it should have been welcome. But fair value accounting, established by US GAAP and IFRS, has received much criticism by the "wrongdoers" who:

- Used their political leverage and their lobbyists to change the accounting rules in their favor.
- Finally succeeded in obliging an independent government body, the FASB, to bend to their *diktat* (more on this later).

As reported by Reuters, on March 11, 2009 in his testimony to congressional hearings, Kevin Bailey, Deputy Director Office of Controller of the Currency (OCC) and regulator of some of the biggest US banks – including JPMorgan Chase, Bank of America and Citigroup – expressed opposition to suspending marking-to-market rules to value bank assets. Bailey also said that as of December 31, 2008 only about 25 percent of OCC-regulated banks' assets were accounted for or subject to fair value measurement. Just think of that:

- Only a quarter of big bank "assets" are subject to marking to market, and
- The toxic waste in the other three-quarters is hidden from view and from public scrutiny.

In America at least, all these bosses of defunct and nearly defunct banks should have been prosecuted on grounds of the Sarbanes–Oxley Act of 2002, which mandates that CEOs and CFO sign, and are personally responsible for, their companies' financial statements. The securitized subprime mortgages that were carried in the banks' books as AAAs and used for tier-1 capital "were worthless even the day they were issued," says John Paulson – a successful hedge fund manager who made a fortune betting on the fact that the unstable edifice of structured products would crumble.[5]

Supposedly to right the balances, on March 23, 2009 Timothy Geithner, the Treasury secretary, revealed his plan for a Public–Private Investment Program (PPIP) aimed at relieving the big banks of their toxic waste. The plan foresees that the US government would loan money under very favorable terms to private investors to induce them to come forward with offers. With $100 billion as first instalment, Geithner put up $1 trillion – which he simply does not have available.

President Obama immediately stated that he was "very confident" this plan would be a success. Lawrence Summers, his economics advisor, pressed the point that "he sees considerable investor interest in the US", but without stating names. Both Summers and Obama are sticking their neck out by betting without any evidence on the success of Geithner's toxic waste plan because:

- The devil is precisely in the details, and
- On April 3, 2009 the financial networks carried the news that "the Fed tries to win over investors afraid of sharks in the TALF aid program" (another "plan" for throwing away US taxpayer dollars).

In an interview he gave on CNN the day PPIP was born, Kenneth S. Rogoff, Professor of Economics at Harvard and former Chief Economist of the International Monetary Fund, said that the US government was taking the lion's share of the risk. Ten days later, some details about PPIP came up but the most basic questions remained unanswered. Is this program going to be:

- Completely voluntary?
- Highly encouraged by the Treasury?
- Mandated to all US banks, no matter the hole it opens to their balance sheet?

In addition, will regulators look at the pricing for loans purchased through PPIP as their clearing level? If such loan sales create a capital hemorrhage to the banks, will the Treasury provide them with additional capital? What are going to be the conditions? The limits? How will favoritism be kept at bay?

Closely associated with these questions is the fact that PPIP is a "non-recourse" give-away plan and, if it fails to redress the banks' deplorable situation, its consequences to the USA and to the global economy will be devastating. Paul Krugman, a Nobel Prize winner economist, Professor at Princeton and *New York Times* columnist, said the non-recourse government loans would allow the private partners to:

- Make large profits if the bets went well, and
- Suffer only limited losses if the bets soured.[6]

In Rogoff's opinion Geithner's March 23, 2009 "plan" is forestalling the inevitable: namely, the nationalization of the big deeply wounded banks. It is simply a complicated diversion, and the government wants it to be complicated so that the taxpayer does not understand the huge amount of money it will cost. Not stated during that interview, but also very important, is that Geithner's "plan" does not differentiate between:

- Those banks that could be saved, and
- Those that have gone beyond repair.

Neither is the government unanimous on the idea that throwing public money at every bank is the best approach. On the day of the plan's announcement, Sheila Bair, FDIC's chairwoman, stated that some banks were already "beyond help of US assistance". Implicit in this statement is the notion that the $1 trillion to be given to the cleaners of the banks' toxic waste may slip down the drain.

Will this $1 trillion, which is bypassing Congress via FDIC, be enough? Ken Rogoff thinks the amount of money that will be necessary to redress the US big banks' wounded balance sheet is not $1 but $8 trillion over three years. That is what it will probably take to clean the mess – provided this proves to be doable – and a quarter of that money may well be the cost of the just announced unsure first phase.

It needs no explaining that the provision of cheap nonrecourse funding to private parties makes some of them salivate. Carlyle, BlackRock and Pimco, among others, are interested in sharing the $1 trillion gift. But banks will be hurt. Richard Bernstein, one of the best analysts on Wall Street, advised investors to take advantage of the banks' equities rally and sell the banks.

Can the US afford to spend this extra $8 trillion Rogoff has projected as being the most likely bill? The answer is far from being positive. According to some estimates, prior to leaving office, the Bush Administration had already committed some $8.5 trillion of public money, to which is added the ballooning of the Fed's balance sheet to over $2 trillion under Dubya's watch.

To this oversized account the Fed still added another $1.15 trillion mid-March 2009 under Obama, while his Administration got nearly $800 for stimulus to the economy – and made noises about needing another $700 billion for TARP, the toxic assets relief. Now with the $8 trillion added it makes a total in excess of $20 trillion, or over 146 percent of US GDP. Add previous public debt to it, and you get a national debt projection in the range of 200 percent to 210 percent of GDP – well beyond Japan's 170 percent which brought the former No. 2 economic powerhouse of the world to its knees.

Too much money has been blown into the wind in a matter of a few years, and this cash bred a great many bad habits, as attested by the spending plans announced by the 23 chiefs of state who participated in the G-20 great love affair (summit) held in London on April 2, 2009. Rather than being a "historic meeting" that second G-20 summit has been distinguished by concentrating on the icing of the cake. Ironically, it has also confirmed the projection made by its critics that nothing could be expected from it. There is always a big gap between:

- What is said in a communiqué, and
- What is being done afterwards.

The G-20 decided to strengthen bank regulation but what has happened that same day has been a disaster for bank regulation in the United States, in the world, and in terms of accounting discipline at large. No matter what the G-20 "decided" under pressure by politicians and the big banks on April 2, 2009 the American accounting standards setters:

- Abandoned the principle of marking to market the banks' toxic waste, and
- Replaced it by marking to myth, leaving it up to the bank management to say what the value of their wounded "assets" are.

This is ridiculous and it looks like a huge hypocrisy when contrasted to the G-20 "decision" to enforce regulation. The change was demanded by members of Congress and by trade groups with the connivance of the Obama Administration, but it has been bitterly denounced by investors and by two former chairmen of the Securities and Exchange Commission.[7] There is no better example of double talk, but an Orwellian euphemism will not change the facts.

Swamping transparency has been a black day for bank regulation, and the deception continues. In terms of tax havens and money-laundering countries, the G-20 divided the world into three groups: white, gray and black. In the black are Uruguay and the Philippines; and in the grey Switzerland, Austria, Belgium, Luxembourg and others – the lamb offered to the sacrificial altar of double talk.

The Jersey Islands and Isle of Man, Britain's famous tax havens, as well as Delaware, New Jersey, Wyoming, Nevada and the US Virgin Islands – which rival familiar offshore financial centers[8] – find themselves in the white list. The irony is that the United States has no strong laws against whitewashing of dirty money, while by some accounts the toughest anti-laundering laws are in Switzerland, which is in the G-20's grey list.

As for the regulation of hedge funds and the urgently needed global bank supervisor, the message is uncertain at best. Far from being the forerunner of a new class of banking regulation, the G-20 communiqué has been characterized by truth-dodging and great uncertainty. Will there be a supranational regulatory agency? An advisory outfit? Or just more handshaking while the rivalries persist?

While what needed to be done has not been done, big spending flourished – except that the G-20 forgot to say who will pay the bill. Bankrupt America, bankrupt Britain or some other bankrupts? "The foreign liabilities of British banks are 400 percent Britain's GDP. All by itself, the Royal Bank of Scotland has liabilities more than the annual GDP," said Lord Lamont[9] in an interview he gave to *Sky News* on March 30, 2009, two days prior to the G-20.

Lamont pointed out that the Labor government is now standing behind all British banks, with ominous results for the taxpayer. Hence the question: Is Gordon Brown also going to underwrite the debts of less developed countries? Or is the American government going to do so, over and above the poorly planned rescue of the US financial industry: stimuli, tax cuts and other goodies of the State Supermarket.[10]

"I don't see that kind of optimism as justified," said Josef Stiglitz in an interview which he gave right after the G-20 communiqué. Stiglitz added that for a number of years the American economy was living beyond its means: debt, debt and debt – and that model is broken.

It needs no explaining that pseudo-summits and hypocrisies – like the April 2, 2009 marking-to-market incident – can accelerate the descent to the abyss and lead to deep global depression, because confidence is totally lost. Nobody is going to be fooled by political promises and communiqués empty of any substance. *Trust* and *confidence* is what it's all about in getting the economies moving again.

Outraged at the excesses that led to the current economic and financial crisis, the market is deeply cynical about the favoritism, wild spending, bailouts, interventions, and indulgencies that form the different governments responses. "Wisdom cannot be bought," says Edith Hamilton. "It is the reward for righteousness."[11] The prerequisite for righteousness is that people are directly accountable for whatever they do, not only in front of God but also in front of the Court on the High Street.

Notes

Preface

1. The focal point of this book.
2. Iceland has done so. Argentina, Ecuador and possibly the Ukraine and Hungary head the list.
3. *Le Monde*, 18 October 2008.
4. Also by being taken to the cleaners by banks and other companies, like GMAC, which have presented no plan for redressing themselves and who have failed to fix their business model until they were on the verge of disaster.

1. The Destruction of the American Dream

1. From an exchange of correspondence.
2. *The Economist*, 15 March 2008
3. Hernando de Soto, *The Mystery of Capital*, Bantham Press/Transworld, London, 2000.
4. The low living standard I saw in 1969 had worsened in 1988, in my second visit to the then Soviet Union. By contrast, in my third visit to Moscow and St Petersburg in 2008 the standard of living had significantly improved – but the abyss between rich and poor had also increased.
5. Curzio Malaparte, *Technique du Coup d'Etat*, Bernard Grasset, Paris, 1931.
6. Golda Meir, *My Life*, G.P. Putnam's Sons, New York, 1975.
7. On the front page, 18-24 October 2008 *The Economist* printed in golden block letters: "Capitalism At Bay". Right? Wrong. Capitalism is still on the high seas and preparing its next debacle.
8. Recently characterized by Dr Alan Greenspan as "the crisis of the century" (without adding that he is its father).
9. Bernard M. Baruch, *Baruch, My Own Story*, Buccaneer Books, Cutchoque, New York, 1957
10. Gross domestic product (GDP) = Consumer spending + Investments by companies + Government expenditures + Exports – Imports.
11. D.N. Chorafas, *The Management of Bond Investments and Trading of Debt*, Butterworth-Heinemann, London, 2005.
12. William Greider, *Secrets of the Temple*, Touchstone/Simon & Schuster, New York, 1987.
13. At the end of 2007, of the $9.7 trillion in total federal government debt outstanding – which in October 2008 was increased to $11.3 trillion because of more deficit financing and the $700 billion bailout plan – $5.1 billion was sold to the public in the form of Treasury bonds and Treasury bills, with about $2.4 trillion of the latter sum owned by foreigners. "Foreign interests have more control over the US economy than Americans," said David Walker, then US Comptroller General (*Executive Intelligence Research*, 25 April 2008).
14. Fannie Mae stands for Federal National Mortgage Association and Freddie Mac for Federal Home Loan Mortgage Corporation. After falling on hard times because of

the meltdown of the US mortgage market and of mismanagement, Fannie Mae and Freddie Mac were taken over by the government on 5 September 2008, and their CEOs were fired.

15. Jeffrey H. Birnbaum, *The Lobbyists*, Times Books, New York, 1992.
16. The word *panic* is derived from Pan, the ancient Greek god who put fear into the heart of humans and caused them to flee.
17. James Grant, *Money of the Mind*, Farrar Straus Giroux, New York, 1992.
18. An end of August 2008 estimate sure to rise well beyond $1 trillion.
19. One of the three largest French credit institutions.
20. Of course the wrong type of trust; not Morgan's.
21. *International Herald Tribune*, 24 May 2008
22. *Executive Intelligence Review*, 25 January 2008
23. *Bank for International Settlements, 78th Annual Report*, Basel, 30 June 2008.
24. Bernard M. Baruch, *Baruch. My Own Story*, Buccaneer Books, Cutchoque, NY, 1957.
25. Big money at the time. A recent example is that at the end of 2007 Goldman Sachs had $1 trillion in assets but only $43 billion in equity.
26. Charles Partee chaired the Fed's Board of Governors' committee on bank supervision.
27. William Greider, *Secrets of the Temple*, Touchstone/Simon & Schuster, New York, 1987.
28. See also in Chapter 9 the *mea culpa* by the same Double Bubble Greenspan (Bubble one: the dotcoms; bubble two: the self-destruction of the banking industry.)
29. "Soros, the Man Who Cries Wolf, Now Is Warning of a Superbubble", by Greg IP, 21 June, 2008
30. Moody's, the rating agency, says that market-implied ratings, like those provided by CDS spreads, tally loosely with credit ratings in roughly 80 percent of all cases. The majority of market participants, however, believe the contrary.
31. By Anil Kashyap and Raghuram Rajan (a former economist of the IMF), of University of Chicago, and Jeremy Stein of Harvard University. Both are great universities. It is not clear to me, however, whether somebody read and cleared that paper for completeness and documentation before it was presented.
32. In October 2008, the Dutch government recapitalized ING, a major banking and insurance company, and Aegon, a global leading Dutch insurer.
33. The hemorrhage of MBIA and Ambac simply does not stop. In the third quarter of 2008 their net losses were, respectively, $870 million and $2.3 trillion.
34. It is indeed a sign of our times that people try to make a career, and gain a Nobel prize if possible, by coming up with just anything without at least studying its further-out consequences. Modigliani and Merton have done so with their hypothesis that it is better to hold debt than equity: Equity gets taxed, debt is not. But what this essentially means is gaming the system by exploiting the tax laws. Debt is no silver bullet, and excessive debt is one of the worst excesses.
35. *The Economist*, 30 August 2008.
36. Wriston was also wrong when he said that countries don't go bankrupt. As Argentina and others have demonstrated, they do.
37. On 5 September 2008 the two huge government-sponsored agencies were taken over by the Treasury to avoid collapse.
38. Of this $58 billion is exposed to subprime securities which have already generated large marking-to-market losses (*The Economist*, 20 September 2008).
39. Also on 10 November 2008 Fannie Mae announced that it had lost an additional $22.5 billion.

40. Which is the philosophy of the cancer cell.
41. Another idea which floated during the 2008 Jackson Hole conference is that of a scheme applied by the Bank of Spain: Commercial banks must hold a higher capital reserve during good times to have an extra buffer in bad times. This has merits, but accounting standards and different national regulations must change to accommodate it. Foreign banks in Spain say that in accounting terms this is a nightmare.
42. This is a step the Swiss regulators took on 1 September 2008.
43. A group of national authorities established by BIS in 1999 to strengthen financial market supervision after the Asian and Russian crises of 1997–1998.
44. Dominique Venner, *Gettysburg*, Editions du Rocher, Paris 1995.
45. This model is not only American, having been adopted by Britain, the euroland, Japan, Australia, and Canada well as being in the process of becoming the model characterizing the major developing economies.
46. An example is the Canadian National Railway project for freight traffic in Chicago.
47. Which stood at €1.25 trillion ($1.88 trillion) at the end of August 2008
48. See note 17 in Chapter 9 below.
49. According to certain economists integrating Fannie Mae's and Freddie Mac's huge liabilities into the US government's balance sheet would endanger the dollar.
50. $11.3 trillion of an estimated $14 trillion GDP in 2008.
51. It can also be called Japan, Inc. style because the Japanese government was the first, among major nations, to hit a public deficit of over 150 percent in its fruitless efforts of the 1990s to jump-start the economy.
52. Government Accountability Office (GAO); an arm of the US Congress.
53. It is indeed regrettable that the 15 November 2008 Washington conference paid no attention to the colossal national debt, though correctly it did attack leverage (Chapter 9).
54. To get Fannie Mae, Freddie Mac, AIG and others nationalized means that they were in such a bad state that nobody wanted to buy them.
55. At 900 basis points for Morgan Stanley, the CDS spread roughly corresponded to a default probability of 13 percent.
56. Even that is only half the $53 trillion of total national debt.
57. Peter S. Goodman, *Is America Too Big to Fail ?* The New York Times, 20 July 2008.
58. Translated from the French text, *Le Monde*, 8 September 2008.
59. Carlo Ponzi of Boston is thought to have been the inventor of pyramiding – paying extravagant dividends to get more deposits and financing these dividends with the new investors' capital till the pyramid collapsed.
60. More than 95 percent of OTC trades have no commercial justification. Banks sell "products" to one another. It is as if GM sold 95 percent of its autos to Ford, and Ford returned the compliment.
61. Louis Levy, *Jean Jaurès*, Calmann-Lévy, Paris, 1946.
62. Golda Meir, *My Life*, G.P. Putnam's Sons, New York, 1975.
63. Still, their most recent bosses were simply replaced with golden parachutes included. Neither they nor those who preceded them – and were responsible for the mess – have been brought to justice.
64. In fact, all of them are responsible but none paid for his or her mistakes.
65. *EIR*, 18 July 2008.
66. Idem.
67. Sterling Seagrave, *The Song Dynasty*, Corgi Books, London, 1996.

2. Macroeconomic Challenges

1. Associated Press "World Leaders at Economic Summit Vow to Cooperate", *New York Times*, 16 November 2008.
2. Statement from G20 Summit.
3. Emphasis added.
4. This text as well as the early part of section 5 reflects the highlights of the European Central Bank's *Financial Stability Review*, December 2004, ECB, Frankfurt.
5. Merrill Lynch, *Economic Commentary*, 11 September 2008.
6. Which, however, is contested by other economists.
7. *Financial Times*, 15 September 2008.
8. Though Citigroup also absorbed $42 billion in Wachovia's liabilities, with a $12 billion grant from the US government.
9. Carmen and Vincent Reinhart, *Capital Flow Bonanzas: An Encompassing View of the Past and Present*, Working Paper 14321, National Bureau of Economic Research, Cambridge MA, 2008.
10. *Financial Times*, 17 September 2008.
11. Corruption and nepotism being among the worst.
12. Dr Ben Bernanke said in 2005 that the US had never had a decline in housing prices on a nationwide basis; but it turned out that it got one under his chairmanship of the Fed.
13. Merrill Lynch, *Global Economics; 124 Banking Crises*, 25 September 2008.

3. Money Supply and Inflation

1. Companies after all are made of people.
2. The importance of monetary policy has been underlined by the 15 November 2008 Washington economic conference. Unfortunately the reference was added "as deemed appropriate to domestic conditions" – which means there will be no international coordination in globalized financial markets.
3. Some consider NGDP as a crude measure of money available to be invested in financial assets. This is not a generally accepted definition.
4. William Greider, *Secrets of the Temple*, Touchstone/Simon & Schuster, New York, 1987.
5. However, when this lavish liquidity finds its way to the market it will create a wave of inflation.
6. ECB, *Monthly Bulletin*, August 2008
7. For instance, in July 2008 in America it reached 5.6 percent, a level which is uncomfortably high. Goldman Sachs reckons that in the third quarter of 2009 the US inflation rate will turn negative (*The Economist*, 15 November 2008).
8. ECB, *Monthly Bulletin*, September 2008.
9. When in 2007 house prices tanked in the US several developers suggested that the Fed should account for housing *deflation*. But they were quick to add that a housing inflation should not be included in the index – a cherrypicking approach which is evidently nonsense.
10. *The Economist*, 5 July 2008
11. *The Economist*, 14 June 2008
12. *The Economist*, 1 November 2008
13. Merrill Lynch, *Metals Strategist*, 13 October 2008.

14. Thereby putting a bottom to the crumbling housing market. Instead the banks will use manna from heaven to pay extraordinary 2008 bonuses to their bosses and traders. A recent US poll documents that the American public is massively against this practice.
15. *The Economist*, 22 March 2008.
16. Central banks have to take unpopular measures to combat inflation. At the end of 1950 Bank Deutscher Länder (predecessor of the Bundesbank) increased interest rates at a time of 11 percent unemployment to combat the inflationary surge created by the Korean war.
17. A significant role can be played by scenario analysis in elaborating the likely but uncertain phases in the evolution of a process or project, as well as in clarifying ideas.
18. Hence the surprise of many Bank of England watchers that on 6 November the Old Lady cut interest rates by 250 basis points, after having already reduced them by 50 bp a fortnight earlier.
19. On 6 November 2008 it was announced that California had money to fulfill its obligations only till February 2009.
20. Merrill Lynch, *Interest Rate Committee Forecast*, 18 April 2008.
21. Brazil, Mexico, and South Korea in 2008 have positive interest rates. China's real lending rate is minus 1 percent; but the US had a negative interest rate of over 5 percent (considering headline inflation) and euroland's interest rate is barely breaking even.

4. The Cost of Money

1. The other levy in the hands of the central bank is minimum reserve ratios on banks' deposits. *If* the monetary authority tightens them, it automatically reduces the supply of credit in the economy; and vice versa. Reserve requirements are not a subject of this book.
2. In 1968 when inflation took off in the US (to be amplified in the 1970s by the oil shocks), the Federal funds rate was about 5 percent; a 4 percent inflation left the real interest rate at practically zero. In 2002 to 2005 the real interest rate was negative, and again in early 2008 in America the Federal funds rate was minus 4 percent as headline inflation increased to about 5 percent.
3. Ironically, the Greek word "eonia" means forever, from eon or aion, which stands for 100 years; an epoch. But as an interest rate acronym it stands for overnight.
4. But they still maintain authority on reserve requirements, which however they are reluctant to use.
5. It is interesting to note that from August 2007 to August 2008 in the global market countries increased the interest rate of their currency: Brazil by 150 basis points (1.5 percent); India and Norway by 125 bp; Australia and Sweden by 100 bp; Indonesia by 75 bp; China by 50 bp. To the contrary, Canada and Turkey joined the US in cutting interest rates by 150 bp and 75 bp respectively.
6. Like the Swiss franc and quite recently the US dollar.
7. Which under current conditions is unrealistic because no hard currency (or government behind it) is able to carry the weight of the global economy.
8. Though the dollar recovered in mid to late September 2008 because of the weakness of the euro. See also sections 7 and 8.
9. Critics say that, rather, they were too big to be saved.
10. *The Economist*, 9 August 2008.

11. *Financial Times*, 17 September 2008.
12. See also the scam of Libor's manipulation, in Chapter 8.
13. High short-term rates could make adjustable and interest-only mortgages onerous whether or not long-term rates move substantially.
14. William Greider, *Secrets of the Temple*, Touchstone/Simon & Schuster, New York, 1987.
15. A swaption is an option on forward swap rates. For a given swap rate, it can be seen as option on a portfolio of forward Libor rates, in the interval spanned by the maturity of the swaption plus the swap's life.
16. In the first week of November 2008, the Group of Seven issued an emergency statement on the yen, warning that "excessive volatility" in currency markets threatens the global economy.
17. *The Economist*, 8 November 2008.
18. Some analysts predicted a dollar/euro exchange rate at 1.10 by mid 2009. We shall see.
19. Merrill Lynch, *US Strategy and Research Special Report*, 8 September 2008.
20. Crédit Suisse, *Research Monthly*, 13 October 2008.
21. And current account deficits widened.
22. Merrill Lynch, *The RIC Report*, 9 September 2008.

5. Leverage Can Be Highly Counterproductive

1. Emphasis added.
2. William H. Husband and James C. Dockery, *Modern Corporate Finance*, R.D. Irving, Homewood, IL, 1957.
3. *Financial Times*, 17 September 2008.
4. By the Federal Reserve, European Central Bank, Bank of England and other central banks each cutting interest rates by 50 bp.
5. In the end Mitsubishi UFJ did put $9 billion into Morgan Stanley for a 21 percent stake, but under improved terms. On 13 October 2008 the US Treasury topped that investment with $10 billion of taxpayer money (Chapter 10).
6. Merrill Lynch, *Monthly Chart Presentation*, 9 October 2008.
7. A 20-year high in volatility was reached on 10 October 2008.
8. D.N. Chorafas, *Economic Capital Allocation with Basle II. Cost and Benefit Analysis*, Butterworth-Heinemann, London and Boston, 2004.
9. More on Basel I and Basel II, particularly Pillars 1, 2, and 3, in Chapter 9.
10. D.N. Chorafas, *The 1996 Market Risk Amendment. Understanding the Marking-to-Model and Value-at-Risk*, McGraw-Hill, Burr Ridge, IL, 1998.
11. James Grant, *Money of the Mind*, Farrar Straus Giroux, New York, 1992.
12. D.N. Chorafas, *Alternative Investments and the Mismanagement of Risk*, Palgrave Macmillan, London, 2003.
13. D.N. Chorafas, *Wealth Management: Private Banking, Investment Decisions and Structured Financial Products*, Butterworth-Heinemann, London and Boston, 2005.
14. *Wall Street Journal*, 13 October 2008.
15. Let me give you Jay Leno's example on how good governments are in arithmetic: "According to a new study, 78 percent of Washington D.C. eighth graders can't do basic math. But President Bush said; 'Let's focus on the positive. Let's look at the 48 percent who can.'"
16. FAS 140 would have forced banks to take previous securitizations back into their books – to a level estimated at $5 billion.
17. *The Economist*, 4 September 2008.

18. Under MMIFF five special purpose vehicles managed by JPMorgan Chase will reportedly buy up to $600 billion in short-term financial paper in dollars denominated issued by highly rated institutions. The curious thing is that, for the time being, the Fed will loan up to $540 billion of that total to the vehicles.
19. Three weeks later, on 18 September, they fell another 23 percent.
20. $A stands for Australian dollar.
21. Hence the Fed's salvage plan referred to in section 5.
22. K. Düllmann, J. Küll, and M. Kunish, *Estimating Asset Correlations from Stock Prices or Default Rates – Which Method is Superior?*, Discussion Paper No. 04/2008, Deutsche Bundesbank, Frankfurt.
23. Losses to be incurred by mortgage lenders after forced sale of underlying housing contract collateral.
24. A *credit default swap* (CDS) is a bilateral financial contract in which the "protection buyer" pays a periodic fee in return for a "contingent payment" by the "protection seller" following a "credit event" of a reference entity – such as a bank or any other company. Should such credit event occur, the settlement can take place in either of two modes: *Physical*, with the protection buyer delivering particular obligation(s) issued by the reference entity; *Cash*, where the protection buyer receives from the protection seller an amount equal to the difference between the market value of defaulted obligation(s) and their par value.
25. Needless to add, nothing has been done since then.
26. For the time being only in the United States, probably before the end of December 2008.
27. *The Economist*, 3 May 2008.
28. The long-term historical default rate average is approximately 5 percent, but it has breached the 10 percent threshold in previous cycles.
29. *The Economist*, 10 October 2008.
30. Companies with assets of over $100 million.
31. *The Economist*, March 21, 2009.

6. Asset Allocation, Credit Regulation, and Banking Supervision

1. "Old coots" in American slang.
2. Becoming by the same token "too big to fail."
3. *The Economist*, 27 September 2008.
4. According to the Bank of England.
5. The ECB, too, was born with political independence written into its constitution; this is however a different case because the euro is a currency without a single country and jurisdiction behind it.
6. Senator Carter Glass shepherded the Federal Reserve Act through Congress in 1913.
7. The last of the Fed's Fannie Mae bonds matured in 2003.
8. Which the Fed presently does, anyway.
9. Even in today's America the suspicion between Wall Street and Main Street continues being strong.
10. Creditworthiness was established and regulated by law in in about 1700 BC by the Code of Hammurabi, written by the great Babylonian emperor. It is however possible that concerns with credit risk date much earlier.
11. The same principles apply to payment and settlement systems used for providing operational support to financial services.
12. In Italian, this word has two meanings: a gambling place and a whorehouse.

13. As an example of financial conglomerates which would fall under neither of former categories of classification, because they extend their activities across them, Kaufman gave Citigroup.
14. BIS, *75th Annual Report.*
15. *The Economist,* 5 July 2008.
16. Established by the Roosevelt Administration in 1934.
17. On 26 May 2008.
18. *The Economist,* 11 October 2008.
19. BIS, *78th Annual Report* (2007/2008).
20. Additionally, one of the conditions of the British government's £50 billion ($80 billion) bank recapitalization scheme is that bankers moderate their pay and bonuses. The Financial Services Authority has warned CEOs that it would look at pay deals that reward short-term profit-seeking.
21. To provide more clarity, the Depository Trust & Clearing Corporation, which runs the central registry for swaps, has just begun publishing weekly data on the largest deals – but these are not broken down by counterparty, as should have been the case.

7. Household Debt and the Housing Market's Debacle

1. Mortgages and car loans are considered to be secured debt. Among them they represented 21 percent of liabilities of US families who filed for bankruptcy in 2007. Another 44 percent was in unsecured debt like credit cards, medical bills, and utility bills. (T.S. Bernard and J. Anderson "Downturn Drags More Consumers Into Bankruptcy", *New York Times,* 16 November 2008. The article does not specify the nature of the other 35 percent.)
2. James Grant, *Money of the Mind,* Farrar Straus Giroux, New York, 1992.
3. When it does not, things turn ugly. People are overburdened and as Dr Martin Feldstein said in an interview he gave to Bloomberg Financial Services on 12 November 2008, household debt has become a big drag on consumer spending.
4. Merrill Lynch, *The White Paper,* Fall 2007.
5. In terms of residential real estate, this goes a long way. In the US alone, $11 trillion are tied up in mortgages, of which $4 trillion are in the banks' books.
6. This is by no means the first appearance of negative equity. Among other cases, it happened fairly frequently in Britain in the 1960s and 1970s with the Labour governments.
7. Typically, adjustable rate mortgages are tied to short-term market interest rates like 6 months Libor, constant Maturity Treasury Index, and Costs of Funds Index.
8. There are no rules regarding percentages of debt payment out of current income, as each case is specific, personalized, and different from others. Thinking aloud, I consider 0 percent to be ideal, 5 percent affordable, and 10 percent an exception absolute maximum.
9. Which led to the banks tightening credit standards for loans. In the week of 15 October 2008 the US Mortgage Applications Index tumbled 16.6 percent on tight lending.
10. Current US law provides for two types of personal bankruptcy protection. With Chapter 13, those who file agree to repay a portion of their debt over the next 3 years, but filers can keep some of their assets like their house. With Chapter 7 debts are forgiven, but assets are liquidated and filers must pass a means test.

11. Jan Hatzius, chief US economist of Goldman Sachs, had estimated in February 2008 that banks and other financial institutions would suffer about $200 billion in real estate losses and respond by cutting their lending by $2 trillion, or about 5 percent of total lending. This looked like a big number, but it was surpassed by the facts.
12. *USA Today*, 18 June 2008.
13. Shortly after a real estate earthquake in the US, and the collapse of Savings and Loans (S&Ls, thrifts, building societies).
14. This is on average – there are some people who are making millions and some even billions.
15. With very minor exceptions in terms of geography.
16. *The Economist*, 2 August 2008.
17. The Economist, *The World in 2008*.
18. Confronted with a free fall in prices, Spanish banks finally started tightening conditions on mortgages; they had no other option as the number of non-performing loans rose, but in the aftermath house sales have been plunging further.
19. *EIR*, 25 July 2008.
20. *The Economist*, 6 October 2007.
21. As of 17 February 2009, coast to coast in the US house prices had dropped by over 20 percent on average, and in come states like California and Nevada by 40 percent. Economists think that nationwide a 40 percent drop is not unlikely.
22. Merrill Lynch, *Interest Rate Committee Forecast*, 18 April 2008.
23. As well as of Britain, Ireland, and Spain.
24. The seriousness of the negative equity problem is dramatized by the fact that, according to a recent US study, writing off negative equity could cost as much as $600 billion (*The Economist*, 25 October 2008).
25. Interest-only mortgage products were originally designed for wealthier households, which tended to use them as a cash management tool, investing the cash freed up during this period at higher return.
26. *EIR*, 5 May 2006.
27. Still another contributor down the same road has been the fact that Britain is considered to have reliable property data, collated and made available by the Investment Property Databank (IPD). IPD is an independent research company whose index tracks the return on property.
28. For instance, lenders have privileged information on the finances of borrowers; and companies that service mortgages have leeway in deciding when a borrower will default.
29. The more classical way of doing this has been by remortgaging or selling part of their homes, but to the opinion of some experts it would not have taken long before derivative financial instruments offered to home owners a way to amplify and leverage this process.

8. *Mea Culpa* and the Abuse of the Virtual Economy's Freedoms

1. Personal bankruptcy filings in the US jumped 8 percent in October from September 2008; and a wholesome 34 percent year-on-year from October 2007.
2. The aftermath has been that self-discipline fainted, the shareholders lost a fortune and in most big banks the only visible equity is taxpayers' money.
3. But he forgot to say that he took no corrective measures after having made that discovery.

4. *International Herald Tribune*, 24 October 2008.
5. In an interview Soros gave to Greg Ip, *Wall Street Journal*, 21 June 2008.
6. Some people say that lobbying epitomizes democracy. That's utterly wrong. Lobbying is a closed society of special interests, buying and selling politicians. Any closed society is antidemocratic. The proof that lobbying has become a cancer is that the European Union now features more than 5,000 lobbyists gravitating around Brussels, promoting special interests and making a good living.
7. Janet Gleeson, *The Moneymaker*, Bantam Books, London, 1999.
8. In November 2008 Saint Gobain, the big conglomerate established by Colbert, was fined by the European Union three-quarters of a billion euros for price fixing.
9. Which, as already noted, in November 2008 represented the astronomical amount of nearly $400 trillion.
10. Only "responsible tax policy"?
11. Jeffrey H. Birnbaum, *The Lobbyists*, Times Books, New York, 1992.
12. Naked short-selling occurs when a trader or investor sell equities that he neither possesses nor is able to borrow from somebody else.
13. In a 12 November 2008 interview by Bloomberg Financial Services.
14. Hernando de Soto, *The Mystery of Capital*, Bantam Press/Transworld, London, 2000.
15. *New York Times*, 19 October 2008.
16. According to the bank's official correction of the original announcement of €600 million in losses.
17. "Je prends mes indemnités ...," which amounted to 3 years of full salary (*Canard Enchaîné*, 22 October 2008).
18. The American grand jury is not a criminal jury. It only instructs and investigates. Its functions roughly correspond to those of the French *juge d'instruction*.
19. *The Economist*, 15 September 2007.
20. James H. Simons and George Soros each earned almost $3 billion in 2007.
21. Jenny Anderson, "Wall Street Winners Get Billion-Dollar Paydays," *New York Times*, 16 April 2008.
22. Over and above that, a mid November 2008 controversy focuses on the allocation of $2 trillion by the Fed characterized by total lack of transparency (Chapter 9).
23. Notice that 3 percent is well below the Basel I capital requirements which stood at 8 percent of which half, hence 4 percent, had to be equity capital.
24. D.N. Chorafas, *IT Auditing and Sarbanes-Oxley Compliance*, Auerbach/CRC, New York, 2009.
25. These 16 banks come from 7 countries, including Britain, the United States, Switzerland, and Germany; and they are asked by BBA at which rate each could borrow a "reasonable amount." Based on their response, BBA eliminates the 4 highest and lowest rates and averages the remaining ones to determine various Libor rates ranging from a day to a year in 10 different currencies.
26. *International Herald Tribune*, 24 May 2008.
27. *EIR*, 25 April 2008.
28. PCAOB is an independent panel formed under Sarbanes–Oxley. Its new guidelines aimed to reduce auditor testing by encouraging certified accountants to rely on work companies have already done – which reduces the sense of an independent audit.
29. With the exception, of course, of *creative accounting*, which is a cheat and illegal.
30. *The Economist*, 20 September 2008.
31. Instituted in 1668, the Riksbank was the first ever central bank in the world.

9. The G-20 Conference, Central Banks, and Garbage Collection

1. "Garbage collection" has been for three decades a technical term in artificial intelligence. In the last couple of years it has transformed itself into a technical term connected to lack of intelligence in banking – and lack of prudence.
2. The group of nations originally called G-20 had 23 members, with plenty of small fry in it. In alphabetic order: Argentina, Bolivia, Brazil, Chile, China, Cuba, Ecuador, Egypt, Guatemala, India, Indonesia, Mexico, Nigeria, Pakistan, Paraguay, Peru, Philippines, South Africa, Tanzania, Thailand, Uruguay, Venezuela, Zimbabwe. Only some of these participated to the 15 November 2008 Washington meeting plus the G-8 and a few others like Saudi Arabia – to a total of 21 countries and 4 international organizations.
3. That would make 13, like Jesus and the apostles in the famous supper.
4. Even if neither Roosevelt nor Churchill were present at Bretton Woods, because of other commitments, everybody knew that White and Keynes spoke for them.
5. By contrast, the supposed BWII was prepared by a mixture of industrial and emerging countries which put together an agenda full of promises and some headlines, in a few frenetic weeks.
6. Provided that absolutely irrelevant references to "the urgency of Doha" and some other issues are left out.
7. *The Economist*, 15 November 2008.
8. D.N. Chorafas, *Modelling the Survival of Financial and Industrial Enterprises. Advantages, Challenges, and Problems with the Internal Ratings-Based (IRB) Method*, Palgrave Macmillan, London, 2002.
9. As has happened with the weak VAR model.
10. Other positives have been outlined in the preceding chapters.
11. The same is true about the inclusion of control over money laundering and confrontation of the terrorist threat. Contrary to the Doha round, these are important goals but they are not crucial objectives of *this* Washington conference.
12. *The Economist*, 15 November 2008.
13. Also curious is the imprecation that "the Financial Stability Forum" (FSF) "must expand urgently." Maybe its current G-7 membership is too narrow, but also the more it "expands," the more ineffectual it will become.
14. Financial Times, February 25, 2009
15. To look ahead, however, Obama has to clean house getting out of the way the remnants of George W. Bush's Administration. Watching the statements (and actions) by these remnants gives the feeling that they have been left behind as rearguard to destroy the Obama Administration.
16. D.N. Chorafas, *Economic Capital Allocation with Basle II. Cost and Benefit Analysis*, Butterworth-Heinemann, London and Boston, 2004.
17. This is written in terms of solvency. Liquidity issues are discussed in the next section.
18. Which, as the economist Nouriel Roubini has remarked, smacks of "socialism for the rich."
19. Macquarie, an Australian investment bank, has been able to secure an ECB loan through a euroland subsidiary against a security backed by Australian car loans.
20. Crédit Suisse, *Global Research Daily, Fixed Income*, 12 November 2008.
21. *The Economist*, 14 June 2008.

22. The central bank however intended to change its money market rules.
23. Also that HBOS and Lloyds will have to downsize the terms of their merger to qualify for capital injections.
24. For US statistics see Chapter 10.
25. *The Economist*, 18 October 2008.
26. They were "smaller" in the sense there was some rationale for them: a severe credit crunch.
27. The Fed will also increase its existing temporary reciprocal currency arrangements (swap lines) with the European Central Bank (ECB) and the Swiss National Bank (SNB), providing up to $30 billion to the ECB and $6 billion to the SNB.
28. Bloomberg.com, 10 November 2008.
29. Originally posted by k4kyv.

10. Trillions of Dollars, Euros, and Pounds Thrown at the Problem

1. This statement characterizes the attitude of politicians and their associates; but there surely is as well a reciprocal attitude on the part of the voters.
2. By West German Chancellor Helmut Schmidt and French President Valéry Giscard d'Estaing. The same reference is valid for the European Monetary System. The latter took effect in 1979.
3. On 18 November 2008 it was stated that America's budget deficit in 2008 stands at $455 billion, and in 2009 it will be at or above $482 billion.
4. The Troubled Assets Relief Act (TARA) of October 2008 by the US Congress, which authorized the Troubled Assets Relief Program (TARP), sections 4 and 5.
5. David March, *The Bundesbank. The Bank That Rules Europe*, Heinemann, London, 1992.
6. Also, Paulson signaled on 16 October 2008 that hedge funds are not *currently* eligible for Federal aid. But what did the Treasury secretary mean by "currently"?
7. Contrary to the ECB, whose charter calls for close watch over monetary stability, the Fed's mission includes both monetary stability and employment.
8. While the first wave of Savings & Loans failures came in the mid 1980s the Resolution Trust Corporation (RTC) was not created to dispose of their assets until 1989.
9. CNNMoney.com, 17 November 2008.
10. *The Economist*, 11 October 2008.
11. *Financial Times*, 11 February 2009.
12. D.N. Chorafas, *Stress Testing for Risk Control Under Basel II*, Elsevier, London and Boston, 2007.
13. *Financial Times*, 18 February 2009.
14. Greenspan presided over two major bubbles: the equity bubble of 2000 and housing bubble of 2007, as well as a couple of minor ones: the equity bubble of 1987 and the debt instruments bubble of 1994.
15. *The Economist*, 31 January 2009
16. 80 percent of this package would focus on interbank lending guarantees, which is the right credit allocation.
17. With this, Ireland became the first euroland member to declare that it would bust the stability-pact ceiling on budget deficits of 3 percent of GDP. In 2009, it expects a deficit close to 6 percent.
18. Later extended to cover the Irish operations of four British banks, mainly in real estate.

19. Hypo Real estate, Germany's second-largest property lender, first obtained Euro 35 billion ($51 billion) in credit guarantees from the government *and* the German banking industry. This sum then had to be increased.
20. Dexia's problems were made worse by its exposure to billions in potential losses at an American subsidiary, Financial Security Assurance, which insured municipal bonds but also had big holdings of mortgage-backed securities.
21. France also provided €10.5 billion to six banks, with half the total going to Crédit Agricole and BNP Paribas.
22. On 15 September 2008, one day after a conference call among central bankers, Fortis announced that it had more than half a billion dollars in the Lehman exposure. The next day it issued a statement that its share price was being exacerbated by emails spreading misinformation.
23. Paribas bought the Belgian operations of Fortis for €14.5 billion ($19.8 billion). Of this €9 billion was paid in stock and the balance in cash. However, this did not make the French bank's fortune and its stock dropped sharply in the Paris bourse.
24. Therefore, valuing ING at €117.65 billion.
25. "Bankassurance" is a term coined to identify a financial conglomerate acting in both banking and insurance. An example is the Dutch ING.
26. So much "stronger" that ING's stock first zoomed up some 20 percent, then shrank 30 percent below its value prior to the €10 billion injection.
27. A practice that has been repeated several times since.
28. During the 15 November 2008 conference Japan also promised $100 billion to the IMF to beef up its finances.
29. *International Herald Tribune*, 18/19 October 2008.
30. See also the references made to Iceland's banks at the end of Chapter 2.
31. In Switzerland, Kaupthing Bank marketed accounts with 4 percent interest rates, compared with the 1.5 percent for Swiss francs, but only 1,700 savers were attracted.
32. The British government froze the assets of Iceland's banks in Britain, and threatened to use anti-terrorist legislation to take over assets of other Icelandic companies in Britain.

Epilog

1. *The Economist*, March 7, 2009.
2. *The Financial Times*, March 24, 2009.
3. RBS has already benefited from over $400 billion in public money. On March 23, 2009 a CNN ticker had it that RBS now faces "director threat" claims.
4. *The Economist*, March 21, 2009.
5. *The Economist*, March 14, 2009.
6. *The Financial Times*, March 24, 2008,
7. *International Herald Tribune*, April 3, 2009.
8. Asian tax havens have also been whitewashed by the great G-20 love affair; Hong Kong and Macao are examples.
9. A former Chancellor of the Exchequer in the Thatcher government.
10. Each of the US, EU and Japan will contribute $100 billion while China throws in $40 billion. With the IMF selling gold to the tune of $250 billion, some $510 billion will be missing from the $1.1 trillion pledge of the G-20 – even if those who pledged money put it on the table, which is far from sure.
11. Edith Hamilton, *The Greek Way*, W.W. Norton, New York, 1930.

Index